Best Bike Rides
Boston

Help Us Keep This Guide Up to Date

Every effort has been made by the author and editors to make this guide as accurate and useful as possible. However, many things can change after a guide is published—roads are detoured, facilities come under new management, phone numbers change, and so forth.

We would love to hear from you concerning your experiences with this guide and how you feel it could be improved and kept up to date. While we may not be able to respond to all comments and suggestions, we'll take them to heart, and we'll also make certain to share them with the author. Please send your comments and suggestions to the following address:

Globe Pequot Press
Reader Response/Editorial Department
P.O. Box 480
Guilford, CT 06437

Or you may e-mail us at:
editorial@GlobePequot.com

Thanks for your input, and happy travels!

Best Bike Rides
Boston

Great Recreational Rides
in the Metro Area

SHAWN MUSGRAVE

FALCONGUIDES

GUILFORD, CONNECTICUT
HELENA, MONTANA
AN IMPRINT OF GLOBE PEQUOT PRESS

FALCONGUIDES®

Copyright © 2014 by Morris Book Publishing, LLC

FalconGuides is an imprint of Globe Pequot Press.
Falcon, FalconGuides, Outfit Your Mind, and Best Bike Rides are registered trademarks of Morris Book Publishing, LLC.

Maps by Trailhead Graphics, Inc. © Morris Book Publishing, LLC

All photos are by the author.

Text design: Sheryl Kober
Layout artist: Justin Marciano
Project editor: Ellen Urban

Library of Congress Cataloging-in-Publication Data

Musgrave, Shawn.
  Best bike rides Boston : great recreational rides in the metro area / Shawn Musgrave.
      pages cm
  Summary: "Best Bike Rides Boston describes 40 of the greatest recreational rides in the Boston area"— Provided by publisher.
  ISBN 978-0-7627-4694-1 (paperback)
  1. Cycling—Massachusetts—Boston Region—Guidebooks. I. Title.
  GV1045.5.M42M87 2014
  796.6'40974461—dc23
                                                                                2014004082

Printed in the United States of America

10 9 8 7 6 5 4 3 2 1

Contents

Overview

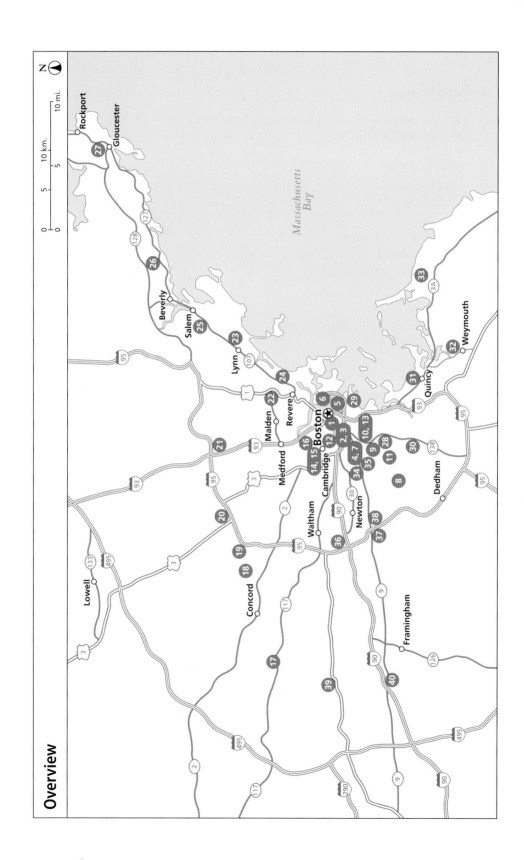

Acknowledgments

No project of this scale is possible without the support, patience, and assistance of many people. While a full list of every person who offered assistance would eclipse the book itself in length, I would like to acknowledge a few in particular who helped make this book happen.

First, I would like to thank the many bicycle clubs, civic associations, and citizen cooperatives that have made Greater Boston and eastern Massachusetts such a fantastic place to ride. Groups like MassBike, Boston Cyclists Union, LivableStreets, Cambridge Bikes, Societies of Spontaneity, Bike to the Sea, and fellow advocates across the Commonwealth routinely put in heroic effort, often at great personal cost. Cyclists in Massachusetts owe these bike warriors a deep debt for the countless hours of legislative advocacy, generous funding, and expert guidance they invest each year to keep Massachusetts at the frontier of bike friendliness. Their passion and dedication laid the foundation for every ride within these pages. While I have done my best to acknowledge particular contributions, there is scarce enough ink to number their hard-won victories.

There are also many fellow cyclists and travelers who gave invaluable advice about routes, points of interest, and logistics, particularly for rides farther from Boston proper. While I caught few of their names and many exchanges were only as long as a stoplight, their knowledge and guidance helped shape this book in countless small ways. Your willingness to chat with a sweaty stranger is endearing and wonderful.

This book would also not be possible at all without the dedication of the FalconGuides and Globe Pequot Press staff, who have worked tirelessly to make the book as clear and accurate as possible.

I would like to thank my Mom and Dad for teaching me to ride a bike in the first place, and for always pushing me to tackle challenges. Gretchen and Jeff, our childhood adventures sparked my passion for biking, even if you both mercilessly clobbered me in every race.

Thanks to Sevan, Lea, Nick, Dan, and Garrett for coming along on a few rides each, even when I was murky on where we were going, how long we'd be gone, or whether the route required mountain bikes.

Teddy, your unflagging encouragement and frank support is sometimes the only thing that sustains my confidence. Ari, you propel my work ethic and creativity like no one else with your enthusiasm and perpetual "Yes And" mindset. Santi, I never could have finished this project without work naps, quesadillas, and fresh-brewed tea.

Introduction

Known around the globe for its sports, seafood, and schools, Boston is also famous for styling itself the "Hub of the Universe," or simply "the Hub." (Don't call it "Beantown." Just don't.) It may not be a city that never sleeps—good luck catching the subway past midnight—and it's certainly not the most polite of towns—wear a Yankees jersey to Fenway at your peril—but Boston has it all: a fascinating history that stretches back to the country's founding, a progressive and dynamic culture that propels it fearlessly forward, and a self-deprecating devotion that kept people flocking to Fenway through an eighty-plus-year pennant drought.

Like many major metro areas across the world, Boston is a city of diverse neighborhoods, each of its districts, boroughs, and blocks boasting its own history and distinct feel. Two points straight across the Charles or Mass Ave can feel worlds or decades apart, rather than fractions of a mile. A ride on the T can carry you from harbor to downtown to wooded fields in the time it takes to scarf down a cannoli. Such variety is one of the best things a city can have, and it's one of the reasons people love calling Boston home.

And with each year, Greater Boston is becoming a better place to bike, both for transportation and for pleasure. Whether it's commuting from Harvard Square to Dorchester, or schlepping up Comm Ave to Newton, cycling is by far the fastest way of getting around. For decades, city planners and citizen advocates have built car-free thoroughfares like the Southwest Corridor Park, Charles River Esplanade, South Bay Harbor Loop, and Minuteman Commuter Bikeway into the fabric of the metro area. And newer routes like the Somerville Community Path, East Boston Greenway, and Northern Strand Community Trail continue to expand and interlink new destinations into the regional network of paths.

Biking also makes it easy to escape downtown and the city's bustle for quieter locales, whether you want to head north to Horn Pond, south to the Blue Hills or Quincy Shore, or west to Hemlock Gorge. A half hour's drive or commuter rail trip will take you even farther, to the picturesque Marblehead, Revere Beach, Assabet River, or World's End. Whatever mood you're in, particular terrain you want to tackle, or type of cyclist you happen to be, there's a ride within easy reach for all.

Happy riding!

About This Book

This book is for people looking to explore the area in and around Boston by mountain, hybrid, or road bike. Most of the rides are between 10 and 30 miles, although there are some rides that are a little shorter or a hair longer. The rides were chosen this way to cater to people who want to do more than a couple miles but aren't looking to pedal arduous circuits of 60 miles, and who appreciate taking in sights along a route. A number of the rides are close together, though, and those who want to put together longer rides can easily combine or modify these paired routes to create new or longer rides.

All of the rides in the book are appropriate for anyone who is healthy and has done some cycling. Each ride includes a description of its length and terrain to give an overall sense for difficulty and time to complete the ride. Keep in mind that some of the shorter rides may still be challenging due to terrain or steep climbs. Before attempting the longer or more difficult rides, it is a good idea to try out some of the shorter and easier rides.

The view from Fan Pier across the water to the harbor front.

ORGANIZATION

Rides in this book are grouped into four geographic areas, all within an hour or so of downtown:

- **Boston and Cambridge**—rides that remain primarily within the city limits of the Hub and the People's Republic
- **North of Boston**—rides that explore areas north of Boston, as close as Somerville or Arlington and as far as Gloucester and Rockport
- **South of Boston**—rides that explore areas south of Boston, as close as Quincy and as far as Scituate
- **West of Boston**—rides that explore areas west of Boston, as close as Newton and as far as Hopkinton

This grouping lets you choose a ride by the area you want to explore, as well as by terrain: Rides within Cambridge and Boston tend to be a little more urban and crowded, and thus require urban cycling skills to navigate popular paths or riding in the street. The remaining rides explore smaller towns, rural parks, and quieter coastline, although parts of these rides may go through small city centers that may still be crowded.

RIDE FORMAT

All the rides in this book have the same format and information. Each ride has a number, name, and a brief summary. Following that is a section that provides more details about the ride, arranged as follows:

Start: The location where the ride begins

Length: The length in miles of the ride

Approximate riding time: An estimate of the time it will take to complete the ride, including stops

Best bike: Suggestions for the type of bike best suited to the ride's terrain and length

Terrain and trail surface: The type of terrain you will encounter on the ride (flat, hilly, etc.) as well as the trail surface (paved, gravel, etc.)

Traffic and hazards: A description of the type of traffic, both car and pedestrian, that you will encounter as well as any other obstacles or potential hazards to look out for along the way

Maps: DeLorme: *Massachusetts Atlas & Gazetteer* maps along with any other worthy maps.

Things to see: A list of some of the things you will see during the ride, including cultural and historical sites, small towns, highlighted neighborhoods, and other points of interest

Getting there: Directions for getting to the starting point

Virtual Rides

If you really want to prepare for the ride and make sure you don't get lost, you can do a quick virtual bike ride to check out the route. Go to Google Maps (www.maps.google.com) and type in the city and state where the ride is starting. You will be presented with a map of the area. If you click on the Satellite button, you will see a satellite view of the area with the roads overlaid on the map. You can zoom in or out and move the map to view the roads of the ride. You can also use the street-view layer to get actual street-level pictures of the roads that you may be riding on. This is a great feature that makes it easy to decide whether it is a good idea to ride a bike on a certain road.

The satellite and street-view images for the area in and around Boston are quite detailed and can give you a good idea of the type of roads you will be navigating. Sometimes you can even tell whether the road has a shoulder. The satellite and street-view images may be a few years old, so they don't necessarily show the current conditions. That said, most roads don't change that often, so the images are usually pretty accurate. The one thing that is hard to tell from the satellite view is the type of terrain and how hard a particular climb is. Google Maps is the next best thing to doing the ride itself and is an invaluable tool for planning a trip.

Following these categories comes a complete description of the ride, along with details about the places and things you will see along the way.

The next section, **Miles and Directions,** is a step-by-step description of the ride with mileage. Immediately following in **Ride Information** you'll find supplemental details about **local events/attractions** that you might be able to incorporate into your outing and lists of public **restrooms** along the route. As you read through each ride, you'll also find highlighted information on nearby bike shops, which may come in handy if you run into trouble along the way.

Another resource for you is the ride map, which gives an overview of the roads along the ride and the surrounding area. The route is clearly marked on the map and includes symbols to mark the start/ end of the ride and the miles at each turn. (See the map legend for a complete list of the symbols used.)

Key to icons used in this edition:

 Roads   Mountain Bike Trails   Paths

The Rides

GETTING TO THE RIDES

If you live in Greater Boston, then getting to the ride can just be a matter of riding to the starting point. If you live in the outlying suburbs or the starting point is too far to ride to, then you'll either have to drive or take mass transit. Because of parking scarcity in the area and the fact that many cyclists don't have cars of their own, most of the rides selected for this book can be accessed by public transit. The Massachusetts Bay Transportation Authority (MBTA, or just "the T"), Boston's mass transit system, is bike-friendly along most lines and allows bicycles on most trains and buses except during morning and evening rush hours. Restrictions are listed below:

Subway ("The T")
- Green Line: Bikes are not allowed on the Green Line at any time.
- Red Line: Bikes are allowed on the Red Line except from 7 to 10 a.m. and 4 to 7 p.m. Monday through Friday, and without restriction on weekends.
- Orange Line: Bikes are allowed on the Orange Line except from 7 to 10 a.m. and 4 to 7 p.m. Monday through Friday, and without restriction on weekends.
- Blue Line: Bikes are allowed on the Blue Line except from 7 to 9 a.m. (inbound) and 4 to 6 p.m. (outbound) Monday through Friday, and without restriction on weekends.
- Silver Line: Bikes cannot be carried onto the Silver Line, but can be loaded into bike racks if they are available.

Bus
Bikes cannot be carried onto MBTA buses, but can be loaded into bike racks if they are available. The vast majority of the MBTA bus fleet has bike racks.

Commuter Rail
- Bike are allowed on all commuter rail lines, as outlined in schedules, except for during peak periods. Look for the bike symbol on each line's timetable.

Note that folding bikes are allowed on all MBTA vehicles, but bikes must be folded before passing fare gates. See the MBTA website (www.mbta.com) for further details on bringing bikes onto public transit, as well as to enroll in the Pedal & Park program for secure bike storage at major stations.

It bears repeating that driving into Boston or Cambridge can be a hassle, particularly for those unused to the particular Bostonian style of street navigation or the maze of one-way streets. Check local news and city social media for updates on traffic and construction projects along particular streets. As in most big cities, plan for extra travel time if attempting to drive during rush hour.

Parking can also be a considerable challenge within Cambridge and Boston, as noted in particular rides. Street parking is limited, and free parking even rarer. If you're commuting in, your best bet may be to park at an outlying MBTA station and take mass transit into the city to save yourself the stress of tracking down a meter.

WHAT TO BRING WITH YOU

Packing a few things to carry on your ride will help you take care of the most common problems. Most of these are available at any of the bike stores mentioned within the ride descriptions.

- For flats: spare tube, tire levers, bike pump, and patch kit
- For miscellaneous mechanical issues: multitool that fits all the screws and nuts on the bike
- For fuel and hydration: water and snacks appropriate to the ride length and locale, particularly if the ride explores more rural areas
- For first aid: antibacterial wipes and adhesive bandages are a godsend for chance falls
- For communication and navigation: cell phone

YOUR MILEAGE WILL VARY

Mileage for the rides are as accurate as possible, but the mileage that you will see on your bicycle computer or personal GPS will most likely be a little higher or lower. This is caused by a couple of factors.

First, most bicycle computers are not as finely calibrated as a car's odometer or most basic GPS units. To calibrate the odometer on your bicycle computer, you have to accurately measure the circumference of the front wheel to a millimeter or small fraction of an inch. If this number is off just a hair, it can significantly alter its accuracy. For example, say that your calibration of your odometer is off by just 0.5 percent. This means that each mile you ride you will be off by 0.05 mile. This may not sound like a lot, but after 10 miles your odometer will be off by 0.5 mile, by 20 miles off by a mile, and by 40 miles off by 2 miles. These small inaccuracies add up!

The other main factor is that you will probably not do the ride exactly as it is mapped out in the description. You may take a wrong turn and have to backtrack, or meander around rest stops, or make any number of little changes to the route that add fractions of a mile here and there. Again, these small changes can add up.

The mileage in the **Miles and Directions** section is best paired with the road signs and landmarks outlined in the ride description and the overview map sketched out for every ride. Trust your instincts, ask for help if you get turned around, and realize that those brief moments of being lost can often be the most fun.

PLANNING FOR SAFETY

Bike riding, particularly in a city, carries its risks. But these risks can be minimized by taking safety into your own hands:

Be visible. The most important safety rule is to always be visible. Whether it's a collision between car and bike, bike and bike, or bike and pedestrian, accidents often boil down to visibility issues. Maximize visibility by wearing bright and reflective clothing, particularly after dusk, and doing your best to stay within line of sight of all vehicles around you.

Signal your intentions. Just as cars must use turn signals and have working brake lights, it's important that cyclists indicate turns, lane changes, and stops. This means using hand signals consistently and clearly. Yelling "left turn" or "stopping" is a great additional tool to help those around you know what you're doing.

Ride predictably. When riding, especially in traffic, it is important to be predictable so other vehicles on the road know where you are going. This means following a straight line when possible, and not weaving in and out around parked cars or changing lanes rapidly. Proper signaling can prevent catastrophic miscommunication.

Wear a helmet. A helmet is the most important piece of safety gear to wear while riding. It's also a good idea to wear glasses to keep the rocks, bugs, and other debris out of your eyes, particularly for longer rides.

Know and obey the law. Every state (and even particular cities) has a set of laws that apply to bicyclists. For the most part, bicyclists must follow the same laws as cars and must obey all traffic signs and signals, but brushing up on a particular area's bike laws can prevent misunderstandings that can lead to tickets and fines and help you know your rights as a cyclist on the streets. Organizations like MassBike (www.massbike.org) and Boston Cyclists Union (www.bostoncyclistsunion.org) have a number of educational resources around bike laws in Massachusetts and Boston.

Ride Finder

BEST SEASIDE RIDES

BEST MOUNTAIN BIKE RIDES

BEST HILL RIDES

BEST RIDES WITH KIDS

BEST SCENIC RIDES

BEST RIDES FROM PUBLIC TRANSIT

Map Legend

(75)	Interstate Highway		✈	Airport
(23)	US Highway		‿	Bridge
(14)	State Highway		■	Building/Point of Interest
(52)	Featured State/Local Road		▲	Campground
	Local Road		†	Church
	Featured Bike Route		🎓	College/University
	Bike Route		❶	Dining
	Railroad		◉	Large City
	Trail		17.1 ◆—	Mileage Marker
	State Line		🏛	Museum
	County Line		🅿	Parking
	Small River or Creek		🎋	Picnic Area
	Marsh/Swamp		○	Small City/Town
	Body of Water		▲	Small Park
	State Park/Forest/Wilderness/ Preserve/Recreational Area		①	Trailhead
	Nontarget State/Country Fill		❓	Visitor/Information Center

Boston and Cambridge

The statue of John Harvard in Harvard Yard is sometimes called the "Three Lies" statue for its mild fibs about Harvard history (Ride 12).

One of the most historic metropolitan areas in the country, Boston and Cambridge are fantastic places to ride around landmarks from the American Revolution, more recent sports legends, and beautiful New England scenery. Whether snaking along the Charles River via the Esplanade, biking the Freedom Trail from the State House to Old North Church, or winding around the dozens of esteemed college campuses, the metro area has a bevy of bikeways for you to explore. The fifteen rides in Boston and Cambridge carve through all twenty-one of Boston's neighborhoods, from Charlestown to Hyde Park, West Roxbury to East Boston. Across the river, you'll see tourist meccas like the four squares and world-famous universities that call the "People's Republic of Cambridge" home, plus less-traveled places like Fresh Pond, the Alewife Linear Park. Welcome to "The Hub of the Universe"!

The Freedom Trail

History buffs flock to Boston to follow the Freedom Trail, a winding tour of the Revolutionary War sites scattered through downtown, the North End, and Charlestown. While portions of the Freedom Trail are difficult to navigate by bike, this ride hits the major highlights on a route that begins and ends on the Boston Common. It also throws in side excursions through the Navy Yard and Beacon Hill that give you a sense for how present-day Boston still reflects its colonial heritage beyond the preserved sites along the trail.

Start: Boston Common Visitor Information Center, 148 Tremont St.

Length: 8.1 miles

Approximate riding time: 2 hours with stops

Best bike: Road bike, mountain bike, or hybrid

Terrain and trail surface: Paved roads through downtown Boston and the North End, as well as sections of paved pathway through urban parks

Traffic and hazards: Tourists are legion along the Freedom Trail, as are families with small children. Joggers also frequent the waterfront paths in Charlestown and the North End. Watch for traffic along Causeway Street, Beacon Street, and Boylston Street in particular.

Things to see: Boston Common, Massachusetts State House, Boston Athenaeum, Museum of African American History, Old City Hall, Old State House, Faneuil Hall, Union Square Oyster House, North End, Paul Revere Mall, Old North Church, USS *Constitution*, Old West Church, Public Garden

Maps: USGS: *Boston South* quad; DeLorme: *Massachusetts Atlas & Gazetteer*, p. 41

Getting there: By car: Parking is available right on the Common. From Copley Square, take Boylston Street east. Stay left on Boylston past

Arlington Street, and turn left onto Charles Street. Park in the Boston Common Garage, immediately on your right. Follow signs to the visitor center on the opposite side of the park, off Tremont Street. **By train:** Take the T Red Line to Park Street. Bikes are allowed on the Red Line, except from 7 to 10 a.m. and 4 to 7 p.m. Monday through Friday, and without restriction on weekends. Exit the station onto Tremont Street and ride southeast to the visitor center. GPS coordinates for starting point: N42 21.325' / W71 03.817'

THE RIDE

The oldest city park in the country, the Common (careful, it's singular, not "the Commons") has been a central fixture for the city since its establishment in 1634 as communal pasture. The Common was used for grazing for nearly two centuries until 1830 and has been the site of countless historic moments: British redcoats made camp here until the outbreak of the revolution, Vietnam protestors gathered thousand-strong in the 1960s, and visiting luminaries like Martin Luther King Jr. and Pope John Paul II made stops on its lawns. It's a fitting start for a ride that explores Boston's rich past.

You'll start in front of the Boston Common visitor center on the southeast edge of the park. Take the paved path just to the left of the visitor center and ride northwest, away from Tremont Street. Turn left at Flag Staff Hill to climb briefly toward the Soldiers and Sailors Monument, a victory column erected in honor of Massachusetts soldiers who died in the Civil War. Continue around the monument to ride down the hill. From mid-April to October you'll find an ornate wooden Herschell carousel at the base of the hill, which was hand carved in the 1940s. On summer nights the carousel lights up the edges of the Frog Pond, another Boston Common landmark and favorite wintertime destination for the city's ice skaters.

Ride straight past the carousel toward the northern edge of the Common, which you'll follow to the Robert Gould Shaw Memorial at the northeast corner of the park. This bronze relief commemorates the Massachusetts Fifty-Fourth Volunteer Infantry, the first African-American volunteer regiment to form in the North during the Civil War. The Fifty-Fourth was also the regiment of Sergeant William H. Carney, who was the first African-American soldier to earn the Medal of Honor.

Carry your bike up the steps just past the monument and across Beacon Street from the Massachusetts State House. Completed in 1798, the Commonwealth's second State House (you'll pass the original in a few minutes) houses

The Boston Common's grassy hills are in the very center of Back Bay.

the legislature and governor's offices. Paul Revere's metalworking company covered the original wooden dome with copper in 1802. After being gilded with twenty-three karat gold leaf in 1874, the dome was painted black during World War II to protect it against bombing raids. The city gilded the State House in gold once again in 1997 at a cost of more than $300,000.

Turning right onto Beacon Street, you'll pass the Museum of African American History and the Boston Athenaeum. An independent membership library, the Athenaeum took up its present residence at 10½ Beacon St. in 1847. The Athenaeum is famous for its serene atmosphere and rare books, boasting at least one tome bound in human skin.

A bit farther on you'll come to King's Chapel. The first Anglican church in New England, the original building was constructed on the Massachusetts Bay Colony public burial ground in 1688 because no one would sell land for the construction of a non-Puritan church. The current stone structure, which was erected around its wooden predecessor, was finished in 1754. The King's Chapel Burying Ground is the oldest cemetery in the city, and thus among the oldest in the United States. It holds the remains of such notable colonial figures as Governor John Winthrop, Puritan minister John Cotton, and Elizabeth Pain, reputedly the inspiration for Hester Prynne in *The Scarlet Letter*.

Just past the chapel lies Boston's Old City Hall, constructed just after the Civil War. Now home to a fine steakhouse and upscale offices, the Old City Hall hosted thirty-eight Boston mayors over its 128 years as the hub of municipal government. The hopscotch mosaic in the sidewalk is a memorial to the Boston Latin School, which met at this site from 1704 to 1748 and which gave School Street its name. Now situated in Mission Hill, Boston Latin was the first public school in the colonies when it was founded in 1635, and is the oldest existing school in the United States today.

Turn left on Washington Street and ride 2 blocks to the ornate Old State House. Worth a stop to walk all the way around, this building has historic significance easily dwarfed by the skyscrapers that encroach on all sides. The Boston Massacre took place here in March 1770 and fueled revolutionary fires with the deaths of five civilian men by British redcoat muskets. The Declaration of Independence was read to throngs of Bostonians from the Old State House balcony on July 18, 1776, after which some impassioned patriots scaled the roof to remove the lion and unicorn, which are symbols of the crown, for burning. After the Revolution, the building served first as the Massachusetts legislature building until 1798, then as Boston's city hall from 1830 to 1841. It was turned into a museum in 1881 and remains the oldest surviving public building in the city.

Turning left on Congress Street brings you shortly to Faneuil Hall, overseen by the

Bike Shop

Urban AdvenTours offers tours and rentals in addition to expert repairs and bike sales. The North End shop is located at 103 Atlantic Ave., Boston; (617) 670-0637; www.urbanadventours.com.

iconic statue of Samuel Adams. Its charming, cobblestoned complex lies just across from the present City Hall, widely reviled for its brutalist design, which was in vogue during its construction in the 1960s. Much easier on the eyes, Faneuil is a testament to the fine details of colonial architecture. Note the gilded grasshopper weather vane atop the main hall. The ornate insect may look small, but it actually spans 4 feet and weighs 80 pounds!

Take a right on North Street and then a quick left onto Union Street to ride past the historic pubs and taverns. The eponymous Union Street Oyster House, famous for its traditional New England seaside fare, is the oldest continuously functioning restaurant in the country, having opened its doors in 1826. The country's first known waitress, Rose Carey, worked in the oyster house in the 1920s. Just next door is the Bell in Hand Tavern, opened in 1795 by Boston's last-known town crier, Jimmy Wilson.

Turning right on Hanover Street, you'll cross the Rose Kennedy Greenway park into the North End, Boston's Little Italy. The mecca for pasta, cannoli, espresso, and all things Italian, the North End is known for its history as much as its cuisine. Follow Hanover past the enticing cafes and trattorias (although a stop at Modern or Mike's Pastry would be entirely appropriate) to the Paul Revere Mall, where you'll find a statue of the famous patriot depicting his Midnight Ride. Walk your bike across the mall courtyard to the Old North Church, the oldest church standing in Boston today. On April 18, 1775, church sexton Robert Newman cemented the church's place in revolutionary history by climbing the steeple to light two lanterns as a signal that the British were marching to Lexington and Concord by sea and not by land. Since the vast majority of the church's parishioners at the time were loyal to the monarchy, Newman's bravery was remarkable. Each year the church commemorates his courage with a lantern ceremony.

The phrase "one if by land, two if by sea" was coined by Henry Wadsworth Longfellow in his poem "Paul Revere's Ride," later retitled "The Landlord's Tale." Each year the Old North Church conducts a reading of this epic homage to Paul Revere as part of its lantern-lighting ceremony.

Continue walking your bike up Hull Street to Copp's Hill Burying Ground, the second oldest in the city. Robert Newman is buried here, as are Puritan ministers Cotton and Increase Mather. Turn right on Snow Hill Street then left on Charter Street to Commercial Street, where you'll turn left again and ride out of the North End. The Great Boston Molasses Flood ripped apart Commercial Street on January 15, 1919, when a molasses tank burst and sent a 15-foot-high wave of 2.5 million gallons of the sticky substance roaring down the street at 35 miles per hour. Twenty-one people died in the accident, which is commemorated with a small plaque a bit up Commercial Street.

Cross over to Charlestown via the west side of the Charlestown Bridge and turn into Paul Revere Park, where you'll follow the waterfront east under the bridge and along the Harborwalk. Within minutes you'll come within view of the Boston Navy Yard and the USS *Constitution,* dubbed "Old Ironsides" for her storied victories in the War of 1812. Launched in 1797, the *Constitution* is the oldest commissioned naval vessel afloat not only in the United States but in the world. The ship still sees action today for ceremonial salutes, when her crew takes her out to Boston Harbor to fire her historic cannons.

Following the boardwalk past the *Constitution* brings you to a series of stunning views of downtown Boston from across the water as well as of East Boston and the Inner Harbor itself. Take First Avenue back toward the Navy Yard, then turn right on Fifth Street to ride away from the waterfront. Carefully cross Chelsea Street and cut under the highway overpass. Turn left to follow Lowney Way past Winthrop Square, where the Bunker Hill Monument comes into view. The site of the first major battle of the American Revolution, the 221-foot granite obelisk actually lies on Breed's Hill. While the Brits ultimately captured the hill, the storied battle opened their eyes to the patriots' resolve to defend the colonies, a bravery captured in the apocryphal order, "Don't fire until you see the whites of their eyes!" The first monument was raised on the hill in 1794 by the King Solomon's Lodge of Masons, which commemorates the battle with a yearly ceremony.

Ride around the monument and continue straight along Pleasant Street past Warren Tavern, a favorite watering hole of Paul Revere and George Washington. Turn left at Main Street, which you'll follow around City Square before turning right onto Chelsea Street and crossing once again to the sidewalk on the west side of the Charlestown Bridge. Ride across the bridge and turn right onto Causeway Street.

In a few blocks you'll see TD Garden, home of the Boston Celtics and Bruins. Built "slightly north" (aka, 9 inches) of the historic Boston Garden in 1993, TD Garden is also the home of the city's Beanpot hockey tournament between Boston University, Boston College, Harvard University, and Northeastern University. Causeway Street becomes Stanford Street as you climb the hill topped by the Old West Church, where Congregational minister Jonathan Mayhew coined the phrase "no taxation without representation" that so pithily summed up many colonists' grievances.

Turn left on Cambridge Street and then right onto Bowdoin Square for a detour through Beacon Hill. Take a right at Deme Street to Hancock Street and then Mount Vernon Street, taking in the meticulously preserved red brick and wrought iron brownstones characteristic of this vibrant neighborhood. Look for lavender-colored glass in the windows, which typically indicates original panes whose materials have changed color after decades of exposure to sunlight. Follow Mount Vernon to River Street and turn left toward Beacon Street, which you'll follow west along the edge of the Public Garden.

Take a left at Arlington Street and again at Boylston Street, entering the Boston Common at the Central Burying Ground to continue through north. Pass the Parkman Bandstand to arrive at the visitor center just off Tremont Street where you began the ride.

MILES AND DIRECTIONS

0.0 Ride northwest along the path to the left of the visitor center.

0.1 Turn left up the hill to the monument, then continue down the other side.

0.3 Continue along the middle path toward the outer edge of the Common.

0.4 Carry your bike up the steps and turn right onto Beacon Street.

0.6 Continue straight onto School Street.

0.7 Turn left at Washington Street.

0.8 Turn right at the Old State House, and follow the path around to turn left onto Congress Street.

1.0 Turn right at North Street, then left onto Union Street and right onto Hanover Street.

1.4 Turn left to walk your bike across the Paul Revere Mall to the Old North Church.

1.5 Walk your bike up Hull Street past Copp's Hill Burying Ground to Snow Hill Street and turn right.

1.7 Turn left at Charter Street then left again onto Commercial Street.

1.8 Ride through the intersection with North Washington Street and turn right to cross the Charlestown Bridge via the foot and bike path.

2.2 Turn left into Paul Revere Park, following the path down the water and under the Charlestown Bridge toward the naval yard.

2.5 Cross the parking lot and follow the waterfront trail past the marina.

2.9 Turn away from the waterfront and then turn right onto Constitution Road, continuing straight onto First Avenue.

3.2 Turn right just past the USS *Constitution* Museum and follow the path out to the end of Mystic Pier 3. Turning back, follow the path right along the waterfront.

4.1 Exit Shipyard Park and turn left onto First Avenue.

4.5 Turn right onto Fifth Street, cross Chelsea Street under the Tobin Memorial Bridge and turn left onto Lowney Way to Winthrop Square.

4.9 Ride up Monument Square and turn right up the hill to the Bunker Hill Monument. Turn left around Monument Square, exiting on Pleasant Street.

5.4 Turn left onto Main Street and follow it past John Harvard Mall and left around City Square.

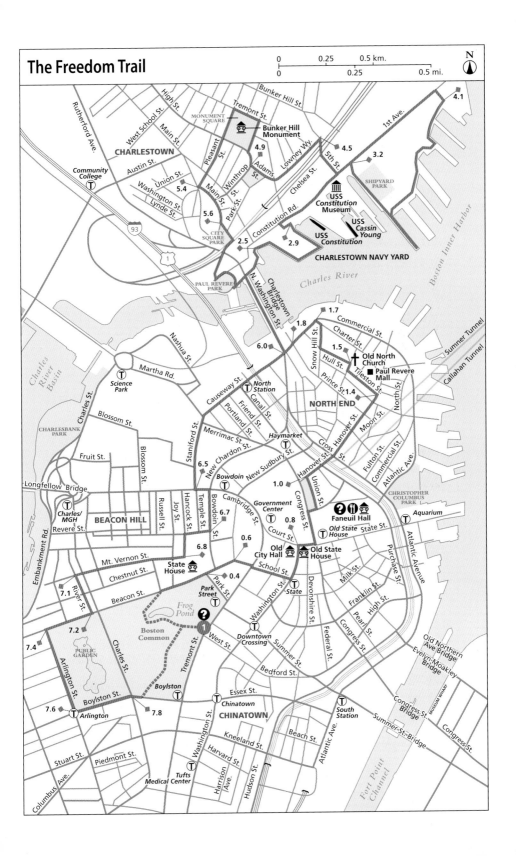

The Freedom Trail

0   0.25   0.5 km.

0   0.25   0.5 mi.

N

CHARLESTOWN

Rutherford Ave.

West School St.

High St.

Main St.

Tremont St.

Bunker Hill St.

MONUMENT SQUARE

Bunker Hill Monument

4.9

4.5

4.1

1st Ave.

3.2

SHIPYARD PARK

Austin St.

Union St.

Washington St.

Lynde St.

Pleasant St.

Winthrop St.

Adams St.

Park St.

5th St.

Chelsea St.

Lowney Wy.

Community College

5.4

5.6

Main St.

93

CITY SQUARE PARK

2.5

Constitution Rd.

2.9

USS Constitution Museum

USS Cassin Young

USS Constitution

CHARLESTOWN NAVY YARD

Boston Inner Harbor

PAUL REVERE PARK

Charlestown Bridge

N. Washington St.

Charles River

1.7

1.8

6.0

Commercial St.

Charter St.

1.5

Old North Church

Paul Revere Mall

Sumner Tunnel

Callahan Tunnel

Snow Hill St.

Hull St.

Prince St.

Tileston St.

1.4

Moon St.

North St.

Charles River Basin

Nashua St.

Martha Rd.

Science Park

Causeway St.

Canal St.

North Station

NORTH END

Hanover St.

Fulton St.

Commercial St.

Atlantic Ave.

CHARLESBANK PARK

Blossom St.

Fruit St.

Blossom St.

Staniford St.

Merrimac St.

Portland St.

Friend St.

Haymarket

Cross St.

Union St.

CHRISTOPHER COLUMBUS PARK

Longfellow Bridge

Charles/ MGH

Revere St.

BEACON HILL

Russell St.

Joy St.

Hancock St.

Temple St.

Bowdoin St.

6.5

Bowdoin

New Chardon St.

New Sudbury St.

Cambridge St.

6.7

1.0

Government Center

0.8

Faneuil Hall

Old State House

State St.

Aquarium

Embankment Rd.

River St.

7.1

Mt. Vernon St.

Chestnut St.

Beacon St.

6.8

State House

0.6

0.4

Court St.

Old City Hall

Old State House

School St.

Devonshire St.

Milk St.

Franklin St.

High St.

Pearl St.

Purchase St.

Atlantic Avenue

7.2

7.4

PUBLIC GARDEN

Arlington St.

Charles St.

Frog Pond

Boston Common

Park Street

West St.

Tremont St.

Washington St.

State

Downtown Crossing

Summer St.

Bedford St.

Federal St.

Congress St.

Old Northern Ave Bridge

Evelyn-Moakley Bridge

Boylston St.

Boylston

7.6

Arlington

7.8

Essex St.

Chinatown

CHINATOWN

Beach St.

Atlantic Ave.

South Station

Congress St. Bridge

MUSEUM WHARF

Congress St.

Stuart St.

Piedmont St.

Columbus Ave.

Washington St.

Kneeland St.

Harvard St.

Harrison Ave.

Hudson St.

Tufts Medical Center

Summer St. Bridge

Fort Point Channel

5.6 Turn right onto Chelsea Street and cross North Washington Street to take the foot and bike path back across the Charlestown Bridge.

6.0 Turn right onto Causeway Street, keeping left at the fork.

6.5 Turn left onto Cambridge Street and then a quick right onto Bowdoin Street.

6.7 Turn right at Derne Street then left onto Hancock Street.

6.8 Turn right onto Mt. Vernon Street.

7.1 Turn left onto River Street.

7.2 Turn right at Beacon Street.

7.4 Turn left onto Arlington Street.

7.6 Turn left at Boylston Street.

7.8 Cross Charles Street into the Common and ride northeast.

8.1 Arrive back at the visitor center on Tremont Street.

RIDE INFORMATION

Local Events/Attractions

Fisherman's Feast: This North End festival held every August was begun in 1910 by immigrants from Sicily. www.fishermansfeast.com

Old North Church: This historic house of worship offers daily tours of the sanctuary. www.oldnorth.com

USS *Constitution*: The museum and ship are open for tours and special exhibits of Old Ironsides. www.ussconstitutionmuseum.org

Boston Harborfest: Boston Harbor Independence Day celebrations during the week of July 4th include the display of the Liberty Tall Ships Fleet. www.bostonharborfest.com

Restrooms

Start/finish: There are public restrooms at the Frog Pond, just north of the Boston Common visitor center.

Mile 0.9: Faneuil Hall has public restrooms.

Mile 6.1: North Station has public restrooms.

Charles River Esplanade

For commuters and recreational cyclists alike, the paved path along the banks of the Charles River is a convenient means of navigating the city. A favorite among runners, cyclists, and picnickers on both sides of the river, the corridor of greenway that lines the Charles offers a tree-lined respite from urban hustle. This ride offers glimpses of historic Cambridge, incredible views of downtown Boston, and a sense for the vastly different atmosphere that lies just across the river.

Start: Edward A. Hatch Memorial Shell, Charles River Esplanade

Length: 12.9 miles

Approximate riding time: 2 hours with stops

Best bike: Road bike, mountain bike, or hybrid

Terrain and trail surface: Mostly paved paths through flat riverside corridor, with occasional patches of uneven pavement. There is also a dirt path that runs alongside most of the paved trail. Road-savvy cyclists may want to ride in the street along portions of Memorial Drive and on crossing the Craigie Drawbridge back into Boston.

Traffic and hazards: Joggers, skateboarders, families with small children, dog walkers, and geese frequent the Esplanade and Charles River trails. Watch for traffic at intersections and while crossing bridges.

Things to see: Edward A. Hatch Memorial Shell, Charles River Esplanade, John W. Weeks Bridge, John F. Kennedy Park, Magazine Beach, Longfellow Bridge, Museum of Science, Community Boating boathouse

Maps: USGS: *Boston South* and *Newton* quads; DeLorme: *Massachusetts Atlas & Gazetteer,* pp. 40–41

Getting there: By car: Parking is very limited near the Hatch Shell. From Copley Square, take Boylston Street east. Stay left on Boylston past

Arlington Street, and turn left onto Charles Street. Park in the Boston Common Garage, immediately on your right. The Hatch Shell is a 0.6-mile ride from the garage. Ride north along Charles Street to Beacon Street. Take a left onto Beacon Street and ride just past Arlington Street to the Arthur Fiedler footbridge, on your right. Cross the footbridge to the Charles River Esplanade, turn right, and follow the path to the Hatch Shell. **By train:** Take the T Red Line to Charles/MGH. Bikes are allowed on the Red Line, except from 7 to 10 a.m. and 4 to 7 p.m. Monday through Friday, and without restriction on weekends. Turn left out of the T station, cross Cambridge Street and Silver Place, and turn right to follow Embankment Road to the footbridge. Cross the footbridge to the Esplanade, and continue straight past the Community Boating boathouse to the Hatch Shell. GPS coordinates for starting point: N42.35732' / W71.07394'

THE RIDE

You'll start at the Edward A. Hatch Memorial Shell, Boston's iconic outdoor concert space that has been a cultural epicenter for the city since the 1940s. Each summer, the Hatch Shell hosts the Boston Pops annual July 4th fireworks concert, as well as a number of free concerts, movie showings, and festivals that draw thousands of Bostonians to the grass oval each week.

From the front of the Hatch Shell, walk your bike north across a small footbridge and ride along the riverbank. This stretch of the Esplanade between the Charles River and the lagoon on the left was added as landfill in the 1950s to offset park space lost to the construction of Storrow Drive. On a given day you might pass sailboats from BU, MIT, and Community Boating on the river, and kayakers or even a gondolier in the lagoon. Keep a sharp eye out for ducks and turtles in the lagoon as you wind past the stand of willows and come to the footbridge that crosses back to the main Esplanade path.

Turn right after the footbridge, then stay left at the fork to continue onto the Dr. Paul Dudley White Bike Path, named for the Harvard-trained

Bike Shop

Back Bay Bicycles is a Boston institution, with an experienced and friendly staff that will care for your equipment and can answer your maintenance questions. The shop also rents bikes by the day. Back Bay Bicycles is located at 362 Commonwealth Ave., Boston; (617) 247-2336; www.backbaybicycles.com.

Views from the Esplanade highlight Boston's union of classic and modern architecture, particularly in Back Bay.

cardiologist and cofounder of the American Heart Association, who was an avid cyclist. The Esplanade continues along Storrow Drive, passing under the Massachusetts Avenue (Mass Ave) Bridge, officially named the "Harvard Bridge" despite leading straight into MIT territory.

The last stretch of the Esplanade will carry you behind Boston University's Charles River campus. On a warm day you might glimpse BU's undergrads laying out on the "BU Beach," so named because cars passing on Storrow Drive reportedly sound like crashing waves with eyes closed and sufficient imagination. The path curves at the BU Sailing Pavilion to pass under the Boston University Bridge. This short wooden boardwalk is one of just a handful of places in the world where a boat can float under a train driven under a car riding beneath an airplane flying overhead.

The path narrows considerably after the bridge as the Charles curves north and Storrow Drive turns into Soldiers Field Road. Here you'll get your first glimpses of historic Cambridge across the water, particularly the iconic red brick and spires of Harvard's undergraduate campus. Follow the river as it curves west again, past the John W. Weeks Bridge that connects the Harvard Business School on the south bank to the rest of Harvard's Cambridge-side campus. As you come to the Anderson Memorial Bridge that leads to Harvard Square via JFK Street, note Harvard Stadium on your left. Every other

November, the storied football rivalry between the Harvard Crimson and the Yale Bulldogs plays out here.

The river meanders south at Soldiers Field, where the path cuts under the Eliot Bridge and into Christian Herter Park. The man-made island in the middle of the park is home to the Publick Theatre, which puts on stellar outdoor plays every summer. You'll pass a number of community gardens and Northeastern University's Henderson before taking the Arsenal Street bridge across the river into Cambridge.

The difference between the Cambridge and Boston sides of the Charles River is marked, particularly on weekends. Turn right after the bridge and continue along the river, passing the Cambridge Boat Club to roll alongside Memorial Drive. On Sundays from early May to mid-November, Cambridge closes Memorial Drive to vehicles from Mt. Auburn Street to Western Avenue so that residents can use the street for skating, biking, and recreation. On warm days, you'll see families playing soccer and field games all along Memorial. The steeples and red brick of Harvard's campus grant this portion of the ride a particularly historic and collegiate air.

The path continues along the north bank of the Charles, passing the iconic Memorial Drive Shell station with its gaudy neon sign built in 1933, one of the few surviving in the metro area. The riverway winds past Magazine Beach, a highly popular swimming spot along the river until the 1950s, when upstream pollution led officials to close the beach and open the public pool for bathers. Magazine Beach is also a popular vantage point to watch the Head of the Charles Regatta, a rowing race which takes place every October.

The Charles River white geese that nest on the Cambridge side of the BU Bridge have been at the center of a number of political controversies over road and infrastructure construction since the 1970s. There have been reported "attacks" on the flock, supposedly financially motivated by those seeking to force the geese from their riverside habitat.

Continuing past the BU Bridge once again, experienced cyclists may want to ride on Memorial Drive for a bit due to uneven pavement. The path improves considerably at MIT's Harold W. Pierce boathouse, just before the Mass Ave Bridge. You'll follow the path along Memorial Drive under the Longfellow Bridge, also called the "Salt-and-Pepper Bridge" for its distinctive towers.

The bike path follows Cambridge Parkway before cutting through a corner park and ending at Commercial Avenue. Turn right onto Commercial Avenue and then right again at Monsignor O'Brien Highway as it passes the Museum of Science with its T-Rex sentinel. Here, again, experienced cyclists may wish to ride in the street rather than on the sidewalk, although either is allowed. If you ride on the sidewalk, take care of heavy foot traffic in front of the museum.

The Craigie Drawbridge, which runs on top of the Charles River Dam, brings you back into Boston. From here you'll also be able to see the Leonard P. Zakim Bunker Hill Bridge, which connects Boston's North End to Charlestown. At ten lanes wide, the Zakim Bridge is the widest cable-stayed bridge in the world. Before its opening in 2003 as part of Boston's infamous "Big Dig" infrastructure modernization initiative, fourteen elephants from Ringling Brothers and Barnum & Bailey Circus marched across the bridge to prove its structural integrity.

Turning right just after the Craigie Drawbridge, you'll rejoin the Esplanade for the final stretch. Across Storrow Drive you'll pass Massachusetts General Hospital, consistently ranked among the top ten medical complexes in the world. The Esplanade path winds past Teddy Ebersol's Red Sox Fields at Lederman Park, which were renovated in 2005 to host youth and community sports leagues. Passing under the Longfellow Bridge once again, you'll approach the docks of Community Boating, which has been providing sailing lessons and boat rentals to the Boston community since 1946.

Just beyond the Community Boating docks and the pair of barrier islands that protect them, you'll come to the back of the Hatch Shell.

MILES AND DIRECTIONS

0.0 Carry your bike across the small footbridge north of the Hatch Shell, and ride west along the path adjacent to the Charles River.

0.7 Cross the footbridge from the barrier island to the main Esplanade stretch and turn right. Keep left to stay on the Dr. Paul Dudley White Bike Path.

1.4 Stay right at the fork to ride adjacent to the river.

2.0 Follow the path as it curves around the Boston University Sailing Pavilion and passes along a brief wooden boardwalk under the BU Bridge.

2.9 Pass the Cambridge Street bridge. Watch out for northbound traffic.

3.1 Pass the Western Avenue bridge. Watch out for southbound traffic.

3.4 Pass the John W. Weeks Bridge. Watch out for pedestrian traffic.

3.7 Pass the Anderson Memorial Bridge. Watch out for traffic traveling in both directions.

4.2 Keep left at the fork to stay on the paved path.

4.3 Turn right just before the Eliot Bridge and take the path that goes under the bridge.

4.8 Turn left to stay on the Dr. Paul Dudley White Bike Path.

5.1 Turn right then make a quick left to stay on the Dr. Paul Dudley White Bike Path.

5.2 Stay left to stay on the paved path.

5.5 Stay left to stay on the paved path.

5.8 Turn right to cross the Arsenal Street Bridge.

5.9 Turn right to remain on the Dr. Paul Dudley White Bike Path.

6.7 Stay left to keep on the paved path.

7.1 Turn right to remain on the Dr. Paul Dudley White Bike Path.

7.9 Keep left.

8.0 Pass the Anderson Memorial Bridge. Stay right to keep on the paved path.

8.3 Pass the John W. Weeks Bridge.

8.6 Pass the Western Avenue bridge.

8.8 Pass the Cambridge Street bridge.

9.4 Cross the street at the BU Bridge and continue on Dr. Paul Dudley White Bike Path. Experienced cyclists may wish to ride in the street along Memorial Drive, although riding on the sidewalk is also permitted.

10.4 Pass the Massachusetts Avenue Bridge.

11.0 Continue on Dr. Paul Dudley White Bike Path to ride under the Longfellow Bridge.

11.3 Turn right to ride adjacent to the river.

11.7 Keep left, then turn right onto Commercial Avenue.

11.8 Turn right at Monsignor O'Brien Highway. Experienced cyclists may wish to ride on the street, although riding on the sidewalk is also permitted. Take care of pedestrian traffic in front of the Museum of Science.

Charles River Esplanade

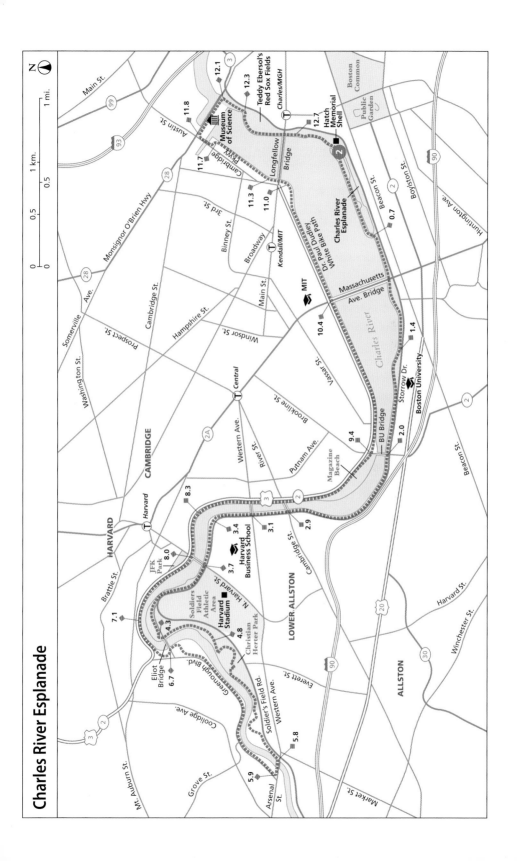

12.1 Turn right before Nashua Street to rejoin the Esplanade.

12.3 Turn right at Embankment Road to ride along the river.

12.7 Stay right at the fork past the Community Boating docks.

12.9 Return to the starting point at the Hatch Shell.

RIDE INFORMATION

Local Events/Attractions

Hatch Shell: This historic outdoor performance venue hosts dozens of free concerts, film screenings, and festivals throughout the spring, summer, and fall, including Boston's July 4th extravaganza featuring the Boston Pops. www .hatchshell.com

Recreation Sundays on Memorial Drive: Every Sunday, from the last Sunday of April to the second Sunday of November, Memorial Drive is closed to traffic between Western Avenue and Mount Auburn Street and open to recreation; the events are organized by the Massachusetts Department of Conservation and Recreation. www.mass.gov/dcr

Sunday Parkland Games: Every Sunday afternoon from mid-June to the end of September, the Charles River Conservancy organizes free park games and exercise classes along the Charles River. www.charlesriverconservancy.org/ParklandGames

Let's Talk About Food Festival: Every June the Museum of Science organizes an outdoor celebration of food, health, cooking, and science, with lectures and demonstrations plus a food-truck food court and cooking Q&As with some of Boston's top chefs. www.mos.org/food

Head of the Charles Regatta: This 3.2-mile rowing race from Boston University's DeWolfe Boathouse to the Eliot Bridge takes place during the second-to-last weekend of October. www.hocr.org

Restrooms

Start/finish: The Hatch Shell has restrooms and water.

Mile 0.5: Dartmouth Street Comfort Station (near the Dartmouth Street footbridge).

Mile 6.5: The Magazine Drive Shell Station has a restroom that is open to the public.

Mile 9.9: There are portable toilets at Teddy Ebersol's Red Sox Fields.

Back Bay, Fenway, and Copley Square

Boston integrates its deep history into its modern landscape better than any other major city in the country. Whether it's in the ornate brownstones throughout Back Bay, the hallowed baseball park in Fenway, or the breathtaking houses of learning and worship around Copley Square, this city is bursting with historic buildings still in active use. This short ride offers an intriguing window to the past through the rich architectural variety for which Boston is famous.

Start: Commonwealth Avenue Mall at Arlington Street, across from the Public Garden

Length: 5.1 miles

Approximate riding time: 45 minutes–1 hour with stops

Best bike: Road bike, mountain bike, or hybrid

Terrain and trail surface: Well-paved urban roads and bike paths

Traffic and hazards: Watch for cars around the busy intersections along Commonwealth Avenue and Boylston Street in particular.

Things to see: Commonwealth Avenue Mall, St. Botolph Club, Algonquin Club, Boston University, Ruggles Baptist Church, Fenway Park, Mother Church (First Church of Christ Scientist), Prudential Center, Lenox Hotel, Boston Public Library, Copley Square, Old South Church, Trinity Church, John Hancock Tower

Maps: USGS: *Boston South* quad; DeLorme: *Massachusetts Atlas & Gazetteer*, p. 41

Getting there: By car: Parking can be very limited in Back Bay. There is street parking along Commonwealth Avenue, or else park in the Boston Common Garage. From Copley Square, take Boylston Street east. Stay left on Boylston past Arlington Street, and turn left onto Charles Street. The garage is immediately on your right. Exiting the garage, ride north along Charles Street to Beacon Street. Take a left onto

Beacon Street and then again onto Arlington Street until you reach Commonwealth Avenue. **By train:** Bikes are not allowed on the Green Line, unfortunately. Take the Orange Line or commuter rail to Back Bay. Bikes are allowed on the Orange Line, except from 7 to 10 a.m. and 4 to 7 p.m. Monday through Friday, and without restriction on weekends. Check the commuter rail timetable for bike details. Exit the station onto Dartmouth Street, and ride north past Copley Square to Commonwealth Avenue. Turn right and follow until Arlington Street. GPS coordinates for starting point: N42 21.221′ / W71 04.310′.

THE RIDE

You'll start at the intersection of Commonwealth Avenue and Arlington Street, just across from the iconic statue of George Washington that stands guard over the Public Garden. The strip of green space that runs from the Public Garden to Kenmore Square is the Commonwealth Avenue Mall, its 32 acres of lawn and paved promenade in the French boulevard style dotted with monuments and a variety of ornamental trees. While bikes are not allowed on the promenade, the bike lanes on either side of the mall afford an ideal view of the park as well as the exquisite buildings that line the street.

As you travel west along Commonwealth Avenue, take in the variety of brownstones: Their building materials, ornamental accents, and moods span the gamut from humble and drab to opulent and brash. Most brownstones are private residences or offices, interrupted periodically by a preserved mansion, academy, or other more public building. Look for the St. Botolph Club and Algonquin Club houses at 199 and 217 Commonwealth Ave., respectively, two homages to Boston's golden age of social clubs at the end of the nineteenth century. The St. Botolph Club was founded in 1880 with an eclectic mix of inaugural members that included painter John Singer Sargent, Henry Cabot Lodge, James Storrow, and Francis Parkman. The Algonquin Club was established a few years later in 1885, its ornate clubhouse designed by the same firm that tackled the Boston Public Library and the Museum of Fine Art, Boston. While originally chartered as gentlemen's clubs, both now accept women as full members.

Just past the Algonquin Club between Fairfield Street and Gloucester Street lies a particular monument of note along the mall: the Boston Women's Memorial. Dedicated in October 2003, the memorial honors the progressive ideas of Abigail Adams, Lucy Stone, and Phillis Wheatley and their contributions to the abolition and suffrage movements. These newest additions to the statuary along Commonwealth Avenue put Adams, Stone, and Wheatley in the company of William Lloyd Garrison, Leif Ericson, and Alexander Hamilton, all of whom also have memorials along the mall.

Turn right onto Hereford Street, passing Marlborough Street's brick-paved and gas-lit sidewalks before turning left onto Beacon Street. Keep right after the Charlesgate overpass as Beacon Street branches into Bay State Road at Boston University's Myles Standish Hall, once a hotel frequented by Babe Ruth before BU bought it for dormitory space in 1949. Bay State Road runs to the heart of BU's Charles River campus, passing dozens of brownstones the university has acquired for use as academic departments and student housing. At the intersection of Bay State Road and Granby Street lies the Boston University Castle, a Tudor mansion originally built in 1915 as a private residence and acquired by BU in 1939. The vine-covered building served as the university president's residence until 1967, and today hosts a variety of academic and social functions.

Turn left onto Granby Street and then right again onto Commonwealth Avenue to ride past the College of Arts and Sciences before turning left onto St. Mary's Street at Marsh Plaza. Turn left onto Mountfort Street and continue onto Park Drive, which leads to the Audobon Circle designed by Frederick Law Olmsted Sr. in 1887 at its intersection with Beacon Street. The Ruggles Baptist Church on the northeastern corner of the circle was completed in 1914 by famed Boston architect Ralph Adams Cram, who also designed the Cathedral of Saint John the Divine in New York City.

Turn left onto Beacon Street and then right onto Miner Street, which cuts behind the Harvard Vanguard hospital. Take a left onto Brookline Avenue, where you'll see the famed green walls of Fenway Park, the oldest professional baseball stadium in active use. Since its first opening day in April 1912, Fenway has been an enduring symbol of Boston's hopes, dreams, and aspirations. Just eight years after opening Fenway, the Red Sox sold Babe Ruth to the New

Bike Shops

Back Bay Bicycles is a Boston institution, with an experienced and friendly staff that will care for your equipment and can answer your maintenance questions. The shop also rents bikes by the day. Back Bay Bicycles is located at 362 Commonwealth Ave., Boston; (617) 247-2336; www.backbaybicycles.com.

Superb Bicycle near Fenway is known for its custom builds and keen focus on the aesthetics of cycling. Superb is located at 842 Beacon St., Boston; (617) 236-0752; www.superbbicycle.com.

The "Mother Church" of Christian Science joins classic architecture with modern structures by I. M. Pei.

York Yankees, thus beginning the more than eighty-year dry spell without a World Series title for Boston due to the "Curse of the Bambino." The Red Sox broke the curse in 2004 with their World Series win over the St. Louis Cardinals, rewarding Sox fans' decades of fanatical and often masochistic support.

Turn right down Landsdowne Street. On a home game day, Landsdowne is packed with fans, food vendors, and ticket hawkers, the crowd a sold-out one without fail. Those who couldn't swing a ticket pack the bars along Landsdowne and Yawkey Way on the other side of the park. At the end of Landsdowne, turn right onto Ipswich Street and follow it to Boylston Street. Turn left and take the curve right onto Park Drive, which you'll follow past the Fenway Victory Gardens before turning left onto Agassiz Road. Take the left at Fenway and a right onto Westland Avenue.

At the intersection of Westland and Massachusetts Avenues you'll see the dome of the "Mother Church," the First Church of Christ, Scientist, which was founded in Boston in 1879 by Mary Baker Eddy. Both the church and the *Christian Science Monitor* news outlet make the Christian Science Plaza one of the most recognizable landscapes in the city. Cross Massachusetts Avenue onto the plaza grounds. While the domed building was erected in 1906, the rest of the plaza, including the reflecting pool, brutalist administration building and Sunday School Building, was designed by famed architect I. M. Pei in the

1960s. The Mother Church is home to the world-famous Mapparium, as well.

Ride along the reflecting pool and turn left on Belvidere Street, curving onto Dalton Street after the Sheraton Boston. Turn right onto Boylston Street and ride toward Copley Square. Just before the square on your right is the Old South Church, its iconic green dome-topped tower completed in 1873. The interior of the church has seen several renovations, including a 1905 overhaul by Louis Comfort Tiffany. The interior was restored to its original design in the 1980s based on archival photographs and paint layer sampling.

On Copley Square itself you'll find the central branch of the Boston Public Library, the McKim Building. Proclaimed a "palace for the people" upon its opening in 1895, the McKim building is the centerpiece of the Boston Public Library system. The BPL is not only the second largest in the United States behind New York City's at nearly nine million print items, but is also notable for being the first such publicly supported library system in the country. The library's internal courtyard, intricate murals, and coffered ceiling are well worth a brief stopover at least.

Just across Copley Square lies the Trinity Church, constructed in 1877 after the Episcopalian congregation's former site on Summer Street burned down in the Great Boston Fire of 1872. Built by Henry Hobson Richardson, Trinity Church launched Richardson's Romanesque style, later adopted by public buildings around the country and characterized by clay roofs and heavy arches. Adjacent to Trinity is the John Hancock Tower, also designed by I. M. Pei's firm in the 1970s. The Hancock Tower is as famous for the hiccups in its construction as for its architectural achievement—the building's opening was delayed several years due to issues with its more than 10,000 window-panes, which had a nasty habit of falling off in heavy winds.

Continue along Boylston Street to Berkeley Street and turn left. Pass Newbury Street, and turn right at Commonwealth Avenue. One block up you'll reach Arlington Street, where you began the ride.

MILES AND DIRECTIONS

0.0 Begin at the intersection of Commonwealth Avenue and Arlington Street, across from the Public Garden.

0.8 Turn right onto Hereford Street.

0.9 Turn left onto Beacon Street.

1.2 Keep right to continue onto Bay State Road.

1.7 Turn left at Granby Street, and then right onto Commonwealth Avenue.

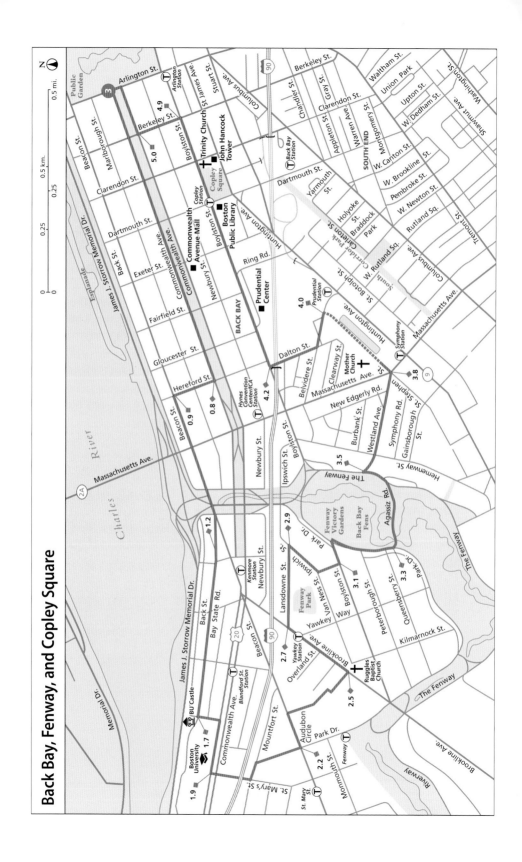

Back Bay, Fenway, and Copley Square

1.9 Turn left onto St. Mary's Street, then left again onto Mountfort Street.

2.2 Turn left at Park Drive, then right onto Miner Street, cutting behind the hospital to continue south on Fullerton Street.

2.5 Turn left onto Brookline Avenue.

2.7 Turn right onto Landsdowne Street.

The Comm Ave Mall connects the Public Garden to the rest of the Emerald Necklace via a shady, statue-lined walking path.

2.9 Turn right onto Ipswich Street.

3.1 Turn left onto Boylston Street, then right to merge onto Park Drive.

3.3 Turn left onto Agassiz Road, and continue onto the Fenway.

3.5 Turn right onto Westland Avenue.

3.8 Cross Massachusetts Avenue onto the Mother Church complex and ride north between the ornate sanctuary and the reflecting pool.

4.0 Turn left onto Belvidere Street, and then right onto Dalton Street at the Sheraton.

4.2 Turn right onto Boylston Street.

4.9 Turn left onto Berkeley Street.

5.0 Turn right onto Commonwealth Avenue.

5.1 Return to the starting point at Arlington Street.

RIDE INFORMATION

Local Events/Attractions

Opening Day: The celebration at Fenway Park for the first home game of the season is an unofficial holiday in Boston. Schoolkids and stockbrokers alike play hooky for Opening Day, usually the first week in April. www.boston.red sox.mlb.com

Mapparium at Mary Eddy Baker Library: This three-story stained-glass globe draws thousands to the Mother Church every year. Admission fees are discounted for students and seniors. www.marybakereddylibrary.org

Art and Architecture Tours at the Central Library: Free hour-long guided tours highlight the architecture of this exquisite landmark, as well as the murals and sculptures that adorn its halls. www.bpl.org/central/tours

Restrooms

Mile 1.9: Boston University has public restrooms and water fountains.

Mile 2.5: There are public restrooms and fountains in the Landmark Center, to your right on Brookline Avenue.

Mile 4.4: The Prudential Center Shopping Plaza has a number of restrooms open to the public.

Mile 4.6: The Boston Public Library has public restrooms.

The Fens to Jamaica Pond

Much like the Esplanade, Boston's Emerald Necklace offers cyclists a paved, tree-lined escape route from the city. This historic string of linear parks is a testament not only to Boston's efforts to integrate green space into its urban planning, but also to the city's strides toward restoring and maintaining natural landscapes for the enjoyment of all. This loop along the Muddy River takes you through the gardens of the Back Bay Fens, Olmsted Park, and around Jamaica Pond before returning to the Fenway for a final stretch past the ornate Museum of Fine Arts.

Start: Agassiz Road and The Fenway, Back Bay Fens

Length: 7.8 miles

Approximate riding time: 1.5 hours with stops

Best bike: Road bike, mountain bike, or hybrid

Terrain and trail surface: Portions of the Back Bay Fens trail are packed gravel or dirt. The Riverway, Olmsted Park, and Jamaica Pond paths are all paved, and the ride follows streets for some portions as well.

Traffic and hazards: Joggers, skateboarders, families with small children, dog walkers, and geese frequent the Emerald Necklace trails. Watch for traffic at intersections and while crossing bridges.

Things to see: Victory Gardens, Muddy River, James P. Kelleher Rose Garden, Leverett Pond, Olmsted Park, Ward Pond, Jamaica Pond, Isabella Stewart Gardner Museum, Museum of Fine Art, War Memorials

Maps: USGS: *Boston South* quad; DeLorme: *Massachusetts Atlas & Gazetteer,* p. 41

Getting there: By car: There is street parking along Fenway near Agassiz Road. From Copley Square, take Huntington Avenue southwest and turn right onto Forsythe Way. Turn right onto Fenway and find a metered spot. **By train:** Take the T Orange Line to Massachusetts

Avenue Station. Bikes are allowed on the Orange Line, except from 7 to 10 a.m. and 4 to 7 p.m. Monday through Friday, and without restriction on weekends. Take Massachusetts Avenue northwest out of the station and turn left at Westland Avenue. Cut through the park at Hemenway Street to the intersection of Fenway and Agassiz Road. GPS coordinates for starting point: N42 20.602′/W71 05.510′

THE RIDE

You'll start at the Back Bay Fens, one of the "jewels" in the Emerald Necklace, a historic string of parks designed by Frederick Law Olmsted. Widely considered the father of American landscape architecture, Olmsted also designed other famous parks, notably New York City's Central and Prospect Parks and the Niagara Reservation; he also designed the landscaping for the United States Capitol in Washington, DC. While the Emerald Necklace was never completed as originally planned by Olmsted in the 1870s, its thousand acres comprise more than half of Boston's parkland. It is also the only linear park system designed by Olmsted that remains intact today, running from the Boston Common in the center of the city all the way to Franklin Park in Jamaica Plain.

From the north shoulder of Agassiz Road and The Fenway, on the eastern edge of the Fens, you'll ride first along the reed-lined gravel path that runs behind the Fire Alarm Office. Stay right at the junction just before the Mother's Rest playground to join the sidewalk and ride across the Boylston Bridge over the Muddy River. Here you'll get your first glimpse of the marshland that makes up the Fens. With the landscape engineering wizardry for which he was so famous, Olmsted transformed the Fens from a foul blight on the landscape into the scenic and popular public space that it remains today. While Olmsted originally designed the Fens to be flushed daily by saltwater tides from the Charles River, the construction of the dam at Craigie Bridge in 1910 transformed it into a freshwater lagoon.

Just past the bridge, you'll turn left onto Path P, which winds through the Fenway Victory Gardens. These gardens were planted by Boston citizens in 1941 to grow vegetables for troops fighting in World War II as well as to supplement the needs of families on the homefront living under rationing. One of only two surviving victory gardens in the country, today the Fenway Victory Gardens are home to community growing space. The dirt path skirts past dozens of plots that host a staggering variety of plants, both edible and ornamental alike.

4

Turn left as you exit the Victory Gardens to continue along the Emerald Necklace sidewalk path. The round hedges on your left mark the James P. Kelleher Rose Garden, which was added to the landscape in 1930 by Olmsted's protege Arthur Shurcliff. This Fenway landmark is absolutely worth a detour (if you're visiting from May to September) for its more than 200 varieties of award-winning roses, including a number that were hybridized especially for the garden. Shurcliff also oversaw the addition of the athletic fields just past the rose garden.

You'll follow the Emerald Necklace path out of the Fens, then ride along Park Drive briefly past Brookline Avenue and the Landmark Center. Cross Park Drive to enter the Riverway section of the Emerald Necklace, which runs along Boston's border with the town of Brookline. Perhaps more than any other segment, the Riverway bears witness to Olmsted's talent for sculpting landscapes to maximum practicality with such subtlety you'd think nature itself accomplished the task. The paved trail, which once functioned as a bridle path, also carries you past two of Olmsted's signature stone bridges. You'll cross Parkway Road and Brookline Avenue before following River Road across Huntington Avenue to the Olmsted Park section of the Necklace.

Keep to the paved path on the right as you come to Leverett Pond, which forms another stretch of the boundary between Boston and Brookline. Like the Riverway path, the Riverdale Parkway was originally a carriage road. Follow the tree-lined trail past Willow Pond and Highland Road, crossing to ride into the street as you catch your first glimpse of Jamaica Pond at Perkins Street.

Unfortunately, bikes are not allowed on the path that runs along the western shore of the pond. Never fear, you'll ride along the waterfront soon enough after skirting the lake street-side for a few minutes. Jamaica Pond is the source of the Muddy River, as well as the largest body of freshwater in the Boston area. Once a wildly popular ice-skating spot in the winters, the pond remains a recreation focal point today as a fishing and boating destination.

Bike Shops

Ferris Wheels Bike Shop has been serving Jamaica Plain since 1982, its dedicated mechanics offering every service from refurbishing to brake checks, and even the occasional pancake breakfast for the cyclists of JP! Ferris Wheels is located at 66 South St., Jamaica Plain; (617) 524-2453; www.ferriswheelsbikeshop.

Giant Cycling World Boston is the first US shop owned by Giant Bicycles. With knowledgeable staff and well-stocked inventory, it's a one-stop solution to your repair or upgrade needs. The store is located at 11 Kilmarnock St., Boston; (617) 424-6400; www.giantboston.com.

The Back Bay Fens are a reminder of how much of Boston was once swampy marsh.

Each October the Jamaica Pond Lantern Parade rings the water in thousands of colorful paper lanterns that illuminate the changing autumn leaves and the entire lakefront.

After turning left onto Francis Parkman, you'll come to the Arborway at the southern edge of Jamaica Pond. Here bikes are allowed on the lakeside paths, which you'll follow alongside Pond Street past the Jamaica Pond boathouse. Brave summer revelers can rent rowboats, kayaks, and sailboats by the hour or day, or admire the spectacular view of the water from the gazebo just next to the dock.

After taking in the pond's beauty, continue on the right-hand path along the Jamaicaway, which leads back to Brookline. You'll pass the open fields and meadows of Jamaica Pond's Sugar Bowl, which hosts outdoor movies and concerts in the summer, as well as the community sports fields on the eastern edge of Olmsted Park. In the final heavily wooded stretch of the path along Leverett Pond, you could easily forget the urban metropolis that surrounds the greenway. Returning to River Road, you'll cross back across Huntington Avenue and backtrack to Brookline Avenue, where you'll turn right and ride on the street until it intersects with Riverway. Cross to the dirt path at the intersection.

Best Bike Rides Boston

The Riverway's dirt path offers a different perspective and new sights as you continue back toward the Fens. You'll pass again under the Bellevue Street bridge, then ride past the dramatic arch of the Chapel Street bridle path footbridge and its adjacent stone gazebo. The Riverway comes to an end at Park Drive, where you'll turn right to follow the Fenway past the campuses of Wheelock College, Simmons College, and Emmanuel College, which together make up the consortium known as the Colleges of the Fenway. Cross at Brookline Avenue to rejoin the Emerald Necklace dirt path as it winds around the southern edge of the Fens, where the ornate facade of the Isabella Stewart Gardner Museum comes into view. Well known for the 1990 theft of works by Rembrandt, Manet, and Degas valued at $500 million, the Gardner Museum has a storied past, fitting for its eccentric namesake founder. In addition to stipulating that her handpicked collection remain permanently displayed without alteration, Gardner's will provided that anyone named "Isabella" should gain free admission to the museum.

Just past the Gardner Museum lies the much larger Museum of Fine Art, where creepily massive bronze baby heads greet visitors outside the museum's Fenway entrance. Home to one of the premier collections in the country, the MFA building bears witness to the swift evolution of architectural vogue, with its neoclassical granite facade, West Wing designed by I. M. Pei, and glass-walled Art of the Americas annex. Hundreds of thousands of visitors pass through the MFA's galleries each year.

Just past the MFA, cross the footbridge to cut through the Fens. You'll pass Boston's memorials to soldiers who died in the twentieth-century wars, including a soaring monument to the fallen of World War II. This contemplative spot lends itself to considering the markedly different tones invoked by each memorial, each fitting to their place in military history: Where the World War II monument is bold and even triumphant in its remembrance, the memorials to those killed in Korea and Vietnam are smaller and less grandiose. The path continues back to Agassiz Road, where you'll turn right and return to the starting point at its intersection with the Fenway.

MILES AND DIRECTIONS

0.0 From the north shoulder of Agassiz Road at The Fenway, ride north along the reed-lined gravel path that runs behind the Fire Alarm Office.

0.1 Keep right at the fork at the Mother's Rest playground and follow the street across the river overpass.

0.3 Turn left onto Path P through the Fenway Victory Gardens.

0.6 Turn left at Park Drive to continue along the Fens path.

1.0 Stay right at the fork to continue along Park Drive.

1.2 Enter Park Drive at Fenway Street, continuing north past Brookline Avenue.

1.3 Cross Park Drive to enter the Riverway section of the Fens, taking the paved path on the right.

2.1 Continue across Parkway Road, carrying your bike across the small flight of steps.

2.2 Turn right onto Brookline Avenue then cross left onto the bike path via the crosswalk.

2.5 Carefully cross Huntington Avenue via the break in the median and enter Olmsted Park, keeping to the far right at Leverett Pond.

3.3 Turn right onto Perkins Street.

3.6 Turn left at Francis Parkman Drive.

4.0 Cross the Arborway onto the Jamaica Pond bike path, keeping right at the fork by the boathouse.

5.6 Exit the park and cross back across Huntington Avenue via the break in the median to River Road.

5.7 Turn right onto Brookline Avenue, then cross left at Riverway onto the unpaved path.

6.1 Cross Pilgrim Road to continue along the unpaved bike path.

6.7 Exit the Riverway and cross to the bike path in the middle of Fenway and Park Drive.

6.8 Cross Brookline Avenue to continue along the bike path.

7.1 Cross Park Drive to continue along the bike path.

7.5 Turn left across the footbridge.

7.6 Turn right at Park Drive and enter Agassiz Road, which you'll ride east.

7.8 Arrive back at the starting point along the Fenway.

The Fens to Jamaica Pond

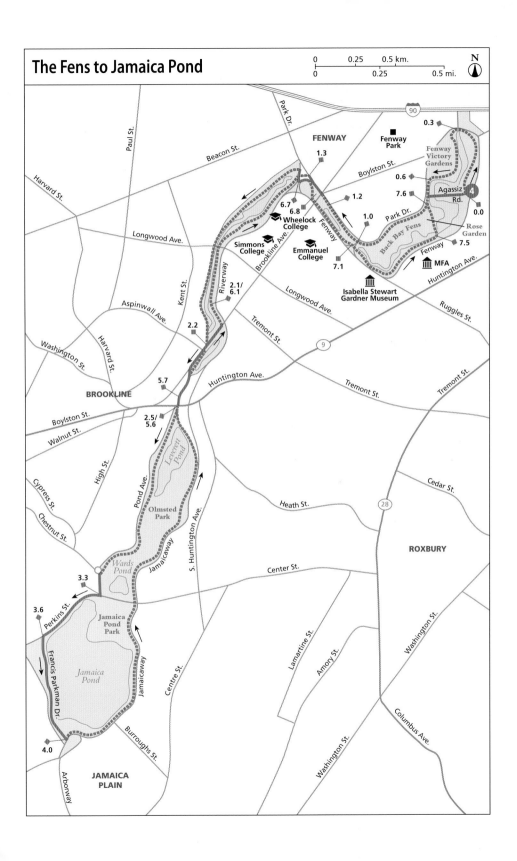

Frederick Law Olmsted oversaw the addition of many carriage roads and bridges to the Fens.

RIDE INFORMATION

Local Events/Attractions

Party in the Park: This annual soiree to support the Emerald Necklace Conservancy happens every spring at the James P. Kelleher Rose Garden. www.emeraldnecklace.org

Jamaica Plain Music Festival: Each summer, the JP Music Fest brings national and local acts together for an outdoor frenzy at Pinebank Field. www.jpmusicfestival.com

Jamaica Pond Lantern Festival: Every October the Jamaica Pond Lantern Parade, sponsored by Friends of Jamaica Pond, rings the water in light. www.friendsofjamaicapond.org

Restrooms

Mile 1.3 and Mile 6.8: The Landmark Center on Park Drive has public restrooms.

Mile 4.3: The Jamaica Pond Boathouse has public restrooms and a water fountain.

Boston Harbor Loop

Boston's harbor is a central dimension of its economy, its culture, and its distinctive character. From the fresh-catch seafood it's offered to local cuisine to its history as a major port, including its recent revitalization as part of the Seaport District, the city's oceanfront location has woven its way through Boston's story since the city's colonial beginnings. As you wind along the harbor's edge and take in the mix of historic and modern buildings that line the shore, enjoy a ride filled with ocean views, boardwalk leisure, and rejuvenating breezes.

Start: Christopher Columbus Waterfront Park

Length: 10.7 miles

Approximate riding time: 1–1.5 hours with stops

Best bike: Road bike, mountain bike, or hybrid

Terrain and trail surface: Well-paved urban roads and bike paths

Traffic and hazards: Joggers, families with small children, and dog walkers frequent the Harborwalk.

Things to see: Christopher Columbus Waterfront Park, Long Wharf, Rowes Wharf, Fan Pier, World Trade Center Pier, Institute of Contemporary Art, Black Falcon Terminal, Moakley Courthouse, Harpoon Brewery, Pleasure Bay, Castle Island, L Street Beach, M Street Beach, Curley Community Center, Telegraph Hill, Boston Tea Party Museum, Boston Children's Museum, Rose Kennedy Greenway, South Station

Maps: USGS: *Boston South* quad; DeLorme: *Massachusetts Atlas & Gazetteer*, p. 41

Getting there: By car: Park in the Harbor Garage next to the New England Aquarium. From downtown, take Boylston Street east onto Essex Street and turn left at Atlantic Avenue. Follow signs to the aquarium and turn right on Milk Street, where you'll see the garage.

Christopher Columbus Park is just on the other side of the Marriott Waterfront Hotel. **By train:** Take the T Blue Line to the Aquarium. Bikes are allowed on the Red Line, except from 7 to 9 a.m. and 4 to 6 p.m. Monday through Friday, and without restriction on weekends. Turn right out of the T station and walk your bike around the Marriott Waterfront Hotel to Christopher Columbus Waterfront Park. GPS coordinates for starting point: N42 21.655' / W71 03.056'

THE RIDE

You'll start at Christopher Columbus Park near the North End, right on the Inner Harbor. Ride toward the water along the path around the Marriott hotel onto Long Wharf. When first built around 1710, Long Wharf extended nearly half a mile from State Street into the harbor and was the busiest pier in the city. Landfill along the shore has since shortened the wharf significantly.

Ride along the wharf onto the wooden boardwalk, which you'll follow around to Central Wharf and the front of the New England Aquarium. The aquarium features marine collections of jellyfish, penguins, and scores of other ocean creatures from the Atlantic and around the world, and draws hundreds of thousands of visitors each year. Take the ramp to the left of the entrance promenade to ride around the aquarium's perimeter, where you'll find the harbor seal exhibit as part of the public plaza. Even those who can't afford the aquarium's pricey admission can still watch the seals play in their transparent tank.

Continue along the other side of Central Wharf and around to India Wharf and Rowes Wharf behind the Boston Harbor Hotel, whose enormous arched entryway hosts music and movie screenings during the summer. Carry your bike up the steps at Northern Avenue and cross the pedestrian bridge to the South Boston Waterfront.

Boston Tea Party Factoid

Many people incorrectly believe that the ships involved in the Boston Tea Party were of British origin. In fact, all three ships were built and commissioned in the colonies. On the night of December 16, 1773, more than 342 chests of tea belonging to the British East India Company were dumped into Boston Harbor over the course of several hours. Two of these ships have been expertly restored at the Boston Tea Party Museum, as a memorial to Boston's long-standing penchant for theatrical and daring political statements.

Columbus Park is the ideal spot to nap off a cannoli from the North End while watching the ships come into the harbor.

Popularly known as the Seaport District, the waterfront in South Boston has benefitted from feverish development and face-lifts over the past two decades. This massive effort has transformed what was once rather desolate prime real estate into a vibrant district of restaurants, museums, and nightlife. Take the path left around Fan Pier Plaza behind the federal Moakley Courthouse, its waterfront face made entirely of glass panes. Follow the water's edge behind the Institute of Contemporary Art, once a "renegade" offshoot of Manhattan's Museum of Modern Art. The first museum built in Boston for more than 100 years, the ICA moved from a Back Bay location on Boylston Street to its newly constructed seaport home in 2006. Its offbeat collections draw ire and admiration alike, as does its brazenly modern building.

Cross through the ICA parking lot on the other side back to Northern Avenue. Turn left onto Seaport Boulevard, then cross onto the World Trade Center Pier. Cross back onto Northern Avenue in front of Boston Fish Pier, where the city's haddock, cod, and all manner of edible sea creatures from around the world come into port. Follow Northern Avenue for a brief departure from the shore, passing the beloved Harpoon Brewery beyond the traffic circle. Turn right at Tide Street and then left on Drydock Avenue toward Black Falcon Pier, where cruise ships and military vessels come in and out of the harbor. Follow Black Falcon Avenue past the cruise terminals, turning left after the last parking lot to follow the waterfront once again.

Cut through the small Marine Industrial Park to turn left and cross the water via Summer Street into the heart of South Boston. Turn left onto East First Street and pass Medal of Honor Park, continuing onto Shore Road with a slight left at Marine Park. At the end of the park you'll see the waters of Pleasure Bay. Enclosed by the Head Island Causeway, Pleasure Bay's protected waters are a favorite swimming and beach leisure spot. Turn left onto William J. Day Boulevard to follow the bay to Castle Island. No longer a true island due to extensive landfill, Castle Island is home to Fort Independence and has been the site of fortifications since the mid-1600s, making it the oldest continuously fortified site build by the English in the United States. The current granite, pentagon-shaped fort was built in the mid-1800s, but gradually fell out of use after the Civil War. Frederick Olmsted Law envisioned connecting Castle Island to the Emerald Necklace via a parkway to be called the Dorchesterway, which never materialized. As the sidewalks around the fort itself do not allow cyclists, walk your bike until you reach the causeway, where you can ride again.

Follow the causeway around the other side of Pleasure Bay and along William J. Day Boulevard once again, past the popular L and M Street Beaches and the Curley Community Center, completed in 1931 by Mayor James Curley as a source of recreation for the working-class residents of South Boston and Dorchester. Cross the boulevard onto I Street to begin the ride back through South Boston. Climb Telegraph Hill through historic Dorchester Heights, passing the Gate of Heaven Catholic Church before turning left onto Emerson Street at East Broadway, then taking a right onto H Street. Turn left onto First Street, which you'll follow to D Street. Take a right onto D Street and ride across the overpass that bridges the Massachusetts Turnpike back into the Seaport District.

Bike Shops

MyBike styles itself as an "untraditional" bike shop because of its concierge "house calls," electric bike offerings, and other add-ons to typical services you'd expect from a full-service bike shop. MyBike is located at 391 West Broadway, South Boston; (617) 202-9720; www.mybike.com **Urban AdvenTours** offers tours and rentals in addition to expert repairs and bike sales. The North End shop is located at 103 Atlantic Ave., Boston; (617) 670-0637; www.urbanadventours.com.

Turn left at Congress Street, which you'll follow past the Boston Fire Museum and Boston Children's Museum and over the Fort Point Channel into the Financial District. Cross Atlantic Avenue onto the Rose Kennedy Greenway, which follows the thoroughfare back toward the North End. Pass through the parkway's public art installations and lawns back toward the aquarium. Just past the Aquarium T station, cross Atlantic Avenue into Christopher Columbus Park, where you began the ride.

MILES AND DIRECTIONS

0.0 From the waterfront at Christopher Columbus Park, head toward the harbor and follow Long Wharf around to Central Wharf and the New England Aquarium.

0.5 Take the ramp next to the aquarium entrance promenade around to the harbor seal exhibit.

0.7 Turn left to ride around India Wharf, continuing past Rowes Wharf behind the Boston Harbor Hotel.

1.1 Carry your bike up the short flight of steps and cross the Northern Avenue pedestrian bridge to the Seaport District.

1.2 Turn left onto the Fan Pier path beside the Daily Catch restaurant, following the waterfront behind the Institute of Contemporary Art.

1.7 Turn right through the parking lot and take Northern Avenue left.

1.9 Take a left onto Seaport Boulevard.

2.0 Cross Seaport Boulevard to the World Trade Center pier.

2.5 Turn left onto Seaport Boulevard.

2.7 Continue straight through the traffic circle onto Northern Avenue.

3.1 Turn right at Tide Street and then left onto Drydock Avenue, then follow Black Falcon Avenue as it loops around the cruise terminal.

3.8 Turn left just past Design Center Place and then right to ride along the water again.

3.9 Cut left through Marine Industrial Park, then cross the water along Summer Street.

4.4 Turn left onto East First Street.

5.0 Continue onto Shore Road with a slight left at Marine Park.

5.2 Cross William J. Day Boulevard and turn left along the Head Island Causeway.

5.6 Walk your bike through Castle Island Park.

6.0 Continue riding along Head Island Causeway.

6.6 Keep right at the end of Pleasure Bay to continue between the harbor front and William J. Day Boulevard.

7.6 Cross William J. Day Boulevard to turn right up I Street.

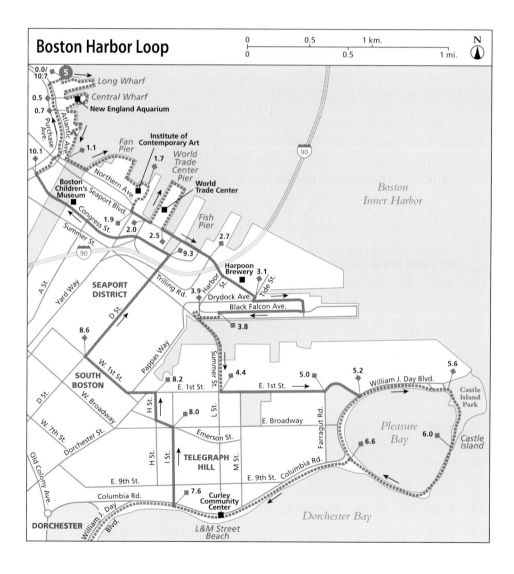

Boston Harbor Loop

8.0 Turn left onto Emerson Street and then right at H Street.

8.2 Turn left onto East First Street.

8.6 Turn right at D Street.

9.3 Turn left at Congress Street.

10.1 Cross Atlantic Avenue to turn right onto the Rose Kennedy Greenway path.

10.7 At the Marriott hotel, cross Atlantic Avenue to Christopher Columbus Waterfront Park.

RIDE INFORMATION

Local Events/Attractions

Boston Harborfest: Boston Harbor's Independence Day celebrations on July 4th or the week of the 4th include the display of the Liberty Tall Ships Fleet. www.bostonharborfest.com

Boston Tea Party Museum: Actors demonstrate this historic revolutionary act steeped in rebellion against unfair taxation. www.bostonteapartyship.com

Harpoonfest and Oktoberfest: The homegrown Harpoon Brewery (617-456-2322) knows how to throw a great party, and beer festivals are its specialty. www.harpoonbrewery.com/festivals

Restaurants

No Name Restaurant: Steeped in mystery, this waterfront seafood house at 15½ Fish Pier in Boston (617-338-7539) is a must-try. www.nonamerestaurant .com

Restrooms

Start/finish: The Marriott Waterfront Hotel has restrooms.
Mile 5.6: Castle Island has restrooms and water fountains.
Mile 7.0: Curley Community Center has restrooms and water.

East Boston Greenway, Belle Isle Marsh, and Deer Island

The East Boston Greenway makes for a quick getaway to the seaside along its paved rail-trail path. After rolling through Bremen Street Park's urban wild, you'll take in the serene and secluded landscape of Belle Isle Marsh. The coastline will then take you through Winthrop and around Deer Island for scenic views of Boston from across the harbor. The last leg of the return ride brings you to Constitution Beach, one of the best vantage points for watching planes coming into Logan Airport across the water.

Start: Lewis Mall Harbor Park, near the Maverick station on the Blue Line and the intersection of Lewis Street and Marginal Street

Length: 17.5 miles

Approximate riding time: 2.5–3 hours with stops

Best bike: Mountain bike or road bike

Terrain and trail surface: Mostly paved roads through flat urban and suburban residential neighborhoods, with occasional small hills in the Winthrop area and around Deer Island. The Belle Isle Marsh Reservation is unpaved but well packed. Some sections of the paved paths along the shoreline can be sandy or wet.

Traffic and hazards: The East Boston Greenway, Belle Isle Marsh, and Deer Island path are closed to vehicles. Most of the streets in between are quiet, although two sections of the route follow busier roads. Watch out for dogs and joggers on the East Boston Greenway, Belle Isle Marsh, Deer Island, and Constitution Beach paths.

Things to see: Lewis Mall Harbor Park, East Boston Greenway, Bremen Street Park, Belle Isle Marsh Reservation, Winthrop Beach, Deer Island, Crystal Cove, Constitution Beach.

Maps: USGS: *Boston South, Boston North, Lynn,* and *Hull* quads; DeLorme: *Massachusetts Atlas & Gazetteer,* p. 41

Getting there: By car: There is limited street parking (both metered and unmetered) in and around Maverick Square. Take the Callahan Tunnel (MA 1A N) toward Logan Airport from downtown Boston. Exit at Porter Street and turn right onto Paris Street. After three blocks turn left onto Winthrop Street and park near Maverick Square. The Lewis Mall runs southwest from the Maverick station to the Lewis Mall Harbor Park. **By train:** Take the Blue Line to the Maverick station in East Boston. Bikes are allowed on the Blue Line, except from 7 to 9 a.m. inbound and 4 to 6 p.m. outbound Monday through Friday, and without restriction on weekends. The Lewis Mall runs southwest from the station to the Lewis Mall Harbor Park. GPS coordinates for starting point: N42 21.98' / W71 02.50'

THE RIDE

East Boston ("Eastie") is one of the most diverse neighborhoods in the metro area. Originally five islands that were connected by landfill in the 1830s, the neighborhood has long been home to immigrants from Ireland, Italy, Russia, and, most recently, all across Latin America. The heart of East Boston is Maverick Square, just a few blocks from the harbor. You'll begin the ride at Lewis Mall Harbor Park at the edge of Maverick's Lewis Mall, from which you can see downtown Boston across the water.

Another two blocks from the harborside lies the beginning to the East Boston Greenway, marked by a pale blue caboose in homage to the path's origins as a railway corridor. Conrail donated the disused corridor to Massachusetts in 1997, and Boston incorporated it into the Bremen Street linear park as part of the infamous "Big Dig" transportation project. You'll pass Logan Airport as you ride through the greenway, which runs alongside the Massachusetts Turnpike overpass. The juxtaposition of the park's open space and greenery against the towering highway is striking. A large map in the center of the park depicts the five original islands that were joined to create East Boston.

From the end of the East Boston Greenway you'll ride through East Boston along Saratoga Street. Note the gold tower atop Orient Heights, the hill to the northeast. This is the back of the 35-foot Madonna Shrine, an Eastie icon built in 1954. The shrine is the national headquarters for the Don Orione order and is a full-size replica of the Don Orione shrine in Rome. While the North End is considered Boston's "Little Italy," the Orient Heights neighborhood is where the first Italian immigrants who came to Massachusetts settled in the 1860s and 1870s.

Continuing onto Bennington Street, you'll pass the Suffolk Downs T station, named for the famous Thoroughbred track, which is just barely visible from the street. World-famous horses like Seabiscuit and Funny Cide have raced at Suffolk Downs, and the Beatles played a set on the track's infield in August 1966. Just past Suffolk Downs lies the entrance to the Belle Isle Marsh Reservation. Boston's last surviving salt marsh, Belle Isle has a mix of saltwater, freshwater, and meadow habitats that are home to songbirds, muskrats, opossums, snapping turtles, and fish. The path around Belle Isle includes two observation points, from which you can take in a full view of the 240-acre reservation.

From the marsh you will cut through the Beachmont neighborhood on the southern edge of Revere. The rocky coastline will take you across the narrow isthmus that connects Winthrop to the mainland. This was one of the first areas settled by the Puritans, who called it Pullen Poynt when they annexed it as a grazing ground in 1630. The modern seaside town is named for Governor John Winthrop, one of the early leaders of the Massachusetts Bay Colony.

You'll pass Winthrop Beach before crossing through a neighborhood to follow Crystal Cove past the Winthrop Yacht Club to Deer Island. Now a peninsula that juts into Boston Harbor, Deer Island was once separated from Winthrop by the Shirley Gut channel, which was filled in by the New England Hurricane of 1938. Since colonial times the island has been used for a number of purposes, some of them fairly sordid. During King Philip's War in the 1670s, the island was an internment camp for Native Americans. Through the 1800s, Deer Island was a quarantine station and hospital for immigrants fleeing Ireland, and from 1896 to 1991 the island housed a low-security prison.

Wastewater to Clean Water

The Deer Island Treatment Center processes more than 350 million gallons of wastewater every day, taking in sewage and runoff and converting it into safe water that is flushed back into the water table and the sea. Wastewater arrives at the plant from forty-three communities in the Massachusetts Bay area and is initially screened through massive grit chambers filled with dirt and sand. Centrifuges then separate out the liquid and pass it through the egg-carton-shaped digesters, where oxygen is added to speed up the elimination of organic matter by microbes. The water then flows into Massachusetts Bay, while any solids are collected and dried into decontaminated fertilizer for agriculture in western Massachusetts.

Deer Island is not only a beautiful landscape, but also a critical cog in Boston's water supply.

Today, Deer Island is part of the Boston Harbor Islands string of parks. Follow the paved path around the island for breathtaking views of the city from across the harbor. The path winds around the Deer Island Water Treatment Plant, whose massive egg-shaped digester facilities and 200-foot wind turbines make it a harbor landmark. Lucky for visitors, the plant gives off no offending odor despite being one of the largest wastewater treatment sites in New England and does not spoil the harbor view from the island's southern tip. The happy marriage of modern technology and natural beauty makes Deer Island a favorite success story among environmental advocates.

From Deer Island you'll pass again around Crystal Cove and through Winthrop, going by the famous Belle Isle Seafood shack as you cross back into East Boston. (Lobster rolls make great fuel for the last leg of the ride!) Turning into Constitution Beach Park, you'll have a fantastic view of Logan Airport just across the water. While Constitution Beach is much smaller and less frequented than nearby destinations like Revere or Winthrop Beach, there's always at least one or two families here watching the planes take off from the Logan tarmac.

After passing through Constitution Beach you'll head back to the East Boston Greenway and Maverick Square.

MILES AND DIRECTIONS

0.0 From the end of the Lewis Mall Harbor Park, ride northeast toward Maverick station and turn right onto Marginal Street.

0.1 Pass Bremen Street and turn left into the East Boston Greenway.

1.2 Turn left to stay on the path.

1.3 Cross the street and turn left onto Neptune Road.

1.4 Turn right onto Saratoga Street.

2.5 Continue straight through the roundabout onto Ford Street, then make a slight left onto Breed Street.

2.6 Turn right onto Ashley Street.

2.7 Turn left onto Bennington Street. Watch out for traffic from both directions.

3.3 Turn right into the Belle Isle Marsh Reservation. Turn right at the roundabout and cross through the parking lot to the trailhead.

3.6 Turn right and continue onto the boardwalk lookout, then return to the main path and turn right. Continue straight until you return to the parking lot.

4.1 Cross the parking lot out of the reservation and turn right back onto Bennington Street.

4.5 Turn right onto Winthrop Avenue.

East Boston Greenway, Belle Isle Marsh, and Deer Island

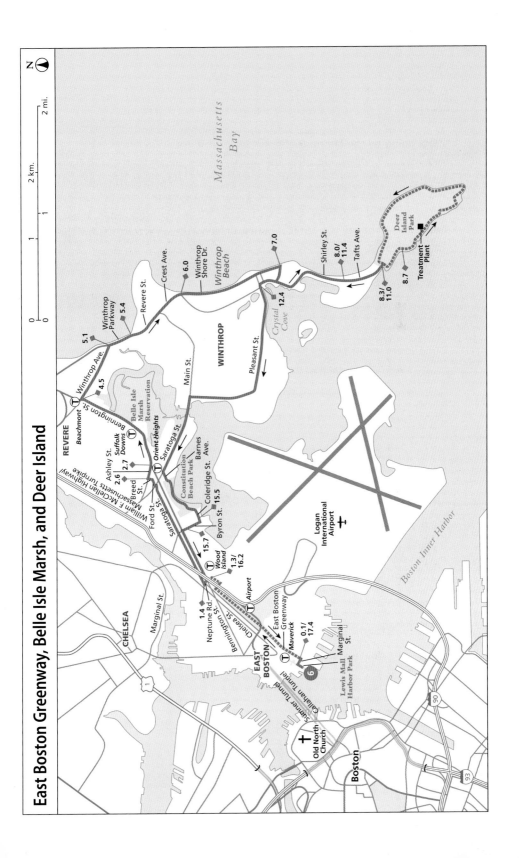

Keep a sharp eye out for the muskrats, opossums, and snapping turtles that make their home in the Belle Isle Marsh.

5.1   Turn right onto Winthrop Parkway.

5.4   Continue straight onto Revere Street, which turns into Winthrop Shore Drive.

6.0   Stay left to remain on Winthrop Shore Drive.

7.0   Turn right onto Beacon Street.

7.1   Turn left onto Shirley Street.

7.9   Turn left onto Elliot Street.

8.0   Turn right onto Tafts Avenue.

8.3   Turn right just past the Deer Island Park entrance onto the paved path.

8.7   Stay right at the fork.

11.0   Turn right into the parking lot and continue back onto Tafts Avenue.

11.4   Turn right onto Shirley Street.

12.4 Turn left onto Washington Avenue, which turns into Pleasant Avenue.

14.0 Turn left onto Saratoga Street.

14.8 Turn left onto Barnes Avenue.

14.9 Turn left into Constitution Beach Park.

15.3 Turn right just after Porrazzo Rink, then turn left onto Coleridge Street and follow it out of the park.

15.5 Turn right onto Byron Street.

15.7 Turn left onto Bennington Street.

16.1 Turn left onto Neptune Road.

16.2 Turn right onto the East Boston Greenway just past the intersection of Neptune Road and Vienna Street.

17.4 Turn right to exit the East Boston Greenway onto Marginal Street

17.5 Return to the Lewis Mall.

RIDE INFORMATION

Local Events/Attractions

ZUMIX Firehouse: This cultural center and gallery hosts live music, films, and dance nights. It's located at 260 Sumner St., East Boston; (617) 568-9777; www .zumix.org.

HarborArts Festival: This celebration of public art each fall features live music and gallery showings of works by the HarborArts collective of sculptor-conservationists, who use monumental sculpture to raise awareness for ocean preservation. www.harborarts.org

Restaurants

Belle Isle Seafood: This popular hole-in-the-wall eatery is famous for its lobster rolls and fried oysters. It's located right on the route at 1267 Saratoga St., East Boston; (617) 567-1619; www.belleisleseafood.com.

Restrooms

Start/finish: Maverick Square has a number of chain restaurants.
Mile 1.0 and 16.4: The Bremen Street Park has public restrooms in the security building.
Mile 8.3: Deer Island Park has public restrooms in the visitor center.
Mile 15.2: Constitution Beach has public restrooms.

Southwest Corridor Park and Jamaica Plain

The Southwest Corridor Park (SCP) cuts through Back Bay and the South End toward Franklin Park and Arnold Arboretum in Jamaica Plain, locally called "JP." The paved corridor provides a welcome alternative to cycling commuters into the city, as well as a scenic jaunt out of downtown. The SCP's straight shot will take you through a number of distinct neighborhoods between Back Bay and JP, including the Northeastern University campus in Mission Hill and Roxbury's Hyde, Jackson, and Egleston Squares. You'll end with a brief tour of Jamaica Plain (and maybe even a stop at the J.P. Licks Ice Cream mothership) before rejoining the SCP for the return leg.

Start: Southwest Corridor Park, across from Back Bay Station

Length: 8.1 miles

Approximate riding time: 1.5–2 hours with stops

Best bike: Road bike, mountain bike, or hybrid

Terrain and trail surface: Paved paths, roads, and bike lanes

Traffic and hazards: Joggers, skateboarders, families with small children, and dog walkers frequent the SCP path. Watch for traffic at intersections and along streets.

Things to see: Southwest Corridor Park, Titus Sparrow Park, Boston Police Department Headquarters, Northeastern University, Roxbury Community College, Islamic Society of Boston Cultural Center, Jamaica Plain, Soldier's Monument, J.P. Licks, Loring-Greenough House

Maps: USGS: *Boston South* quad. DeLorme: *Massachusetts Atlas & Gazetteer*, p. 41

Getting there: By car: There is limited street parking in Back Bay or the South End near the SCP trail, but garage parking is available at Tent City on Dartmouth Street. **By train:** Take the T Orange Line or commuter rail to Back Bay station. Bikes are allowed on the Orange Line, except from 7 to 10 a.m. and 4 to 7 p.m. Monday through Friday, and without restriction on weekends. Check the commuter rail timetable for bike directions. Exit the station onto Dartmouth Street—the SCP begins just across the street. GPS coordinates for starting point: N42 20.821' / W71 04.589'

THE RIDE

Today, the Southwest Corridor Park that runs through Back Bay, the South End, Roxbury, and Jamaica Plain is a well-traveled but serene stretch dotted with small parks and green space. But the corridor's history is rooted in dramatic protest and civil disobedience. In the 1960s, housing in the neighborhoods along the corridor were razed to make way for an expansion of I-95 into downtown Boston. Hundreds of protests and angry meetings with state development offices culminated in Bostonians lying down on the ground in front of bulldozers in opposition to the destruction of their homes for the eyesore of a polluting expressway. Their "people before highways" demonstrations prompted Massachusetts governor Francis Sargent to cancel the highway project in favor of developing the city's mass transit infrastructure and open space. The Southwest Corridor Park parallel to the expanded Orange Line was opened in 1987.

You'll start the ride at the eastern end of the Southwest Corridor Park, just across from the Back Bay Train Station. Appropriate to the protest that led to the creation of the corridor, its head lies next to the Tent City apartment development, the site of gentrification protests in the 1960s. In April 1968, hundreds of residents who had been displaced by city development projects occupied a parking lot where the apartments now stand, demanding an end to the city's demolition of older, affordable housing in favor of luxury units and shopping space. Led by organizer Mel King, who would later win a seat in the Massachusetts legislature, the protestors erected a "tent city" on the lot as a visual demand for city hall to include affordable housing in its development plans.

From Tent City you'll ride west along the Southwest Corridor Park, cutting through the South End via the corridor's garden-lined path. At West Newton Street you'll enter Titus Sparrow Park, named for the South End resident and tennis aficionado who helped found the first African-American nonprofit tennis club in the country, the Sportsmen's Tennis Club, in Dorchester. Sparrow was also the first black umpire in the United States Tennis Association. Today his namesake park behind the Union United Methodist Church hosts summertime concerts and youth sports leagues in reflection of Sparrow's commitment to community building through recreation.

After passing the park and crossing Massachusetts Avenue, you'll see a sign for Pierre Lallement Southwest Corridor Bike Path as you continue west along the trail. Born in France in 1843, Pierre Lallement developed the velocipede transmission and pedal system typically credited to Pierre Michaux and the Olivier brothers, who were acquaintances of his in Paris. Lallement crossed to America in 1865 and secured a US patent for his design but died unrecognized and penniless in Boston in 1891, just blocks from the corridor path. The path was rededicated in his honor in 1993 as part of the International Cycling History Conference held in Boston that year, in recognition of his and Boston's place in cycling history.

You'll follow the corridor along Columbus Avenue as it crosses through the Northeastern University campus. Established in 1898 at the nearby Huntington Avenue YMCA, Northeastern began as an "evening institute" to teach immigrant men introductory courses in law, engineering, and finance. The university continued to be associated with the Boston Young Men's Christian Association until formally separating in 1948. Northeastern University is particularly notable as a pioneer in cooperative education, which combines classroom learning with work experience for academic credit.

Bike Shops

Bikes Not Bombs is a nonprofit bike shop in Jamaica Plain that collects used bikes to ship to less-developed countries in Africa, Latin America, and the Caribbean. The expert mechanics also refurbish and repair every type of bike imaginable for their retail shop, which supports the shop's economic development and local youth programs. The BNB shop is located at 284 Amory St., Jamaica Plain; (617) 522-0222; bikesnotbombs.org.
Community Bike Supply in the South End does it all, from tune-ups and flat repair to overstock sales on high-end gear. The shop is located at 496 Tremont St., Boston; (617) 542-8623; www.communitybicycle.com.
Ferris Wheels Bike Shop has been serving Jamaica Plain since 1982, its dedicated mechanics offering every service from refurbishing to brake checks, and even the occasional pancake breakfast for the cyclists of JP! Ferris Wheels is located at 66 South St., Jamaica Plain; (617) 524-2453; www.ferriswheelsbikeshop.

PIERRE LALLEMENT BIKE PATH
SOUTHWEST CORRIDOR RESERVATION

dcr ✿ MASSACHUSETTS DEPARTMENT OF
CONSERVATION AND RECREATION

Inventor Pierre Lallement moved to Boston from France, and this path honors his contributions to modern cycling.

Just past the university campus and the headquarters of the Boston Police Department you'll cross into the Roxbury neighborhood of Boston. One of the first towns founded in the Massachusetts Bay Colony, Roxbury was its own municipality until its annexation to Boston in 1868. Touted by the city as the "heart of black culture in Boston," Roxbury received the influx of African Americans from the South in the 1940s and 1950s and was the training ground for such notable civil rights leaders as Malcolm X and Martin Luther King Jr. Today, the neighborhood is also home to a diverse immigrant community drawing from Latin America and the Caribbean. The corridor follows the border of Roxbury and Mission Hill as you ride southwest past Malcolm X Boulevard, where you can see the minaret and dome of the Islamic Society of Boston Cultural Center.

Continuing on, you'll pass Jackson Square and the Stony Brook MBTA station, which marks the transition from Roxbury into Jamaica Plain, or "JP." A string of garden parks runs from Boylston Street to the end of the corridor at New Washington Street. These community gardens provide plots for residents of the surrounding neighborhoods to grow vegetables and ornamentals.

Exit the Southwest Corridor Park, turn right onto New Washington Street then take your first right to ride along South Street into JP proper. One of the first areas of Boston to be settled, today JP is an eclectic neighborhood with a considerable immigrant population and active arts scene. JP is also a hotbed of civic activism on a diverse range of issues and home to an array of summer music, art, and earth festivals. Continuing up South Street to Centre Street, you'll pass the Loring-Greenough House, which was constructed by a British naval commodore in 1760 and confiscated as Tory property at the outset of the Revolutionary War. The house served as a military hospital during the war, making it the only such facility surviving in the Boston area today. The Jamaica Plain Tuesday Club purchased the house in 1924 for restoration, and today it houses a fine collection of art and period furnishings. Just across from the Loring-Greenough house lies Soldier's Monument, a memorial to the Civil War fallen.

The storefronts and restaurants along Centre Street provide a prime illustration of JP's hodgepodge. Riding north, you'll pass an Irish pub, an Indian bistro, and a burrito joint within three blocks. Just a couple blocks on, a giant cow's head protruding from a redbrick building will alert you to the location of the original J.P. Licks ice cream shop and factory. Bostonians tend to be polarized devotees to either J.P. Licks or fellow hometown creamery Emack & Bolio's, both of which make a wonderful scoop. At the J.P. Licks mothership, you can get a first taste of new flavors and products.

Once you've hit your dairy quota and rewarded yourself for a fine ride, follow Centre Street back to Jackson Square, where you'll rejoin the Southwest Corridor Park for the return leg to Back Bay.

MILES AND DIRECTIONS

0.0 From the end of the Southwest Corridor Park across from Back Bay Station, ride southwest.

0.5 Go up the ramp and cross Massachusetts Avenue to continue along the SCP path.

0.6 Keep left to stay on the SCP path.

0.7 Turn left onto Camden Street, then right to ride along Columbus Avenue. Watch signs indicating which sides of the path are for pedestrians and cyclists.

1.2 Cross Ruggles Street to continue along SCP path.

2.2 Cross Centre Street to continue along the SCP path.

2.9 Stay left past New Minton Street to continue along the SCP path.

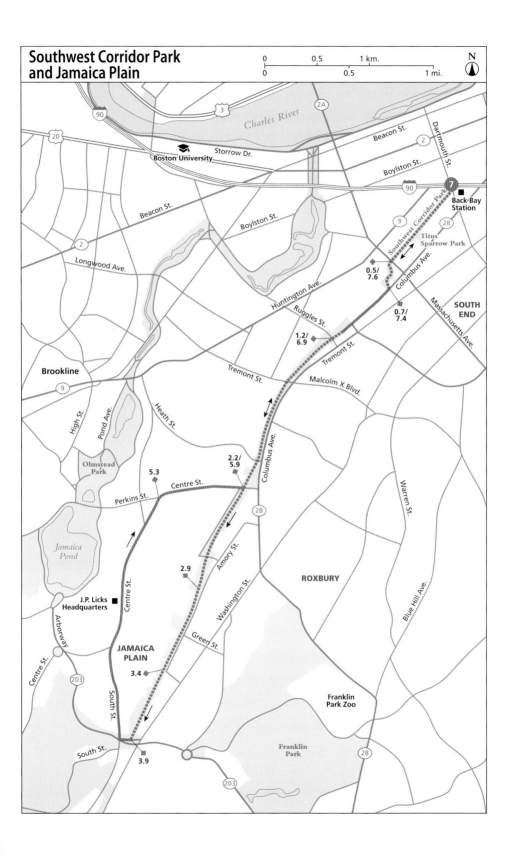

Southwest Corridor Park
and Jamaica Plain

0   0.5   1 km.

0   0.5   1 mi.

N

Charles River

90

20

3

2A

Storrow Dr.

Boston University

Beacon St.

Dartmouth St.

2

Boylston St.

90

7

Back Bay
Station

Beacon St.

Boylston St.

9

Southwest Corridor Park

28

Titus
Sparrow Park

2

Longwood Ave.

Huntington Ave.

0.5/
7.6

Columbus Ave.

SOUTH
END

Ruggles St.

0.7/
7.4

Massachusetts Ave.

1.2/
6.9

Tremont St.

Brookline

9

High St.

Pond Ave.

Heath St.

Tremont St.

Malcolm X Blvd.

Olmstead
Park

Centre St.

Perkins St.

5.3

2.2/
5.9

Columbus Ave.

Jamaica
Pond

28

Amory St.

2.9

ROXBURY

Warren St.

J.P. Licks
Headquarters

Centre St.

Washington St.

Blue Hill Ave.

Arborway

Green St.

JAMAICA
PLAIN

3.4

Centre St.

203

South St.

Franklin
Park Zoo

South St.

3.9

Franklin
Park

28

203

3.4 Follow the SCP path to the right of the open field past Williams Street.

3.9 Exit the SCP via the ramp and turn right onto New Washington Street, then take your first left.

4.4 Follow South Street right around the Soldier's Monument, and continue straight onto Centre Street.

5.3 Keep right to follow Centre Street.

5.9 Cross Centre Street to rejoin the SCP path heading north.

7.4 Turn left onto Camden Street, then right onto the SCP.

7.6 Cross Massachusetts Avenue to continue along the SCP.

8.1 Arrive back at the starting point at Back Bay Station.

RIDE INFORMATION

Local Events/Attractions
Roxbury International Film Festival: Originally the Dudley Film Festival when established in 1999, this festival of independent film puts Boston on the cinematic map each year. www.roxburyinternationalfilmfestival.org

Jamaica Plain Music Festival: Each summer, the JP Music Fest brings national and local acts together for an outdoor frenzy at Pinebank Field. www.jpmusicfestival.com

Restrooms
Start/finish: The Boston Public Library in Copley Square, just three blocks north on Dartmouth Street from the SCP trail, has restrooms and water.

Mile 5.3: Centre Street in Jamaica Plain has many shops and restaurants with restrooms.

Millennium Park

The Boston Common, Cambridge Common, Emerald Necklace, the Arboretum. These are the parks that first come to mind when you think of Boston, each one with a historic and storied past. But one newcomer deserves recognition among the metro area's parks: West Roxbury's Millennium Park. This ride reaches Millennium's serene landscape of hilltops amid reclaimed woodlands all the way from Back Bay via the Southwest Corridor, Roslindale, and West Roxbury. Be sure to pack a kite!

Start: Southwest Corridor Park, across from Back Bay Station

Length: 18.2 miles

Approximate riding time: 2–2.5 hours with stops

Best bike: Road bike, mountain bike, or hybrid

Terrain and trail surface: A mix of paved car-free bike path and paved urban roads

Traffic and hazards: Watch for traffic along roads, particularly at Massachusetts Avenue, Forest Hills, and VFW Parkway. Joggers, dog walkers, and families with small children frequent the Southwest Corridor Park and Millennium Park.

Things to see: Southwest Corridor Park, Titus Sparrow Park, Boston Police Department Headquarters, Northeastern University, Roxbury Community College, Islamic Society of Boston Cultural Center, Jamaica Plain, Adams Park, Millennium Park

Maps: USGS: *Boston South* and *Newton* quads. DeLorme: *Massachusetts Atlas & Gazetteer*, p. 40–41

Getting there: By car: There is limited street parking in Back Bay or the South End near the SCP trail, but garage parking is available at Tent City on Dartmouth Street. **By train:** Take the T Orange Line or commuter rail to Back Bay station. Bikes are allowed on the Orange Line, except from 7 to 10 a.m. and 4 to 7 p.m. Monday through Friday, and without restriction on weekends. Check the commuter rail timetable for bike directions. Exit the station onto Dartmouth Street—the SCP begins just across the street. GPS coordinates for starting point: N42 20.821' / W71 04.589'

THE RIDE

You'll start at the end of the Southwest Corridor Park, just across from Back Bay Station. While this corridor may seem serene today, its history is rooted in dramatic protest and civil disobedience. In the 1960s, housing along the corridor was leveled for an expansion of I-95 into downtown Boston. After hundreds of protests, angry meetings, and a handful of Bostonians lying in the bulldozers' path, Massachusetts governor Francis Sargent canceled the highway project. Instead, he developed the city's mass transit infrastructure and open space, which culminated in the 1987 opening of the Southwest Corridor Park parallel to the expanded Orange Line.

Follow the park away from Back Bay Station, through the South End via the corridor's garden-lined path. At West Newton Street you'll enter Titus Sparrow Park, named for the South End tennis aficionado who helped found the first African-American nonprofit tennis club in the country, the Sportsmen's Tennis Club in Dorchester. Sparrow was also the first black umpire in the United States Tennis Association. Today his namesake park hosts summertime concerts and youth sports leagues in homage to Sparrow's commitment to community through recreation.

After carefully crossing Massachusetts Avenue, you'll see a sign for Pierre Lallement Southwest Corridor Bike Path as you continue west. Born in France in 1843, Pierre Lallement developed the velocipede transmission and pedal system often credited to Pierre Michaux and the Olivier brothers, who were his acquaintances in Paris. Lallement crossed to America in 1865 and secured a US patent for his design, but died penniless in Boston, just blocks from the corridor path, in 1891. The section of the path near to his Boston home was rededicated in his honor in 1993 as part of the International Cycling History Conference held in Boston that year, in recognition of his and Boston's place in cycling history.

You'll follow the corridor along Columbus Avenue as it skirts through the Northeastern University campus. Established in 1898 at the nearby Huntington Avenue YMCA, Northeastern began as an "evening institute" to teach

Each year the kite festival takes advantage of Millennium Park's hilltop winds.

immigrant men, and today is notable as a pioneer in cooperative education that combines classroom learning with work experience.

Just past the university campus and the headquarters of the Boston Police Department you'll cross into the neighborhood of Roxbury. One of the first towns founded in the Massachusetts Bay Colony, Roxbury was its own municipality until 1868. Touted as the "heart of black culture in Boston," Roxbury received the influx of African Americans from the South in the 1940s and 1950s. It was also the training ground for such notable civil rights leaders as Malcolm X and MLK. Today, the neighborhood is also home to a diverse immigrant community from Latin America and the Caribbean. Ride southwest past Malcolm X Boulevard, where you can see the dome of the Islamic Society of Boston Cultural Center to your left.

Continuing on, you'll pass Jackson Square and into Jamaica Plain, or "JP." A string of gardens runs from Boylston Street to the end of the corridor at New Washington Street. Exit the Southwest Corridor Park, turn right onto New Washington Street and take your first left to ride along the edge of the Arnold Arboretum into Roslindale. Another of Boston's classic streetcar suburbs, this area was originally called South Street Crossing until the 1860s, when it was renamed for a town just south of Edinburgh in Scotland as part of its application for a federal post office district. Turn right at Adams Park in Roslindale's central shopping district onto South Street. Keep right at Robert Street and turn left onto South Street again just past Fallon Field, which offers a brief preview of the hillside landscape that awaits at your destination.

Continue left onto Centre Street, the major thoroughfare of the West Roxbury neighborhood. Although often confused with Roxbury, West Roxbury seceded in 1854 and was annexed to Boston in 1874. A predominantly Irish-American neighborhood and home to many of the city's firefighters, police officers, and civil servants, West Roxbury has a place in national history as the location of the Brook Farm commune near Millennium Park. Unitarian minister George Ripley and his wife Sophia founded Brook Farm in 1841 as a Transcendental Movement experiment in communal living and agriculture. While the enterprise lasted only six years before its bankruptcy in 1847, the community's goal of establishing a self-sustaining, egalitarian society attracted the likes of Margaret Fuller, Ralph Waldo Emerson, Henry David Thoreau, and Nathaniel Hawthorne. Hawthorne based his book *The Blithedale Romance* on his experiences as a founding member of Brook Farm, and today the site is on the National Historic Register.

Bike Shops

Adi's Bike World has been serving West Roxbury since 2001, its professional bassoonist owner an enthusiastic resource for repairs and advice. Adi's Bike World is located at 231 Grove St., West Roxbury; (617) 325-2453; www.adisbikeworld.net.

Bikes Not Bombs is a nonprofit bike shop in Jamaica Plain that collects used bikes to ship to less-developed countries in Africa, Latin America, and the Caribbean. Its expert mechanics also refurbish and repair every type of bike imaginable for their retail shop, which supports the shop's economic development and local youth programs. The BNB shop is located at 284 Amory St., Jamaica Plain; (617) 522-0222; bikesnotbombs.org.

Busted Knuckle Bikes is West Roxbury's headquarters for new bikes and all manner of repairs. Busted Knuckle is located at 2066 Centre St., West Roxbury; (617) 942-2900; www.bustedknucklebikes.com.

Ferris Wheels Bike Shop has been serving Jamaica Plain since 1982, its dedicated mechanics offering every service from refurbishing to brake checks, and even the occasional pancake breakfast for the cyclists of JP! Ferris Wheels is located at 66 South St., Jamaica Plain; (617) 524-2453; www.ferriswheelsbikeshop.com.

Follow Centre Street past Lagrange Street, then stay right at the fork to continue along Spring Street past the Boston Veterans Affairs Hospital. Turn right onto the Veterans of Foreign Wars Parkway, then left at Charles Park Road to arrive at Millennium Park. An incredibly recent development, Millennium Park lies atop reclaimed landfill landscaped with dirt from Boston's "Big Dig" downtown tunnel project in the late 1990s. Millennium Park's more than 6 miles of paved trails, vast fields, hilltop views, and access to the upper Charles River made it an instant favorite upon its opening in 2000. Widely known as one of the best places to fly a kite in the city, the park even hosts an annual festival that features everything from traditional four-panes models to elaborate trick kite designs.

Enter your destination and pass the West Roxbury High School athletic fields on the right. Any of the hillside's paths make for excellent views in every direction, from the city to the northeast, Blue Hills to the southeast, and Newton's hills to the north and west. When you've taken your fill of kites and vistas, exit the park where you came in and head back down Charles Park Road, then turn right at VFW Parkway. Cut left through the Boston VA Hospital rather than brave the tricky intersection, and turn left back onto Spring Street. Continue straight onto Centre Street and track back to take a right onto Belgrade Avenue. Stay right at Corinth Street and turn left at Washington Street back through Roslindale. Turn right at New Washington Street and cross to the Southwest Corridor Park. Follow the SCP back to Back Bay Station, where the ride began.

MILES AND DIRECTIONS

0.0 From the end of the Southwest Corridor Park across from Back Bay Station, ride southwest.

0.5 Go up the ramp and cross Massachusetts Avenue to continue along the SCP path.

0.6 Keep left to stay on the SCP path.

0.7 Turn left onto Camden Street, then right to ride along Columbus Avenue. Watch signs indicating which sides of the path are for pedestrians and cyclists.

2.9 Stay left past New Minton Street to continue along the SCP path.

3.4 Follow the SCP path to the right of the open field past Williams Street.

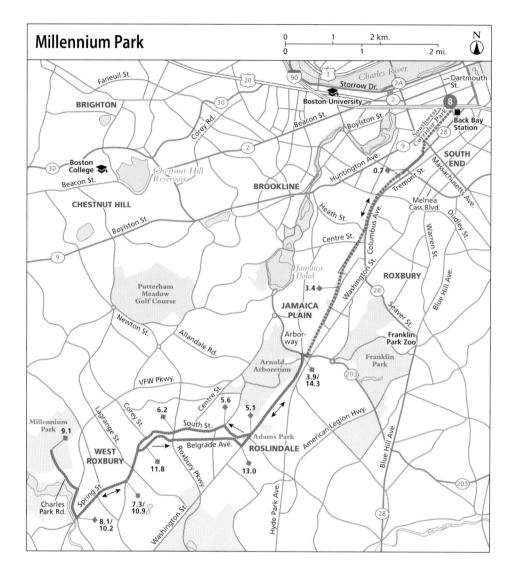

Millennium Park

0   1   2 km.

0   1   2 mi.

N

Faneuil St.

BRIGHTON

20

90

3

Charles River

Storrow Dr.

2A

Dartmouth St.

Boston University

2

8

30

Corey Rd.

Beacon St.

Boylston St.

Back Bay Station

2

9

SOUTH END

30

Boston College

Chestnut Hill Reservoir

Huntington Ave.

0.7

Tremont St.

Massachusetts Ave.

Beacon St.

BROOKLINE

Southwest Corridor Park

28

Melnea Cass Blvd.

Dudley St.

CHESTNUT HILL

Heath St.

Washington St.

Columbus Ave.

ROXBURY

Warren St.

Blue Hill Ave.

9

Boylston St.

Centre St.

Jamaica Pond

3.4

28

Putterham Meadow Golf Course

JAMAICA PLAIN

Seaver St.

Franklin Park Zoo

Newton St.

Allandale Rd.

Arbor-way

Franklin Park

VFW Pkwy.

Arnold Arboretum

3.9/ 14.3

203

Corey St.

Centre St.

5.6

5.1

Millennium Park

9.1

Lagrange St.

6.2

South St.

American Legion Hwy.

Blue Hill Ave.

WEST ROXBURY

Belgrade Ave.

Roxbury Pkwy.

Adams Park

ROSLINDALE

11.8

13.0

Charles Park Rd.

Spring St.

7.3/ 10.9

Washington St.

Hyde Park Ave.

203

8.1/ 10.2

28

3.9   Exit the SCP via the ramp and turn right onto New Washington Street, then take an immediate left.

4.2   Keep left to stay on Washington Street.

5.1   Turn right at Adams Park onto South Street.

5.3   Keep right at Robert Street.

5.6   Turn left onto South Street.

6.1   Continue left onto Centre Street.

6.2 Take the second exit out of the traffic circle to continue along Centre Street.

7.3 Stay right at the fork to continue along Spring Street.

8.1 Turn right onto the Veterans of Foreign Wars Parkway.

8.5 Turn left onto Charles Park Road

9.1 Arrive at Millennium Park and turn around.

9.8 Turn right onto Veterans of Foreign Wars Parkway, then cut southeast through the Boston VA Hospital at the break in the median.

10.2 Turn left onto Spring Street.

10.9 Continue straight onto Centre Street.

11.8 Turn right onto Belgrade Avenue and keep left to stay on Belgrade Avenue.

12.8 Turn right onto Corinth Street.

13.0 Turn left onto Washington Street.

14.3 Turn right onto New Washington Street and cross to the Southwest Corridor Park.

18.2 Arrive back at Back Bay Station.

RIDE INFORMATION

Local Events/Attractions
Boston Area Sport Kite Championships & Festival: Millennium Park's open hills are an ideal location for a kite festival! www.kite.org
Roxbury International Film Festival: Originally the Dudley Film Festival when established in 1999, this festival of independent film puts Boston on the cinematic map each year. www.roxburyinternationalfilmfestival.org

Restrooms
Start/finish: The Boston Public Library in Copley Square, just 3 blocks north on Dartmouth Street from the SCP trail, has restrooms and water.
Mile 5.1 and 13.0: The shopping district at Adams Park has a number of shops and restaurants with restrooms.

South End, Roxbury, and Franklin Park

One of Boston's most diverse and historic neighborhoods, Roxbury is also a fascinating conduit from the city to the greener suburbs beyond. This ride winds from the South End along the main stretches of Roxbury via Tremont Street and Columbus Avenue, all the way to Franklin Park tucked away on the neighborhood's southernmost edge. From dense urban blocks to rolling woods, craggy hills, and country-club landscapes, you'll get a chance to see the many facets of this eclectic borough.

Start: Tremont Plaza, Arlington Street and Tremont Street, South End

Length: 9.5 miles.

Approximate riding time: 1–1.5 hours with stops

Best bike: Road bike, mountain bike, or hybrid

Terrain and trail surface: Well-paved urban roads and bike paths, with brief patches of dirt and gravel trail in Franklin Park

Traffic and hazards: Watch for traffic along Tremont Street, Columbus Avenue, and Warren Street, in particular, as well as at intersections and traffic circles.

Things to see: South End, Cyclorama, Roxbury, Islamic Society of Boston Cultural Center, Franklin Park, Scarboro Pond, Franklin Park Zoo, Twelfth Baptist Church, Dudley Square, Cathedral of the Holy Cross

Maps: USGS: *Boston South* quad; DeLorme: *Massachusetts Atlas & Gazetteer,* p. 41

Getting there: By car: Parking can be very limited in the South End. There is metered street parking along Massachusetts Avenue and side streets. **By train:** Take the 9 or 43 bus to Tremont Street, near Tremont Plaza at Arlington Street. Bikes are allowed on all buses with bike racks, without restriction. GPS coordinates for starting point: N42 20.839' / W71 04.126'

THE RIDE

You'll start in Boston's South End, at the Tremont Plaza where Tremont Street and Arlington Street intersect. This area was once tidal marsh and was filled from the 1830s to the 1870s with gravel from Needham and submerged timbers. The South End neighborhoods you'll pass as you head southwest on Tremont Street were developed in the mid-nineteenth century, and their architecture reflects the popular style of that era. The rows of red-bricked brownstones with a mixture of renaissance revival, European-inspired facades, and cast-iron railings are considered a hallmark of classic Bostonian architecture today. By many estimates, the South End holds the most Victorian brownstones of any area in New England. While originally envisioned as an affluent residential area close to downtown, the South End became a center for the settlement houses that sprang up to provide social services through the 1920s, and a number of settlement societies persist to this day in the neighborhood for low-income outreach.

In the last forty years, though, the South End has gradually conformed more to its designers' original plans for high-culture and high-society residents, its quaint streets now filled with sidewalk cafes, offbeat artisan shops, and world-class restaurants. Revitalization projects have brought historic and artistic landmarks back to the South End as well, one example being the restoration of the Cyclorama Building on your right at Milford Street. The building's huge dome was second only to the US Capitol building when it was first constructed in 1884 to house a massive circular mural, or cyclorama, of the Battle of Gettysburg. The building was one of a string of highly popular cycloramas installed across the country, its paintings a popular tourist destination for a short while before the fashion for such murals died out. The building

Bike Shops

Bikes Not Bombs is a nonprofit bike shop in Jamaica Plain that collects used bikes to ship to less-developed countries in Africa, Latin America, and the Caribbean. Their expert mechanics also refurbish and repair every type of bike imaginable for their retail shop, which supports the shop's economic development and local youth programs. The BNB shop is located at 284 Amory St., Jamaica Plain; (617) 522-0222; bikesnotbombs.org.

Community Bike Supply in the South End does it all, from tune-ups and flat repair to overstock sales on high-end gear. The shop is located at 496 Tremont St., Boston; (617) 542-8623; www.communitybicycle.com.

The zoo was one of the last features of the park to be finished.

then housed roller-skating rinks, boxing facilities, horse tracks, and carousels, in turn, before becoming an industrial space at the turn of the century and a flower exchange in the 1920s. The Boston Center for the Arts acquired the space in 1970 and has converted the massive dome into its centerpiece venue.

Follow Tremont Street past rows of brownstones and across Massachusetts Avenue to its merger into Columbus Avenue a bit past Melnea Cass Boulevard, which marks the boundary between the South End and Roxbury. One of the first towns founded in the Massachusetts Bay Colony, Roxbury was its own municipality until its annexation to Boston in 1868. Touted by the city as the "heart of black culture in Boston," Roxbury received the influx of African-Americans from the South in the 1940s and 1950s and was the training ground for such notable civil rights leaders as Malcolm X and Martin Luther King Jr. Today, the neighborhood is also home to a diverse immigrant community drawing from Latin America and the Caribbean.

Follow Columbus Avenue past Roxbury Community College and the minaret and dome of the Islamic Society of Boston Cultural Center, where you can ride either in the street or along the Southwest Corridor bike path. Stay on Columbus as it diverges from the park's greenway deeper into Roxbury. At Egleston Square, stay right onto Washington Street. Just past the athletic fields, turn left onto Williams Street. You may see a Sam Adams Brewery Tour trolley stopped in front of Doyle's Cafe on your left—the restaurant was the first to serve Sam Adams beer on tap starting in 1986. Franklin Park is straight ahead, past Forest Hills Street. Enter the park via the paved path.

At more than 500 acres, Franklin Park is the crown jewel in Frederick Law Olmsted's Emerald Necklace string of parks, and the architect's last significant project before his death in 1903. Olmsted wanted to sculpt a green space to soothe urban dwellers and settled on Franklin Park to be primarily "country park" land with winding hills to hide the surrounding metropolis views. Just a bit inside the park's Wilderness section lies the Ninety-Nine Steps, one of the staircases Olmsted built into the hillsides of his opus out of native Roxbury puddingstone. The steps are next to Ellicott Arch, which carries the path beneath Jewish War Vets Drive and is made of the same native rock. You can also see puddingstone in the many boulders scattered throughout the park, which show off the rock's unique mix of quartzite, granite, and sandstone. Keep right after the arch and ride around Ellicottdale and the Shattuck Picnic Grove, staying to the left of the tennis courts and riding straight into the woods.

Turn right to ride around Scarboro Pond, the park's only body of water, which was installed by popular demand for a waterway. It is fed from Jamaica Pond by underground pipe and was once a popular ice-skating spot. Today, it is prime bird-watching grounds and a popular fishing hole. The hill to the west of the pond was originally intended to hold a dairy with sheep and cattle under Olmsted's original designs. Follow the pond's shore then continue along the path as it curves back to Circuit Drive and turn left to ride past the William J. Devine Golf Course. This section was originally the Country Park meadow which Olmsted designed as the park's centerpiece, its broad and winding hills meant to hide the city skyline and create a green oasis free from urban stresses. In 1896, the area was converted into a golf course, the second-oldest public course in the country. Ride along the edge of William J. Devine Golf Course, turning right past the parking lot that marks the end of the park.

Keep right as you pass Franklin Park Zoo, which opened in 1912. Olmsted originally planned a more naturalistic area for native animals rather than a traditional zoo with exotic creatures. The zoo was originally free of charge for all until hard economic times beginning in the Depression and through World War II ushered in admission fees. The zoo features giraffes, zebras, lions, gorillas, and more than 200 species in total.

Take a left at Blue Hill Avenue to head back to the South End. Stay left at the fork to continue onto Warren Street, which you'll follow past the Twelfth Baptist Church before Dudley Square. This landmark in the civil rights struggle hosted such prominent abolitionists as William Lloyd Garrison and Frederick

Douglass, as well as civil rights leaders like Martin Luther King Jr. Pass Dudley Square and Melnea Cass Boulevard to continue straight onto Washington Street. At Monsignor Reynolds Way you'll pass the gorgeous and imposing Cathedral of the Holy Cross, Boston's primary cathedral and seat of the Roman Catholic Archdiocese of Boston.

Take a left at East Berkeley Street and then a right onto Tremont Street to arrive at Tremont Plaza, where the ride began.

MILES AND DIRECTIONS

0.0 From Tremont Plaza at the corner of Tremont and Arlington Streets, ride south along Tremont Street through the South End.

1.7 Continue straight onto Columbus Avenue.

2.3 Keep left to stay on Columbus Avenue.

2.9 Turn right onto Washington Street.

3.7 Turn left onto Williams Street.

4.0 Cross Forest Hills Street into Franklin Park.

4.1 Turn right after the tunnel and ride along the path to the left of the tennis courts.

4.5 Turn right to ride along Scarboro Pond.

4.7 Keep left to continue along the pond shore.

5.0 Turn left onto Circuit Drive.

5.6 Turn right past the golf course parking lot and keep right at the fork.

5.8 Turn left onto Blue Hill Avenue.

6.3 Turn left onto Warren Street.

7.7 Keep left along Warren Street past Dudley Square.

7.9 Continue straight onto Washington Street.

9.2 Turn left onto East Berkeley Street.

9.4 Turn right onto Tremont Street.

9.5 Arrive back at Tremont Plaza at Arlington Street.

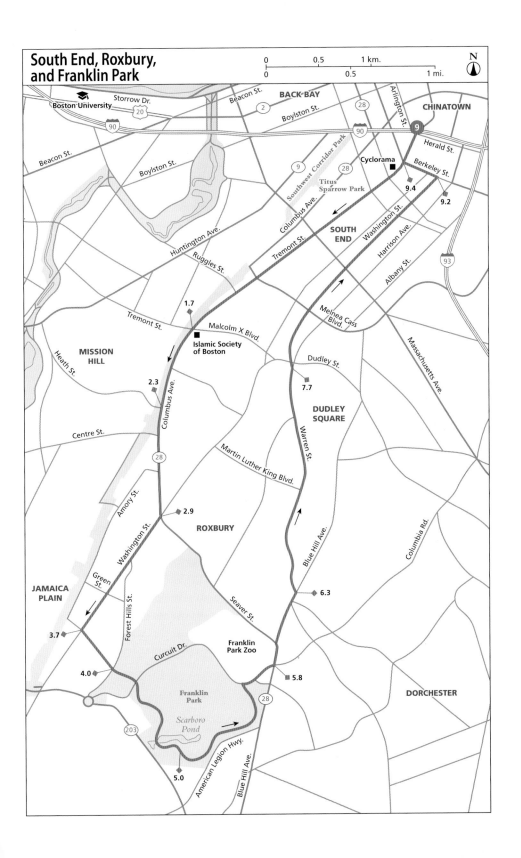

South End, Roxbury, and Franklin Park

| 0 | 0.5 | 1 km. |
| 0 | | 0.5 | 1 mi. |

N

BACK BAY

Storrow Dr.

Beacon St.

Boylston St.

Boston University

90 20

2

28

Arlington St.

CHINATOWN

90

9

Herald St.

Beacon St.

Boylston St.

9

Southwest Corridor Park

28

Cyclorama

Berkeley St.

9.4

Boylston Ave.

Titus Sparrow Park

9.2

Columbus Ave.

SOUTH END

Washington St.

93

Huntington Ave.

Tremont St.

Harrison Ave.

Ruggles St.

Albany St.

1.7

Tremont St.

Melnea Cass Blvd.

Malcolm X Blvd.

Massachusetts Ave.

MISSION HILL

Islamic Society of Boston

Dudley St.

Heath St.

2.3

7.7

Columbus Ave.

DUDLEY SQUARE

Centre St.

Martin Luther King Blvd.

Warren St.

28

Amory St.

2.9

Columbia Rd.

ROXBURY

Washington St.

Blue Hill Ave.

Green St.

6.3

JAMAICA PLAIN

Forest Hills St.

Seaver St.

3.7

Franklin Park Zoo

4.0

Curcuit Dr.

5.8

DORCHESTER

Franklin Park

28

Scarboro Pond

203

American Legion Hwy.

Blue Hill Ave.

5.0

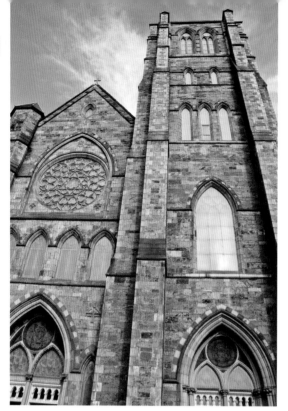

The Cathedral of the Holy Cross was the largest Catholic church in New England until the mid-1960s.

RIDE INFORMATION

Local Events/Attractions

Roxbury International Film Festival: Originally the Dudley Film Festival when established in 1999, this festival of independent film puts Boston on the cinematic map each year. www.roxburyinternationalfilmfestival.org

Franklin Park Kite and Bike Festival: A yearly tradition in Roxbury with roots back to 1969, this celebration allows revelers to explore the park's skies and bike paths the weekend after Mother's Day. www.franklinparkcoalition.org

Elma Lewis Playhouse in the Park: This series of outdoor summer concerts once featured Duke Ellington and other national acts, and its stage in the ruins of Overlook Shelter continues to bring world-class performances to Roxbury. www.franklinparkcoalition.org

Restrooms

Start/finish: The South End is full of shops and cafes with restrooms, as is Roxbury.

Mile 5.6: There are public restrooms and fountains in the golf course clubhouse of Franklin Park.

South Bay Harbor Trail

Boston's density and bustle can make it easy to forget just how close every single one of its neighborhoods and suburbs is to the ocean shoreline. This ride traces the path to the sea from the border of South End and Roxbury, spanning five neighborhoods as it winds toward Fan Pier in the Seaport District. If nothing else, this quick ride along the South Bay Harbor Trail is a fantastic reminder that, no matter where in the city you are, the waterfront is never more than a few minutes' ride away!

Start: South Bay Harbor Trail, Columbus Avenue and Melnea Cass Boulevard, Roxbury

Length: 6.9 miles

Approximate riding time: 1.5 hours with stops

Best bike: Road bike, mountain bike, or hybrid

Terrain and trail surface: A mix of paved paths, street bike lanes, and boardwalk, with occasional patches of uneven pavement

Traffic and hazards: Joggers and dog walkers frequently use this trail. Watch for traffic at intersections and while crossing bridges.

Things to see: Northeastern University, SoWa Open Market, Gillette World Headquarters, Fort Point Channel, Boston Children's Museum, Fan Pier, Moakley Courthouse, Institute of Contemporary Art, South Station, Chinatown Gate, Armory Castle at Park Plaza

Maps: USGS: *Boston South* quad. DeLorme; *Massachusetts Atlas & Gazetteer*, p. 41

Getting there: By car: There is street parking available along Columbus Avenue. Take Massachusetts Avenue south to Columbus Avenue and turn right. **By train:** Take the T Orange Line to Ruggles. Bikes are allowed on the Orange Line, except from 7 to 10 a.m. and 4 to 7 p.m. Monday through Friday, and without restriction on weekends. Exit the station toward the Northeastern University campus and take the bike path along Columbus Avenue northeast to Melnea Cass Boulevard. GPS coordinates for starting point: N42 20.177′ / W71 05.249′

THE RIDE

You'll start at the South Bay Harbor Trail head, at the northeast corner of Columbus Avenue and Melnea Cass Boulevard, close to the Ruggles T station and Northeastern University. Completed in 2010, the South Bay Harbor Trail connects the landlocked neighborhoods of Roxbury and the South End to Boston Harbor. Ride east along the trail, which runs parallel to Melnea Cass Boulevard. Named for community and civil rights activist Melnea Cass, the boulevard makes up the border between Boston's South End and Roxbury neighborhoods. Continue past Massachusetts Avenue, where the trail follows the Mass Ave Connector and runs along the I-93 Frontage Road.

Turn left at Albany Street and then right onto Malden Street and right again at Harrison Avenue. Just after Perry Street you'll pass the SoWa (South of Washington Street) Artists Guild and Marketplace, where every Sunday in the summer and fall an eclectic mix of artisans, food vendors, and craft dealers converge for the SoWa Open Market. Once a mill and warehouse district, today SoWa is known for its galleries, artist workshops, and restaurants. Follow Harrison Avenue to Traveler Street and turn right, crossing I-93 into South Boston, then left onto Dorchester Avenue.

Dorchester Avenue takes you past the world headquarters of the Gillette Company to the Fort Point Channel, which was shaped by the massive landfill project that expanded Boston's landmass to its current breadth. Turn right at the channel and follow its edge north around the Binford Street Park. Continue straight along the waterfront, riding through the passage under Summer Street. Carry your bike up the stairs and across Congress Street to the Children's Wharf Park that surrounds the Boston Children's Museum and its iconic giant Hood milk bottle.

Pass under Seaport Boulevard and up the ramp by The Barking Crab and continue north to Fan Pier Plaza, which runs behind the Moakley Courthouse. Admire the views of the Boston waterfront, the harbor, and East

Fort Point Channel

The Fort Point Channel takes its name from the fort that once stood atop Fort Hill's landmass jutting into the sea and guarded Boston in the colonial era. The fort and its hill were razed between 1866 and 1872 during a redevelopment and landfill project by the Boston Wharf Company, which also erected many of the buildings that stand along the channel today. The Fort Point Channel refashioning offered the city many lessons in shaping the Seaport District in the twentieth century.

The trail winds between the Gillette World Headquarters and Fort Point Channel.

Boston. This is the terminus of the South Bay Harbor Trail, just a short ride from Roxbury.

For the return leg, round Fan Pier past Louis toward the Public Green, where music plays around the clock. Turn right onto Northern Avenue and cross the pedestrian bridge. Turn left at Atlantic Avenue and take Oliver Street north to Purchase Street, where you'll turn left. Ride alongside the Rose Kennedy Greenway past South Station. First built in 1899, the station is one of the central hubs for buses and trains in the city. The clock on top of the station's face is styled after London's Big Ben, and has a 400-pound mechanism that makes it the largest operating hand-wound clock of its kind in New England. The stone eagle that adorns the clock weighs over 8 tons.

Bike Shop

Community Bike Supply in the South End does it all, from tune-ups and flat repair to overstock sales on high-end gear. The shop is located at 496 Tremont St., Boston; (617) 542-8623; www.communitybicycle.com.

Continuing past South Station, you'll pass Chinatown Park and the China Gate Plaza, which leads into Chinatown. The center of Asian-American life in New England, Chinatown is a destination for all manner of Asian cuisine and cultural life. Turn right onto Kneeland Street and continue to Charles Street, where you'll turn right and then left onto Park Plaza. Take a left at Columbus Avenue and ride southwest back toward Roxbury and the South End.

In a few blocks you'll come to the Armory of the First Corps of Cadets, a historic castle that is today home to the Smith & Wollensky restaurant. Chartered in 1741 as the bodyguard squadron for the governor of the Massachusetts Bay Colony, the First Corps mustered to aid in the Revolutionary War, subsequent civil unrests like Shays' Rebellion, and both world wars. A bit farther along Columbus Avenue, now deep into the South End, you'll see Harriet Tubman Square, the statue of the famous runaway slave enshrined among red-bricked brownstones.

Ride along Columbus Avenue past Massachusetts Avenue and along the Northeastern University campus. At the intersection of Columbus Avenue and Melnea Cass Boulevard, you'll reach the starting point for your ride.

MILES AND DIRECTIONS

0.0 From the southeast corner of Columbus Avenue and Melnea Cass Boulevard, follow the South Bay Harbor Trail south and then east as it curves along Melnea Cass Boulevard.

0.9 Cross Massachusetts Avenue and continue along the shoulder bike path, which follows I-93 for a stretch.

1.6 Curve left along the sidewalk at Albany Street and cross onto Malden Street.

1.8 Turn right onto Harrison Avenue.

2.2 Turn right at Traveler Street and pass under I-93.

2.6 Turn left at Dorchester Avenue.

2.7 Turn right onto the South Bay Harbor Trail just past the Gillette World Headquarters.

3.3 Continue through the covered ramp along the waterfront.

3.4 Carry your bike up the steps and cross Congress Street, then continue to ride past the Boston Children's Museum.

3.5 Exit the waterfront via the ramp and ride left past The Barking Crab restaurant onto Fan Pier.

4.0 Turn right onto Northern Avenue and ride across the pedestrian bridge past the courthouse.

South Bay Harbor Trail

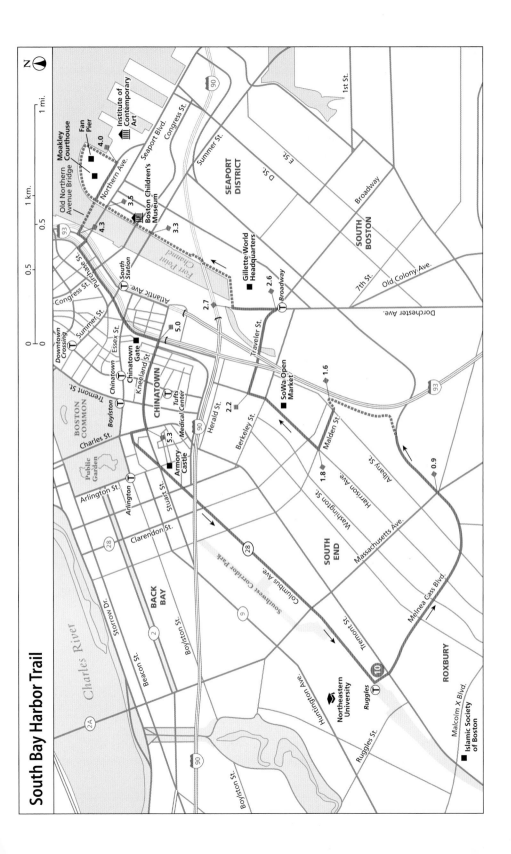

4.3 Turn left after the bridge and cross Atlantic Avenue, turning left onto Purchase Street, keeping right through the financial district and past South Station.

5.0 Turn right onto Kneeland Street.

5.3 Follow the street right onto Charles Street, then turn left at Park Plaza.

5.4 Turn left onto Columbus Avenue and continue through the South End.

6.9 Arrive back at your starting point at Melnea Cass Boulevard.

RIDE INFORMATION

Local Events/Attractions

Roxbury International Film Festival: Originally the Dudley Film Festival when established in 1999, this festival of independent film puts Boston on the cinematic map each year. www.roxburyinternationalfilmfestival.org

SoWa Open Market: This outdoor bazaar is a mecca for foodies, vintage shoppers, and arts enthusiasts alike. www.sowaopenmarket.com

Boston Harborfest: Independence Day celebrations that take place the week of July 4th in and along Boston Harbor include the display of the Liberty Tall Ships Fleet. www.bostonharborfest.com

Restrooms

Start/finish: Northeastern University has public restrooms and water on campus.

Mile 4.7: South Station has public restrooms.

Arboretum, Roslindale, Stony Brook, and Franklin Park

Just outside the city lie a number of parks that rival even the Public Garden and Boston Common in natural beauty, serene landscapes, and creative incorporation of nature into urban infrastructure. This hilly ride explores three of such woodsy escapes on the southern outskirts of Boston: the Arnold Arboretum, the Stony Brook Reservation, and Franklin Park. A fantastic picnic ride for a spring or fall afternoon, this ride is the perfect mix of tree-lined paths and forest jaunts to cure even the deepest urban blues.

Start: Arnold Arboretum visitor center, Arborway Gate, Jamaica Plain

Length: 14.6 miles

Approximate riding time: 1.5–2 hours with stops

Best bike: Road bike, mountain bike, or hybrid

Terrain and trail surface: Well-paved urban roads and bike paths

Traffic and hazards: Joggers, families with small children, and dog walkers are frequent visitors to all three parks, especially the Arboretum. Watch for uneven terrain along the Stony Brook paths, and for traffic on busy roads in Roslindale and Jamaica Plain.

Things to see: Arnold Arboretum, Peters Hill Overlook, Bussey Hill, Stony Brook Reservation, Turtle Pond, Franklin Park, Forest Hills Cemetery.

Maps: USGS: *Boston South* and *Newton* quads; DeLorme: *Massachusetts Atlas & Gazetteer*, p. 40–41

Getting there: By car: Parking is available outside the Arboretum gate and along the park perimeter. From downtown Boston, take Huntington Avenue southwest to Jamaicaway, which curves south around Jamaica Pond to become Pond Street and then Arborway. **By train:** Take the

T Orange Line to Forest Hills Station. Bikes are allowed on the Orange Line, except from 7 to 10 a.m. and 4 to 7 p.m. Monday through Friday, and without restriction on weekends. Exit the station onto Washington Street and ride north, then turn left on Arborway. The Arnold Arboretum gate is 0.8 mile on the left. GPS coordinates for starting point: N42 18.440′ / W71 07.210′

THE RIDE

You'll begin the ride at the visitor center just inside the Arnold Arboretum's Arborway Gate. Established in 1872 as another link in Boston's Emerald Necklace, the Arnold Arboretum is a partnership between the city and Harvard University. Its living botanical collections draw scientists from all over the world as well as more casual admirers of the more than 1.3 million specimens contained on the Arboretum's 281 acres. At once a research center and a well-traveled green space, the Arboretum is beloved by tourists and locals alike.

The visitor center hosts rotating exhibitions of art and history related to botany and its extensive collections of trees, shrubs, and various flora, which provide excellent context for the extraordinary variety of plants you'll see along the ride. If you're curious about any plant, there's an excellent chance it is tagged or labeled with genus, species, and global region of origin. The Arboretum's specimens hail from every corner of the world, from giant trees to delicate flowers and vines. The park's meticulous manicuring and landscaping showcase this diversity exquisitely, so take your time as you ride to get the full effect, letting your curiosity guide you.

Ride south from the visitor center along the Meadow Road, passing stands of tulip trees, lindens, and cork trees on your right and willows and maple on your left as you come to the Bradley Rosaceous Collection, a 5-acre garden section of the park. This carefully selected collection of rose-family plants arranged around two small ponds features more than 800 plants, including a cherry promenade that bursts to life every spring with pale pink blossoms. Turn right at the fork and then right again to follow Bussey Hill Road up Bussey Hill. Named for New England merchant, amateur arborist, and philanthropist Benjamin Bussey, who donated the bulk of the present park's land to Harvard College in 1861, Bussey Hill commands some of the most impressive views of the Arboretum. On your way to the hill's summit you'll pass lilacs, birches, and elms, some of which were planted by Bussey himself to adorn his mansion, which sits on the south side of his namesake hilltop.

Ride back down the hill and turn left, following Valley Road until its intersection with Beech Path, where you'll turn right. Continue along Hemlock Hill Road, past stands of junipers and pines in the conifer section, until you reach the Bussey Street Gate. Cross into the southern segment of the Arboretum, the Peters Hill tract, which was added to the park in 1894. Follow Peters Hill Road to the right and climb to the top of the hill, the highest point in the Arboretum and one of the tallest in the metro area at 240 feet. Peters Hill offers fantastic views of the Boston skyline, as well as of the Arboretum's groves and ponds. Follow Peters Hill Road all the way around the hill's base, past oaks, hawthorns, and crab apples, to exit the Arboretum via the Poplar Gate onto South Street.

Follow South Street to Washington Street, which cuts through the suburb of Roslindale. Skirt the triangular Adams Park via South Street and Poplar Street, continuing on Washington Street toward the second park on the ride: the Stony Brook Reservation. Press through the constant incline along Washington Street until you reach Enneking Parkway, where you'll turn left into the reservation. One of the five original parks created by the Metropolitan Park Commission in 1894, the Stony Brook Reservation is 475 acres of tree-covered hills, rock outcroppings, and wetlands. Follow Enneking Parkway past Turtle Pond, a popular fishing spot for its sunfish and perch stocks.

Just past the pond, take the paved Overbrook Path into the hilly woods, passing the steep Overbrook Ledge and a couple of smaller ponds as you ride through the woods. While the path is paved, take care of uneven patches along the trail, which is not maintained as often as the parkway. At the trail's intersection with West Boundary Road on the edge of the forest, turn left onto Gavin Path to follow the reservation's boundaries until Dedham Parkway,

Bike Shops

Bikes Not Bombs is a nonprofit bike shop that collects used bikes to ship to less-developed countries in Africa, Latin America, and the Caribbean. The expert mechanics also refurbish and repair every type of bike imaginable for their retail shop, which supports the shop's economic development and local youth programs. The BNB shop is located at 284 Amory St., Jamaica Plain; (617) 522-0222; bikesnotbombs.org.

Ferris Wheels Bike Shop has been serving Jamaica Plain since 1982, its dedicated mechanics offering every service from refurbishing to brake checks, and even the occasional pancake breakfast for the cyclists of JP! Ferris Wheels is located at 66 South St., Jamaica Plain; (617) 524-2453; www.ferriswheelsbikeshop.

The view of the Boston skyline is worth the trek up Peters Hill.

where you take a left. Follow Dedham Parkway onto Enneking Parkway and then East Boundary Road.

At Gordon Avenue, take a right and then a quick left onto Child Street, a left at Chestnut Street and a right onto Braeburn Road. Ride along the edge of the George Wright Golf Course, a public course named for the nineteenth-century sportsman who anchored the Boston Red Stockings team from 1871 to 1878, winning six pennants in eight seasons. Wright was pivotal in bringing golf to Boston after requesting "experimental" permission from the Boston Park Permission to hit golf balls in Franklin Park. Wright also donated the 156 acres that would become his namesake course.

Ride along Poplar Street past the golf course, continuing onto Canterbury Street and then the American Legion Highway. Turn left at Canterbury Street and then take the second right off of Bourne Street into the St. Michael Cemetery, established in 1905 as a burial ground for Boston's growing Italian population. Follow the main path as it curves right, and exit right out onto Walk Hill Street. Turn left and then take your first right into the adjacent Forest Hills Cemetery. Designed in 1848 drawing on the Mount Auburn Cemetery in Cambridge, Forest Hills is the burial site for numerous famous Bostonians and historical figures, including William Lloyd Garrison, E. E. Cummings, Eugene O'Neill, Jacob Wirth, and Reggie Lewis, as well as a number of Massachusetts politicians and artists. Executed anarchists Nicola Sacco and Bartolomeo Vanzetti were cremated here in 1927 before their ashes were returned to Italy. Take the second right onto Maple Avenue and ride past historic graves dating back dozens of decades to the eerie *Girl in Glass* sculpture at Elm Avenue, an icon of the cemetery. Turn left onto Elm Avenue and ride toward Lake Hibiscus, where you'll turn right onto Lake Avenue. Follow the signs to the exit, turning right onto Consecration Avenue and riding past the flagpole to the ornate main cemetery entrance.

Take Forest Hills Avenue past Morton Street onto Cemetery Road, turning right onto Forest Hills Street after the overpass. At Williams Street, turn right into Franklin Park. At more than 500 acres, Franklin Park is the crown jewel in Frederick Law Olmsted's Emerald Necklace, and the architect's last significant city park project. Olmsted wanted to design a green space to soothe urban dwellers, and settled on Franklin Park to be majority "country park" land with winding hills to hide the surrounding metropolis views.

Ride straight into the park, crossing North Jewish War Vets Drive and staying left at the fork to continue north along the edge of the William Devine Golf Course. Cross Circuit Drive to enter The Wilderness, a less manicured forest section of the park. Keep left at the first fork and wind around the Wilderness Picnic Grove, then loop back toward North Jewish War Vets Drive and follow the parallel bike path north to Pierpont Road, which carries you past Overlook Ruins, The Steading woods, and White Stadium to Walnut Avenue, where you'll turn left out of the park.

Continue along Sigourney Street, then Glen Road and Green Street past the Green Street station and Johnson Park to Centre Street, which runs through the Jamaica Plain neighborhood. Turn left onto Centre Street and ride past the Soldier's Monument to Arborway, where you'll turn left and ride back to the Arboretum main entrance, where you began the ride.

MILES AND DIRECTIONS

0.5 Turn left at Forest Hills Road, then curve left again onto Bussey Hill Road.

0.8 Follow Bussey Hill Road up the hill to the summit, then back down to this junction, where you'll continue left.

1.7 Take Hemlock Hill Road right.

2.0 Cross Bussey Street and follow Peters Hill Road to the right.

2.4 Turn left onto the path to the top of Peters Hill, then return to this junction and continue left.

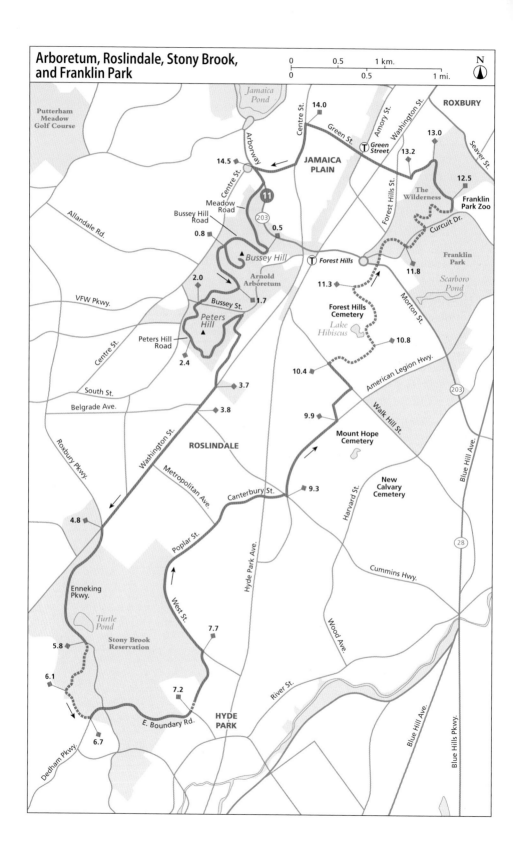

Arboretum, Roslindale, Stony Brook, and Franklin Park

| 0 | 0.5 | 1 km. |
| 0 | 0.5 | 1 mi. |

N

Jamaica Pond

Putterham Meadow Golf Course

ROXBURY

Centre St.
14.0
Green St.
Amory St.
Washington St.
13.0
Green Street
13.2
Arborway
JAMAICA PLAIN
14.5
Centre St.
Forest Hills St.
12.5
The Wilderness
Franklin Park Zoo
Meadow Road
11
Bussey Hill Road
203
0.8
0.5
Circuit Dr.
Allandale Rd.
Bussey Hill
Arnold Arboretum
Forest Hills
Franklin Park
2.0
1.7
11.8
VFW Pkwy.
Bussey St.
11.3
Scarboro Pond
Peters Hill
Forest Hills Cemetery
Lake Hibiscus
Morton St.
Peters Hill Road
10.8
2.4
Centre St.
10.4
American Legion Hwy.
203
3.7
South St.
9.9
Walk Hill St.
Belgrade Ave.
3.8
Mount Hope Cemetery
Washington St.
ROSLINDALE
Harvard St.
New Calvary Cemetery
Blue Hill Ave.
Roxbury Pkwy.
Metropolitan Ave.
Canterbury St.
9.3
4.8
Poplar St.
Hyde Park Ave.
Cummins Hwy.
28
Enneking Pkwy.
West St.
Wood Ave.
Turtle Pond
7.7
5.8
Stony Brook Reservation
6.1
7.2
River St.
HYDE PARK
6.7
E. Boundary Rd.
Blue Hill Ave.
Dedham Pkwy.
Blue Hills Pkwy.

2.9 Turn right off Peters Hill Road toward the Poplar Gate, where you'll turn right onto South Street.

3.7 Turn right onto Washington Street.

3.8 Turn left onto Poplar Street, then right at Washington Street after passing Adams Park.

4.8 Turn left onto Enneking Parkway.

5.8 Turn right off the road onto the paved Overbrook Path.

6.1 Turn left onto Gavin Path to ride along the edge of the park.

6.7 Exit the park and ride left onto Dedham Parkway, then continue straight onto Enneking Parkway.

7.2 Turn right at Gordon Avenue and then left onto Child Street.

7.3 Turn right at Chestnut Street and then left onto Braeburn Road.

7.5 Keep left onto Myopia Road.

7.7 Turn left onto West Street, which becomes Poplar Street and then Canterbury Street past Grew Avenue.

9.3 Carefully merge onto American Legion Highway, headed northeast.

9.9 Turn left onto Canterbury Street, then turn right into St. Michael Cemetery, continuing straight to the curve on the opposite side of the yard and then exiting. Turn left onto Walk Hill Street.

10.4 Turn right into Forest Hills Cemetery, then take your second right onto Maple Avenue and follow the curve.

10.8 Turn left onto Elm Avenue at the *Girl in Glass* sculpture, turn right onto Lake Avenue at Lake Hibiscus and then a quick right onto Consecration Avenue, following the signs to the exit.

11.3 Exit the cemetery onto Forest Hills Avenue and continue straight at Morton Street onto Cemetery Road.

11.7 Turn right onto Forest Hills Avenue and enter Franklin Park at Williams Street.

11.8 Follow the path as it crosses Circuit Drive, and then back across again into The Wilderness section of the park. Keep right at all forks.

12.5 Stay left toward the parking lot and follow the path left along Pierpont Road and then Pier Point Road.

13.0 Turn left onto Sigourney Street.

13.2 Turn right onto Glen Road, continuing straight on Green Street past Washington Street.

14.0 Turn left onto Centre Street.

14.2 Stay right at the monument to stay on Centre Street.

14.5 Turn left onto Arborway.

14.6 Turn left and cross Arborway to return to the starting point at the Arnold Arboretum visitor center.

RIDE INFORMATION

Local Events/Attractions

Lilac Sunday: Every May, the Arnold Arboretum celebrates its lilac collection with live music, family activities, and a special day of picnicking on the grounds. www.arboretum.harvard.edu

Forest Hills Cemetery Lantern Festival: Hundreds come to light paper lanterns on Lake Hibiscus each July in a ceremony that draws its inspiration from the Japanese Bon Festival, a day when a door opens between the realms of the living and dead. www.foresthillscemetery.com

Franklin Park Kite and Bike Festival: A yearly tradition in Roxbury with roots back to 1969, this celebration allows revelers to explore the park's skies and bike paths the weekend after Mother's Day. www.franklinparkcoalition.org

Restrooms

Start/finish: The Arnold Arboretum visitor center has restrooms and water.
Mile 3.7 to 4.8: There are a number of fast-food restaurants and shops along Washington Street with restrooms and water.
Mile 12.9: The White Stadium has restrooms that are open to the public.

The Seven Campus Ride

In addition to its sports and seafood, Boston is world renowned for its institutes of higher learning, and for good reason: There are more than a hundred colleges and universities in Greater Boston, from tiny conservatories to multicampus research behemoths! This ride explores seven of the principal campuses around Boston, including the five largest—Boston University, Harvard University, Northeastern University, Boston College, and University of Massachusetts, Boston—plus two of its most distinctive campuses, Tufts University and the Massachusetts Institute of Technology. You'll tour the metro area through the eyes of the hundreds of thousands of students who call Boston home!

Start: Massachusetts Institute of Technology, 77 Massachusetts Ave., Cambridge

Length: 28.2 miles

Approximate riding time: 3–3.5 hours with stops.

Best bike: Road bike or hybrid

Terrain and trail surface: Paved urban roads and bike lanes

Traffic and hazards: Watch for traffic, particularly along Massachusetts Avenue, Beacon Street, and Old Colony Avenue, as well as at bridges and traffic circles.

Things to see: Massachusetts Institute of Technology, Tufts University, Harvard University, Boston College, Northeastern University, University of Massachusetts–Boston, Boston University

Maps: USGS: *Boston North, Boston South, Lexington,* and *Newton* quads; DeLorme: *Massachusetts Atlas & Gazetteer,* p. 41

Getting there: By car: Parking can be very limited in MIT territory. There is street parking along parts of Massachusetts Avenue, or else park in the garage at Star Market. Take Massachusetts Avenue to Cambridge and turn left onto Sidney Street, then left again onto Green Street. The garage is past the hotel, on your right. Exiting the garage, take a left onto Landsdowne Street and a right on Massachusetts Avenue to arrive at the ride start in front of 77 Massachusetts Ave. on the MIT campus. **By train:** Take the Red Line to Kendall, which allows bikes except from 7 to 10 a.m. and 4 to 7 p.m. Monday through Friday, and without restriction on weekends. Exit the station onto Main Street and ride west, turn left onto Vassar Street and left again onto Massachusetts Avenue to arrive at the ride start in front of 77 Massachusetts Ave. on the MIT campus. GPS coordinates for starting point: N42 21.550′ / W71 05.613′

THE RIDE

You'll start at Massachusetts Institute of Technology, in front of its landmark dome near the Mass Ave bridge over the Charles River. MIT was incorporated in 1861 in a bid to keep Massachusetts at the frontier of industry through research and practical training in the industrial sciences. From its start as "Boston Tech," MIT has followed a polytechnic style of education steeped in both laboratory and classroom learning. The school moved to its current campus on the Cambridge side of the Charles in 1916 after failed proposals to merge with Harvard. Its multifaceted campus showcases every architectural style from neoclassical to postmodern, a reflection of the cutting-edge thinking for which MIT's student body prides itself. The dome before you is Building 7, which holds the school's architecture and urban planning departments as well as a number of libraries. Just across the street lie the main MIT student center and athletic facilities.

Follow Massachusetts Avenue away from the river and turn right onto Vassar Street. The orange and silver building rising on your right is the State Center, which was designed by Frank Gehry in 2004. It sits on the former site of the famous Building 20, a temporary wooden structure thrown up during World War II to house a number of defense research projects. It wasn't until World War II that MIT truly ascended to the global stage, and the work at Building 20 is what put the school on the map through development of microwave radar and other technologies critical to the war effort. While Building 20 was meant to be temporary, it remained standing from 1943 through 1998. Behind the State Center is a complex of MIT buildings dedicated to a variety of research endeavors, including biological, chemical, and computer laboratories. Continue straight past Main Street onto Galileo Galilei Way through Kendall Square, then turn left at Broadway to exit MIT territory.

MIT's Building 7 is one of the primary structures on campus, housing a number of libraries and student centers.

Next up is Tufts University, a few miles away on the line between Somerville and Medford. Turn right onto Hampshire Street at Reardon Square and ride northwest through Cambridge. At Inman Square, continue straight onto Beacon Street as you cross into Somerville. Continue until Park Street and turn right, then take a left onto Somerville. Stay right at the fork with Elm Street, which you'll follow until Willow Avenue and turn right. Take a left on Broadway to Powder House Square, where Tufts will come into view just as you pass the historic Powder House Park on the left, where colonial militiamen kept gunpowder and weapons. Take the second exit out of the rotary onto College Avenue.

Established in 1852 after Charles Tufts donated 20 acres of land on the Somerville-Medford border to the Universalist Church, Tufts University is among the top universities in the world, with a gorgeous campus to match its reputation. Turn left on Professors Row, which divides the upper and lower campus, then take the paved path on the right onto President's Lawn, carrying your bike up the short stairs to Ballou Hall. Turn right and ride past the Goddard Chapel, in which you can find the "Easter Lilies" Tiffany stained-glass window. Continue onto the library roof, where you'll find one of the most impressive views of Greater Boston outside the city itself. Tufts is located on one of the highest points in the metro area, a feature that sets it apart from every other campus in Boston.

From the roof ride across the Green, past the statue of the Tufts mascot elephant, Jumbo. Circus showman P. T. Barnum was among the school's most generous benefactors and an original trustee. When Barnum's elephant died in a train accident, he had the mascot's hide stuffed and installed on campus in the natural history museum he had bankrolled. Barnum's museum burned to the ground in 1975, but Jumbo remains the mascot of Tufts in homage to his support.

Turn left at Packard Avenue to leave the Tufts area back toward Cambridge. At the end of Packard Avenue at Broadway, take the paved path across the street, through the Powder House Community School parking lot. Continue past Holland Street onto Cameron Avenue, then turn left onto Massachusetts Avenue. Ride past Porter Square to the crown institute of Boston: Harvard University.

Harvard is the oldest higher education entity in the United States and needs little introduction. From its establishment in 1636 to the present, no school in the world inspires the level of esteem as does this eminent university, its iconic crimson shield recognized across the globe as a symbol of first-class academics and professional alumni of highest caliber. As you approach Harvard Square, the redbrick buildings of the university come into view, particularly on the left as you pass Cambridge Common and draw nearer to Harvard Yard, the school's epicenter. From its humble beginnings out of the estate of John Harvard with nine students, Harvard has climbed to the top tier of universities, being one of the five largest institutions in Boston and the best-funded university in the world. Follow Massachusetts Avenue past Harvard Yard and the undergraduate dormitories, as it continues into Brattle Street and then Eliot Street. Turn right onto JFK Street to head back across the river toward Harvard Business School and Harvard Stadium, where every other November the Harvard-Yale game pits the two Ivy League football teams against each other in an epic rivalry that dates back to 1875.

Continue on North Harvard Street to Cambridge Street and turn right, riding over the I-90 overpass and into Allston-Brighton. Take a left onto Winship Street, which becomes Chestnut Hill Avenue. Take a right at South Street onto Commonwealth Avenue, where you'll first see the iconic spire of Boston College. Turn left onto Thomas More Road and enter its campus.

The Jesuit school of Boston College was established in 1827 in Boston's South End. The anti-Catholic Massachusetts legislature barred BC's charter until 1863, and it wasn't until fifty years later that the school moved to Chestnut Hill. In its initial decades, BC focused its outreach on sons of Irish workers with an emphasis on theology and the classics. Today, the school is a major research institution that draws students and researchers from across the globe. The tall spire for which BC is known is Gasson Hall, named for BC President Thomas Glasson, who led the school's move to Chestnut Hill. The tower epitomizes the collegiate gothic architecture that BC pioneered and was built from stone quarried on-site for its 1913 opening. To this day, BC is home to one of the largest Jesuit communities in the world. Boston College is also known for its sports, particularly its rabid football and hockey fans. Along with Harvard, Boston University, and Northeastern, BC competes each February in the Beanpot hockey tournament, a Boston tradition that dates back to the 1950s.

Take Thomas More to Chestnut Hill Drive, then turn left at Beacon Street to round Chestnut Hill Reservoir. Take a right up Chestnut Hill Avenue and then a left at Boylston Street, riding straight to Huntington Avenue in Mission Hill, the stomping ground of the Northeastern University Huskies as well as a handful of smaller schools like the Massachusetts College of Art and Design and Wentworth Institute of Technology.

Take a right at Ruggles Street, then turn briefly onto the Southwest Corridor path as it cuts through Northeastern's campus. Established in 1898 at the nearby Huntington Avenue YMCA, Northeastern began as an "evening institute" to teach immigrant men introductory courses in law, engineering, and finance. It is particularly notable as a pioneer in cooperative education, which combines classroom learning with work experience for academic credit. You'll ride through Northeastern briefly before taking the South Bay Harbor Loop right along Melnea Cass Boulevard until it curves around to Massachusetts Avenue. Turn right, then left, onto Columbia Road and right at the rotary onto William T. Morrissey Boulevard in Dorchester, where the University of Massachusetts, Boston will come into view. Take a left onto the Harborwalk just after Bianculi Boulevard to enter campus.

It's no joke that Boston really is a college town: While the total population in the metro area is a bit over one million, total enrollment at area colleges hovers at 250,000. In the summer, neighborhoods like Allston, Mission Hill, and Harvard can feel eerily quiet!

UMass Boston was established in 1964 in the midst of the civil rights movement and intense social upheaval, and moved to its current location on Dorchester's Columbia Point in 1974. It is the only public university in Boston, and in recent years has opened a residential campus for its historically commuting-only students. Interestingly, it shares the Columbia Point peninsula with Boston College High School next door. Follow the coastline to get a sense of this gorgeous seaside campus. Rounding the peninsula, you'll also pass the adjacent JFK Presidential Library. Continue briefly onto the gravel path of the Harborwalk, then turn left at the T to Mt. Vernon Street, where you'll ride right out of UMass Boston.

Take Old Colony Avenue right and ride through South Boston, past Joe Moakley Park and onto Dorchester Avenue. Take a left at West Fourth Street to cross into the South End via East Berkeley Street and continue into Back Bay. Follow Berkeley Street to Beacon Street and turn left.

Bike Shops

Ace Wheelworks is as much about supporting the local bicycling community as providing high-quality repairs, parts, and equipment. Their shop is located at 145 Elm St., Somerville; (617) 776-2100; www.wheelworks.com.

Bicycle Belle specializes in city, cargo, and vintage bicycles, and is located at 368 Beacon St., Somerville; (617) 661-0969; bicyclebelle boston.com.

Cambridge Bicycle has a staff experienced in custom builds and all manner of repairs. The shop is located right by MIT campus, at 259 Massachusetts Ave., Cambridge; (617) 876-6555; www.cambridge bicycle.com.

The Cambridge Bicycle Exchange at Porter Square has been selling, renting, and repairing bikes for more than twenty years. Their shop is located at 2067 Massachusetts Ave., Cambridge; (617) 864-1300; www.cambridgebicycleexchange.com.

International Bicycle has a full selection of new bikes, equipment, and apparel, plus a full-service department of expert technicians. The shop is located at 89 Brighton Ave., Allston; (617) 783-5804; www.inter nationalbike.com.

Landry's Bicycles has been a family-owned bike business since 1922, gaining the trust of avid cyclists at its four locations in Boston, Natick, Norwood, and Westboro. The Boston shop is close to the ride route at 890 Commonwealth Ave., Boston; (617) 232-0446; www.landrys.com.

MyBike styles itself as an "untraditional" bike shop because of its concierge "house calls," electric-bike offerings, and other add-ons to typical services you'd expect from a full-service bike shop. MyBike is located at 391 West Broadway, South Boston; (617) 202-9720; www.mybike.com.

Paramount Bicycle Repair is a household name in Somerville for its high-quality repairs and built-to-order bikes. Their shop is located at 104 Bristol Rd., Somerville; (617) 666-6072; www.paramountbicycle.com.

At Charlesgate Road, you'll spy the first signs of Boston University. Keep right after the overpass as Beacon Street branches into Bay State Road at Boston University's Myles Standish Hall, once a hotel frequented by Babe Ruth before BU bought it for dormitory space in 1949. Bay State Road runs to the heart of BU's Charles River campus, passing dozens of brownstones the university has acquired as academic departments and student housing over the decades since its founding in 1839 as a Methodist theological center. The school has its roots in Beacon Hill, but moved to its current location along the Charles River after 1937.

At the intersection of Bay State Road and Granby Street lies the Boston University Castle, a Tudor mansion originally built in 1915 as a private residence and acquired by BU in 1939. The vine-covered building served as the university president's residence until 1967 and today hosts a variety of academic and social functions. Turn left at Granby and then right again onto Commonwealth Avenue, which runs past the BU College of Arts and Sciences on your right, and iconic Warren Towers dormitory on the left side of the street. Like many colleges in Boston, BU began as a commuter school but gradually developed its residential offerings, which range from large dormitories like Warren Towers, to the brownstones you passed along Bay State Road, to retrofitted homes in the southern part of campus. A bit farther on is Marsh Plaza, its marble foundation and ornate towers and architectural details a common draw for tourists and one of the first features of the Charles River Campus to be completed during the 1940s. Note how students avoid walking over the large medallion of the BU seal behind the commemorative dove statue donated in honor of Martin Luther King Jr., an alum of the BU School of Theology: Campus superstition holds that walking on the medallion curses you to late graduation.

Turn right at the Boston University bridge to cross back into Cambridge, savoring the particularly impressive view of downtown as you come to Memorial Drive for the final stretch back to MIT. Turn right and follow the bike path along the river to the Massachusetts Avenue bridge, where you'll turn left via the crosswalk. Ride until you once again reach the domed Building 7, where your ride began.

MILES AND DIRECTIONS

0.0 Begin at MIT in front of its landmark dome at 77 Massachusetts Ave. Ride away from the river along Massachusetts Avenue and turn right at Vassar Street.

0.4 Continue straight onto Galileo Galilei Way.

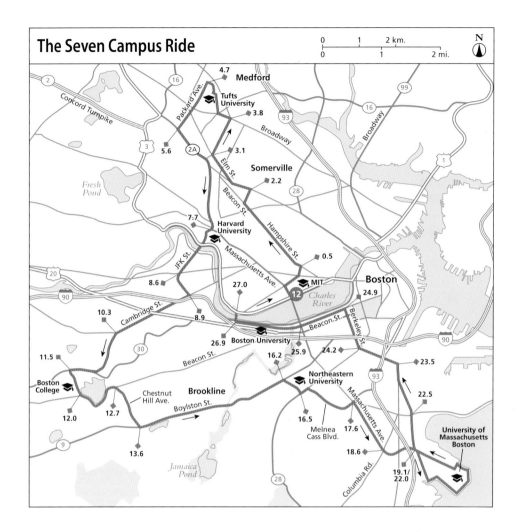

The Seven Campus Ride

0   1   2 km.
0   1   2 mi.

N

0.5 Turn left onto Broadway.

0.6 Keep right onto Hampshire Street.

1.4 Continue straight onto Beacon Street.

2.0 Turn right onto Park Street.

2.2 Turn left onto Somerville Avenue.

2.6 Keep right to continue onto Elm Street.

3.1 Turn right onto Willow Avenue.

3.8 Turn left onto Broadway.

4.0 Enter the traffic circle at Powder House Square and take the second exit onto College Avenue.

4.3 Turn left onto Professors Row.

4.5 Turn right onto the path across the lawn, turn right at Goddard Chapel, and proceed to the Tisch Library roof.

4.6 Follow the path past Ballou Hall around the Tufts Green.

4.7 Turn left onto Packard Avenue.

5.2 At the end of Packard Avenue at Broadway, take the paved path across the street, through the Powder House Community School parking lot.

5.3 Continue past Holland Street onto Cameron Avenue.

5.6 Turn left onto Massachusetts Avenue.

7.7 Turn right onto JFK Street.

8.6 Keep left to continue on North Harvard Street.

8.9 Turn right onto Cambridge Street.

9.5 Continue straight onto Cambridge Street.

10.3 Turn left onto Winship Street, which becomes Chestnut Hill Avenue.

10.9 Turn right onto South Street.

11.1 Turn right onto Commonwealth Avenue.

11.5 Turn left onto Thomas More Road.

12.0 Turn left onto Beacon Street.

12.7 Enter the traffic circle at Cleveland Circle and take the first exit onto Chestnut Hill Avenue.

13.6 Turn left onto Boylston Street.

16.2 Turn right onto Ruggles Street.

16.5 Cross to the Southwest Corridor Park next to Ruggles Station.

16.7 Turn right onto the South Bay Harbor Loop.

17.6 Turn right onto Massachusetts Avenue.

18.6 Turn left onto Columbia Road.

19.1 Enter the rotary and take the first right onto William T. Morrissey Boulevard.

19.8 Turn left onto the boardwalk around Columbia Point.

21.2 Turn left off of the gravel path and turn right onto Mt. Vernon Street.

22.0 Turn right onto Old Colony Avenue.

22.5 Enter the rotary and take the second exit to continue along Old Colony Avenue.

23.5 Turn left onto West Fourth Street.

24.2 Continue straight onto Berkeley Street.

24.9 Turn left onto Beacon Street.

25.9 Keep right onto Bay State Road.

26.4 Turn left onto Granby Street, then right onto Commonwealth Avenue.

26.9 Turn right across the Boston University Bridge.

27.0 Turn right onto the Charles River Greenway.

28.0 Turn left onto Massachusetts Avenue.

28.2 Arrive back at 77 Massachusetts Ave. at MIT.

RIDE INFORMATION

Local Events/Attractions

Pi Day: Every March 14, in honor of the mathematical operator, MIT's nerdier students and faculty organize events centered around pi(e). www.mit.edu

Harvard Museum of Natural History: This world-class museum features exhibits that are as much about the museum's history as natural history itself. www.hmnh.harvard.edu

John F. Kennedy Presidential Library and Museum: The archives of JFK and Ernest Hemingway, as well as exhibitions about these two titans in very distinct cultural spheres, draw thousands of visitors a year to Columbia Point next to UMB. www.jfklibrary.org

Restrooms

There are public restrooms at every campus, as well as at any number of shops and restaurants in between.

Massachusetts Avenue to Arlington Reservoir

One of Boston's main thoroughfares, Mass Ave connects Dorchester in the city's south to northerly neighborhoods such as Cambridge, Arlington, and beyond. It is also eminently bike-friendly, with dedicated and well-paved bike lanes along much of this central artery! This ride follows Mass Ave past the stunning diversity that Greater Boston offers, from urban center and commercial hub to rolling suburbia and waterfront parkland. If you want to get a real sense for what Boston and its outliers are all about, Mass Ave is a great place to start.

Start: Thomas J. Kane Square, Dorchester, Boston

Length: 22.6 miles

Approximate riding time: 2.5–3 hours with stops

Best bike: Road bike or hybrid

Terrain and trail surface: Well-paved urban roads with dirt trail around Arlington Reservoir

Traffic and hazards: Watch for traffic along Massachusetts Avenue, particularly at major intersections, rotaries, and the Massachusetts Avenue Bridge. The Arlington Reservoir is also particularly popular with hikers, joggers, dog walkers, geese, and families with small children.

Things to see: Dorchester, South End, Christian Science Plaza, Massachusetts Avenue Bridge, MIT, Harvard Square, Harvard Yard, Porter Square, Alewife Brook, Jerry Cataldo Reservation, Arlington Reservoir, Reservoir Beach

Maps: USGS: *Boston North, Boston South,* and *Lexington* quads; DeLorme: *Massachusetts Atlas & Gazetteer,* p. 41

Getting there: By car: Take Massachusetts Avenue south to Dorchester. There is parking available at the Stop & Shop just before Thomas J. Kane Square. Exit the lot left onto Massachusetts Avenue and continue south to the ride start at Columbia Road and Massachusetts Avenue. **By train:** Take the Red Line or commuter rail to JFK/UMass Station—bikes are allowed on the Red Line, except from 7 to 10 a.m. and 4 to 7 p.m. Monday through Friday, and without restriction on weekends. Exit the station onto Columbia Road and turn right, riding until the ride start at Columbia Road and Massachusetts Avenue. GPS coordinates for starting point: N42 19.242' / W71 03.693'

THE RIDE

You'll start at Thomas J. Kane Square in the Dorchester neighborhood of Boston, where Massachusetts Avenue begins. The largest of the city's boroughs, Dorchester was founded a few months before Boston in 1630 and annexed to the city in 1870. That first Dorchester settlement was constructed not far from Kane Square, as the Puritans who established it landed just east of here at Columbia Point, where the University of Massachusetts, Boston, stands today. Every year on the first Sunday in June, the Dorchester Day parade and festivities commemorate the settlement's founding.

A popular summer retreat in the mid-1800s, Dorchester became a center for social activism in the twentieth century, fostering such abolitionists as William Monroe Trotter, who helped found the Niagara Movement with W. E. B. DuBois. Leading suffragette Lucy Stone, who was the first woman from Massachusetts to earn a college degree, lived in Dorchester while orchestrating the first women's rights convention in Worcester and tirelessly recruiting compatriots to the cause, including Susan B. Anthony. Stone's daughter, Alice Stone Blackwell, recorded her teenage perspective of growing up in Dorchester in a book she titled *Growing Up in Boston's Gilded Age*. The civil rights struggle also gained a foothold in the Dorchester neighborhoods where African Americans had flocked during the Great Migration from the South. Martin Luther King Jr. drew many of the movement's leaders to the apartment in Dorchester where he lived while completing his PhD at Boston University.

Follow Mass Ave northwest, turning right briefly onto Theodore Glynn Way as Mass Ave becomes one-way for a short stretch, then take the first left onto Southampton Street to rejoin Massachusetts Avenue and cross Melnea Cass Boulevard into the South End. This area was once tidal marsh, filled in from the 1830s to the 1870s with gravel from Needham and submerged timbers. The South End neighborhoods you'll pass as you ride along Massachusetts Avenue were developed in the mid-nineteenth century, and their architecture reflects the popular style of that era. The rows of red-bricked brownstones with a mixture of renaissance revival and European-inspired facades, cast-iron railings, and a scattered number of carriageways are all now considered hallmarks of classic Bostonian architecture. By many estimates, the South End holds the most Victorian brownstones of any area in New England. In the last forty years, though, the South End has gradually conformed more to its designers original plans for high-culture and high-society residents, its quaint streets now filled with sidewalk cafes, offbeat artisan shops, and world-class restaurants.

Pass Tremont Street and Huntington Street into Back Bay, another segment of the city that was filled out of water and marshland. At the intersection of Westland and Massachusetts Avenues you'll see Symphony Hall to your left, built in 1900 for the Boston Symphony Orchestra and also home today to the Boston Pops Orchestra. Its acoustics are consistently rated among the best of any hall in the world, and its ornate interior amplifies the beauty of the music you'll hear inside. Just across the street is the equally intricate dome of the "Mother Church," the First Church of Christ, Scientist. The headquarters of the

Bike Shops

Back Bay Bicycles is a Boston institution, with an experienced and friendly staff that will care for your equipment and can answer your maintenance questions. The shop also rents bikes by the day. Back Bay Bicycles is located at 362 Commonwealth Ave., Boston; (617) 247-2336; www.backbaybicycles.com.

The Bike Stop is conveniently located right along the Minuteman path and carries a full selection of bikes for sale and rent. The Bike Stop is located 43R Dudley St., Arlington; (781)-646-7867; www.abike stop.com.

Cambridge Bicycle has a staff experienced in custom builds and all manner of repairs. The shop is located right by the MIT campus at 259 Massachusetts Ave., Cambridge; (617) 876-6555; www.cambridge bicycle.com.

The Cambridge Bicycle Exchange at Porter Square has been selling, renting, and repairing bikes for more than 20 years. Their shop is located at 2067 Massachusetts Ave., Cambridge, (617) 864-1300; www .cambridgebicycleexchange.com

Quad Cycles, just blocks from the Minuteman path in Arlington Heights, has been offering professional cycling advice and repairs since owner Rustem Gode moved from Cambridge in 2000 to open his own shop. Quad is located at 1043 Massachusetts Ave., Arlington; (781) 648-5222; www. quadcycles.com.

Harvard Square is one of the centers of Cambridge culture and nightlife, particularly for residents of the Yard.

Church of Christ, Scientist, which was founded in Boston in 1879 by Mary Baker Eddy, the Christian Science Plaza is also home to the Christian Science Monitor news outlet. While the domed building was erected in 1906, the rest of the plaza was designed by famed architect I. M. Pei in the 1960s. Pei's contributions include the reflecting pool to the right of the dome, the brutalist-style administration building behind the dome, and the fan-shaped Sunday School Building. The Mother Church is home to the world-famous Mapparium, as well.

Continue along Mass Ave through the territory of the Berklee College of Music, the largest independent college of contemporary music in the world. Its focus on jazz and modern American music are a contrast to the conservatory model centered on classical music, and Berklee alumni have racked up more than 200 Grammys across a wide swath of genres. Pass Hynes Convention Center and press across the Mass Ave Bridge, officially named the Harvard Bridge despite running straight into the MIT campus. The bridge was first constructed in 1891, while MIT did not move to its campus along the Charles River until 1916. Savor the spectacular view of downtown and the Boston skyline as you cross into Cambridge, noting the numbers painted along the pedestrian sidewalk. These are the bridge's measurements in smoots, a unit established by MIT's Lambda Chi Alpha fraternity in 1958. The fraternity used its shortest pledge that year, Oliver Smoot, to measure the bridge, laying him out across its span for a total length of 364.4 smoots (plus or minus one ear). Mr. Smoot later became president of the International Organization for Standardization, as it happens.

Reaching the Cambridge side, you'll immediately pass the iconic MIT buildings at 77 Mass Ave as you push on into Central Square toward Harvard. Keep right at the fork as the red brick of the oldest college in the country come into view. From its establishment in 1636 to the present, no school in the world inspires the level of esteem held by this world-famous university. Mass Ave curves around the school's epicenter at Harvard Yard, where you'll find the undergraduate residential colleges and famous statue of its benefactor John Harvard, whose toe applicants rub in hopes of an extra boost on their admissions review.

Carefully continue straight through the rotary past Harvard Yard toward Porter Square and North Cambridge. At Alewife Brook Parkway you'll cross over the small brook into Arlington.

When English colonists first settled here in 1635, they named their new village Menotomy, an Algonquian word meaning "swift running water." Squaw Sachem of the Massachusett tribe sold her ancestral land for 10 pounds and an agreement that granted her a new woolen coat each year until she died. The town name was changed in April 1867 to honor those buried at Arlington National Cemetery in Virginia. You'll quickly ride past Arlington High School and into a hilly residential stretch, keeping left at the fork to stay on Mass Ave. Turn right at Bow Street and cross the Minuteman Commuter Bikeway, turning right again onto the dirt path immediately after crossing Mill Brook. Follow this wooded trail behind the row of houses and through the marshy Jerry Cataldo Reservation to your destination at Arlington Reservoir.

Turn left onto the dirt trail that rings the reservoir, which was created by damming the Cuckmere River in 1871. The reservoir is today a nature reserve and no longer part of the water supply. Keep a sharp eye out for the many bird species that frequent the reservoir, including cormorants, swallows, and geese. Round the north shore of the reservoir to where the path turns left onto Lowell Street at Reservoir Beach, among the most popular swimming holes in Greater Boston. Its spectacular backdrop certainly puts it among the most picturesque of places to cool off from a long ride!

When you're ready to head back to Boston, follow Lowell Street south from Reservoir Beach to Park Street and turn right, then turn left onto Massachusetts Avenue once more. Retrace your path through Arlington and Cambridge to Harvard Square, where you'll leave Mass Ave briefly to curve right onto Brattle Street past Harvard Yard. Keep left at the fork at Brattle Square and ride straight onto Mount Auburn Street, which flows back into Mass Ave.

Watch for cranes and songbirds along the Arlington Reservoir path.

Cut back through Central Square and MIT, across the Mass Ave Bridge to the Boston side, where a straight shot along Mass Ave brings you back to Thomas J. Kane Square in Dorchester, where the ride began.

MILES AND DIRECTIONS

0.0 Begin at Thomas J. Kane Square and ride north along Massachusetts Avenue.

0.8 Follow Theodore Glynn Way to the right where Mass Ave becomes one-way.

0.9 Turn left onto Southampton Street and keep right to rejoin Massachusetts Avenue.

2.8 Cross the Massachusetts Avenue Bridge (officially the Harvard Bridge).

4.5 Keep right to stay on Massachusetts Avenue.

5.1 Keep left at the fork and take the first exit out of the rotary to stay on Massachusetts Avenue.

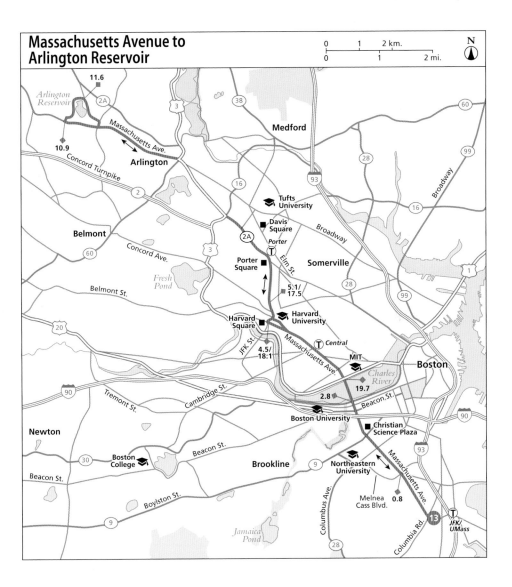

Massachusetts Avenue to Arlington Reservoir

0   1   2 km.
0   1   2 mi.

N

Arlington Reservoir

11.6

2A

3

38

60

Medford

Massachusetts Ave.

10.9

Concord Turnpike

Arlington

Concord Ave.

Belmont

60

Belmont St.

Fresh Pond

2

16

Tufts University

Davis Square

Porter

2A

Porter Square

T

Elm St.

Broadway

Somerville

28

99

5.1/ 17.5

Harvard Square

Harvard University

T Central

MIT

Charles River

Boston

JFK St.

Massachusetts Ave.

4.5/ 18.1

19.7

2.8

Beacon St.

90

Tremont St.

Cambridge St.

Boston University

Christian Science Plaza

93

90

Newton

30

Boston College

Beacon St.

Brookline

9

Northeastern University

Massachusetts Ave.

Beacon St.

Boylston St.

9

Jamaica Pond

Columbus Ave.

Melnea Cass Blvd.

0.8

28

Columbia Rd.

13

T
JFK/ UMass

99

1

20

7.3 Cross Alewife Brook Parkway into Arlington.

10.1 Keep left to stay on Massachusetts Avenue.

10.9 Turn right onto Bow Street and cross the Minuteman Commuter Bikeway, then turn right again onto the dirt path immediately after Mill Brook.

11.2 Turn left to ride around Arlington Reservoir.

11.6 Take the dirt path left back up to Lowell Street and turn right past Reservoir Beach.

12.1 Turn right onto Park Avenue.

12.3 Turn left onto Massachusetts Avenue.

17.5 Follow Brattle Street to the right at Harvard Square.

17.7 Keep left onto Mount Auburn Street, then continue straight past JFK Street.

18.1 Continue straight to rejoin Massachusetts Avenue.

19.7 Cross the bridge back into Boston.

22.6 Finish at Thomas J. Kane Square.

RIDE INFORMATION

Local Events/Attractions

Dorchester Day: This annual parade and revelry the first Sunday in June marks the establishment of the Dorchester settlement in 1630. www.dotday parade.com

City of Cambridge Dance Party: Each summer the city shuts down Massachusetts Avenue in front of Cambridge City Hall for an all-ages dance party. www.cambridgema.gov

Harvard Square: There's a festival of some sort or another in Harvard nearly every month, between its pedigree of cultural epicenters and the adjacent university. www.harvardsquare.com

Restrooms

As Massachusetts Avenue is a major thoroughfare from Boston all the way to Arlington, there are shops and restaurants all along the route with restrooms and water, particularly in the larger squares.

Cambridge Bow-Tie Ride

Often derided as the "People's Republic of Cambridge," the city across the Charles from Boston is as historic and diverse as its more populous neighbor. Appropriate to its famous blue-blood pedigree and Ivy League focal point, the city's borders form the shape of a bow tie, which this ride follows around its major highlights. From the Cambridge Common, Tory Row, and Harvard Yard, to the working-class neighborhoods of North Cambridge, to the tech havens of MIT and Kendall Square, this bow-tie loop explores the many faces of densely populated Cambridge.

Start: Cambridge Common, in front of the Civil War Memorial

Length: 10.2 miles

Approximate riding time: 2–2.5 hours with stops

Best bike: Road bike, mountain bike, or hybrid

Terrain and trail surface: Primarily paved roads and bike lanes, with stretches of paved paths

Traffic and hazards: Watch for cars along streets, in particular along Fresh Pond Parkway, Memorial Drive, and Broadway, as well as joggers, skateboarders, families with small children, and dog walkers along paths.

Things to see: Cambridge Common, Harvard Square, Harvard University, Fresh Pond, Longfellow National Historic Site, Danehy Park, Fort Washington Park, Massachusetts Institute of Technology, Cambridge Public Library

Maps: USGS: *Boston North, Boston South,* and *Lexington* quads; DeLorme: *Massachusetts Atlas & Gazetteer,* p. 41

Getting there: By car: Parking can be tricky around Harvard Square, although you can find street spots. The Harvard Parking Garage is usually a good bet as well. From Boston, take Massachusetts Avenue to Memorial Drive and turn right. Take JFK Street right, and take a left onto Eliot Street, where you'll see a garage on your immediate right. There is also parking at the Charles Hotel. From the garage, take JFK Street north to Massachusetts Avenue and cross left at Harvard Yard to Cambridge Common. **By train:** Take the T Red Line to Harvard Square. Bikes are allowed on the Red Line, except from 7 to 10 a.m. and 4 to 7 p.m. Monday through Friday, and without restriction on weekends. Exit the station to Church Street and walk your bike north along Massachusetts Avenue to the Cambridge Common. GPS coordinates for starting point: N42 22.577' / W71 07.212'

THE RIDE

Start just across from Harvard Yard at Cambridge Common, in front of the Civil War Memorial to Abraham Lincoln. Popular legend has anointed the Cambridge Common as the place where George Washington assumed command of the Continental army, although this has never been substantiated. Exit the park onto Garden Street and turn right, then take a left onto Mason Street at the First Church in Cambridge, which, true to its name, holds the first congregation established in the city, which was called "Newtowne" until 1638. For its first three years until 1636, the First Church was led by Rev. Thomas Hooker, who would leave it to found the Colony of Connecticut. Anne Hutchinson was also tried at the meetinghouse of the First Church, although its present building was not built until 1872.

Turn right onto Brattle Street at the street's Tory Row section, a district of houses which were confiscated from their Loyalist owners at the outbreak of the American Revolution. Tory Row's most famous estate is the Longfellow House, once the confirmed headquarters of General Washington as well as the personal home of poet Henry Wadsworth Longfellow for more than fifty years until his death in 1882. Continue along Brattle Street, winding past numerous grand estates, many of which have plaques explaining their particular context in Cambridge history. Turn right onto Aberdeen Avenue at the Mount Auburn Cemetery, whose historic paths unfortunately do not permit bicycles. The 174-acre cemetery is credited as the original "garden cemetery," and set off the parks and gardens movement that saw the rise in popularity of similar cemetery landscapes, as opposed to its predecessor burial ground design.

Follow Aberdeen to Huron Avenue and turn right, then cross onto the pathway around Fresh Pond and follow it north along Fresh Pond Parkway. The 155-acre Fresh Pond Reservoir has served as Cambridge's principal water supply since 1852, when the city was granted eminent domain over the pond.

Cross to Bay State Road just after the traffic circle and enter Danehy Park, which was built on the city's reclaimed landfill. The 50-acre park was covered with fill dirt and blasted rock fragments from the excavation of MBTA Red Line tunnels from 1978 to 1983, and opened in 1990 as a recreation center for the city. Follow the trail left around the soccer field and loop around the track, then turn left at the trail fork toward the parking lot. Exit the park and turn left onto Sherman Street, then turn right onto Pemberton Street. You've crossed briefly into North Cambridge, a more blue-collar section of the city. Take the tunnel right just across from Rindge Field and turn left to Raymond Street, which you'll follow south to Walden Street and turn right. Take another left at Newell Street and a right onto Huron Avenue, then take a left at Spark Street to ride south.

Pass Brattle Street and turn left at Foster Street and right onto Willard Street, which carries you past Longfellow Park. Cross Mt. Auburn Street and Memorial Drive to ride along the Charles River, where you'll turn left. Pass John F. Kennedy Park and John F. Kennedy Street, to continue along the riverfront past Harvard's redbrick dormitories at last to Hingham Street, where you'll cross and then take a right onto Putnam Avenue. Follow Putnam Avenue as it curves through the Cambridgeport neighborhood of southern Cambridge, turning left onto Albany Street. In a block you'll pass Fort Washington Park, site of one of the oldest surviving fortifications from the Revolutionary War.

Just a couple blocks farther brings you to the campus of the Massachusetts Institute of Technology, or MIT, which was incorporated in 1861 and moved to Cambridge in 1916. MIT rocketed into the top echelons of higher learning during World War II, when scientists and engineers flocked to the campus in pursuit of various defense-funded projects, including developing

Bike Shops

Broadway Bicycle School is a cooperative shop with a wide range of class offerings in bike maintenance, mechanics, and safety, with a community focus that has made it a much-beloved resource since 1972. Broadway Bicycle is located at 351 Broadway, Cambridge; (617) 868-3392; www.broadwaybicycleschool.com.

Cambridge Bicycle has a staff experienced in custom builds and all manner of repairs. The shop is located right by the MIT campus at 259 Massachusetts Ave., Cambridge; (617) 876-6555; www.cambridge bicycle.com.

Quad Bikes is a nonprofit shop run for the Harvard community, but open to the public as well. The shop is located at 51 Shepard St., Cambridge; (617) 496-5955; www.quadbikes.org.

radar. Follow Albany Street to Massachusetts Avenue and turn right, then take a quick left at Vassar Street and follow it to Kendall Square, passing the hard-to-miss Stata Center, its warped facade designed by Frank Gehry. Once a salt marsh, today Kendall Square hosts more than 150 biotechnology and information technology firms, many of them MIT spin-off enterprises and most fed by MIT-led innovation. Turn right at Main Street, then left at Ames Street and left again onto Broadway to leave Kendall Square for the Area IV neighborhood.

Follow Broadway past Prospect Street and the City Hall Annex to the Cambridge Public Library complex, which also houses the Cambridge Rindge & Latin School. The complex expertly integrates modern steel-and-glass exteriors with stone columns and granite facades in an ode to Cambridge's past and future. Cross the complex heading north and turn left onto Cambridge Street to pass into the Harvard University campus.

The undisputed oldest academic institution in the United States, Harvard was founded in 1636. Named for the minister John Harvard who bequeathed half his fortune and entire scholarly library to the foundling college, Harvard now boasts eleven separate academic units, most of which ring its central campus and Harvard Yard. The university's accomplishments fill volumes, and numerous graduates, including eight US presidents and seventy-five Nobel Laureates, demonstrate the quality of education it offers. Follow Cambridge Street through its tunnel and around the traffic circle, crossing back into Cambridge Common, where you began the ride.

MILES AND DIRECTIONS

0.0 Exit the Cambridge Common at the corner of Massachusetts Avenue and Garden Street and turn right.

0.1 Turn left onto Phillips Place at the First Congregational Church, then turn right onto Brattle Street.

1.4 Turn right onto Aberdeen Avenue.

1.6 Turn right onto Huron Avenue.

1.8 Cross left onto the path along Fresh Pond Parkway.

2.3 Cross Concord Avenue at the crosswalk and turn right onto the bike path, then take a left onto Bay State Road.

2.5 Turn left into Danehy Park, taking the path at the northwest corner of the parking lot continuing straight at the junction to ride around the athletic fields.

2.7 Continue straight to ride around the running track.

Cambridge Bow–Tie Ride

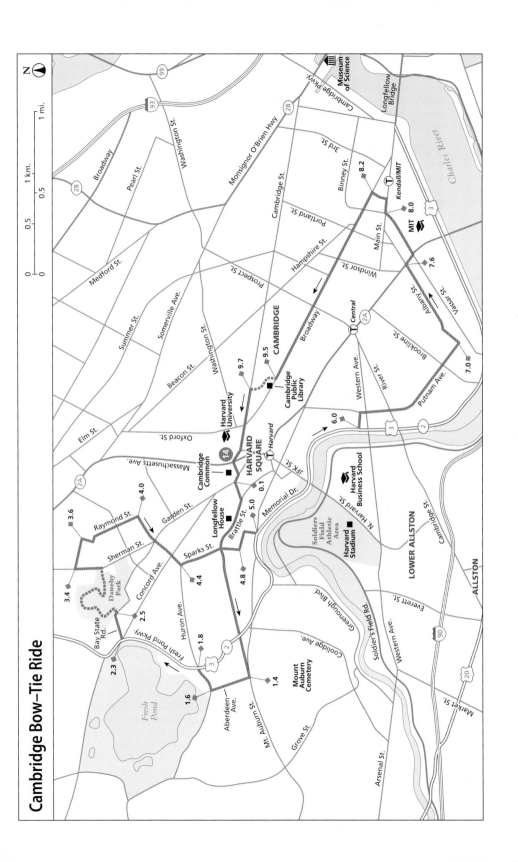

Mount Auburn Cemetery is admired around the world for its artful landscaping and historic grave sites.

3.1 Turn left and ride past the baseball fields toward the parking lot, turning left onto Sherman Street.

3.4 Turn right onto Pemberton Street.

3.6 At Yerxa Road, take a right through the tunnel and take a left through the parking lot, then a right onto Raymond Street.

4.0 Turn right onto Huron Avenue.

4.4 Turn left onto Sparks Street.

4.8 Turn left at Foster Street and then right onto Willard Street.

5.0 Cross Mt. Auburn Street and Memorial Drive to ride the path along the Charles River.

6.0 Cross Memorial Drive onto Hingham Street, then take a right on Putnam Avenue.

7.0 Turn left onto Waverly Street.

7.1 Turn right onto Albany Street.

7.6 Turn right onto Massachusetts Avenue, then left at Vassar Street.

8.0 Turn right onto Main Street, then left at Ames Street.

8.2 Turn left onto Broadway.

9.5 Turn right into the Cambridge Public Library complex, and ride north between the library and high school to Cambridge Street.

9.7 Turn left on Cambridge Street, keeping right at the fork after the tunnel to cross Massachusetts Avenue via the crosswalk.

10.2 Return to the starting point on Cambridge Common.

RIDE INFORMATION

Local Events/Attractions
Recreation Sundays on Memorial Drive: Every Sunday, from the last Sunday of April to the second Sunday of November, Memorial Drive is closed to traffic between Western Avenue and Mount Auburn Street and open to recreation. Events are organized by the Massachusetts Department of Conservation and Recreation. www.mass.gov/dcr

Cambridge Bike Tours: The community Cambridge Bikes association hosts a number of bike tours of the city each year (including its iconic Bow Tie ride along the Cambridge city border, which provided much inspiration for this ride). www.cambridgebikes.org

Mount Auburn Cemetery: This National Historic Landmark is one of the most beautiful garden cemeteries in the country, its grounds sprinkled with ornate monuments and diverse fauna. www.mountauburn.org

Sunday Parkland Games: The Charles River Conservancy organizes free park games and exercise classes along the Charles River every Sunday afternoon from mid-June to the end of September. www.charlesriverconservancy.org/ParklandGames

MIT Mystery Puzzle Hunt: Every January over MLK Day weekend, MIT hosts a team puzzle competition to locate a coin hidden on the university campus. Founded in 1981, the hunt draws more than 1,000 people to MIT each year. www.mit.edu/~puzzle

Restrooms
Start/finish: The Harvard Square Coop near Cambridge Common has restrooms that are open to the public.
Mile 3.2: Danehy Park has restrooms near the Sherman Street parking lot.
Mile 9.5: There are public restrooms in the Cambridge Public Library.

Somerville Community Path, Alewife Linear Park, and Fresh Pond

The cycling community has had a strong voice in the development of Cambridge and Somerville. This concerted bike advocacy has paid off in the construction of interlinked paths that connect the two cities to each other as well as to the statewide network of bike trails. The Somerville Community Path, Alewife Linear Park, and Fresh Pond Reservation Loop make for an easy excursion through Somerville's Davis Square and around the Fresh Pond reservoir in North Cambridge. This route hits a coveted sweet spot: the intersection of bike-friendly urban planning and the tranquil beauty of natural landscapes.

Start: Somerville Community Path, Cedar Street between Morrison Avenue and Alpine Street

Length: 8.0 miles

Approximate riding time: 1–1.5 hours with stops

Best bike: Road bike or mountain bike

Terrain and trail surface: Paved paths through Somerville and Cambridge, with occasional sections of gravel or hard-packed dirt around Fresh Pond

Traffic and hazards: Joggers, families with small children, and dog walkers use this route as well. Watch for traffic at intersections.

Things to see: Somerville Community Path, Davis Square, Somerville Theatre, The Rosebud, Alewife Linear Park, Fresh Pond, Fitchburg Cutoff Bike Path

Maps: USGS: *Boston North* and *Lexington* quad; DeLorme: *Massachusetts Atlas & Gazetteer*, p. 41

Getting there: By car: Street parking is available in the blocks near the Somerville Community Path head on Cedar Street. From downtown

Boston, cross to Cambridge via the Monsignor O'Brien Highway and continue north onto McGrath Highway (MA 28). Turn left at Broadway and take a left on Cedar Street past Magoun Square and Trum Field. The entrance to the path is between Morrison Avenue and Alpine Street.

By train: Davis Square Station along the T Red Line lies between the head of the Somerville Community Path and Alewife Station. To get to the head of the Somerville Community Path, take the T Red Line to Porter Square. Bikes are allowed on the Red Line, except from 7 to 10 a.m. and 4 to 7 p.m. Monday through Friday, and without restriction on weekends. Exit the station onto Massachusetts Avenue and ride north, turning right on Davenport Street. Take a left at Elm Street and a right on Willow Avenue to Highland Avenue. Turn right and then left at Cedar Street. GPS coordinates for starting point: N42 23.645' / W71 06.677'

THE RIDE

You'll start at the eastern end of the Somerville Community Path (SCP), a paved rail-trail that runs through Davis Square and connects to the Alewife Linear Park trail. The product of years of advocacy and sweat from the Somerville cycling community, the SCP is a prime example of incorporating bikes as a pragmatic cog in urban transportation infrastructure.

From its eastern head at Cedar Street between Highland Avenue and Broadway, you'll head west along the SCP's tree- and lantern-lined path. The SCP offers a unique vantage point to take in Somerville's staggered development across the past couple of decades—the city's trademark triple deckers abut the trail, punctuated by modern condos, commercial strips, and lots awaiting development.

It's a short ride from the SCP head at Cedar Street to its terminus just past the Bikeway Community Garden at Grove Street, a block away from Davis Square. Well-known for its hellish central intersection, Davis Square is nonetheless a beloved destination and a cultural hub for neighboring parts of Cambridge and Somerville. Landmarks like the Somerville Theatre and The Rosebud historic diner have drawn crowds to this part of Somerville for years, and each October the HONK! Street Band Festival fills Davis with the clamor of competing drums, brass, and tambourines.

A bit past Grove Street, you'll follow signs to walk your bike on the approach to the infamous six-way intersection. Take Dover Street then turn right along Meacham Road, where you'll see Seven Hills Park behind the MBTA station. This marks the beginning of the Alewife Linear Park, which runs from Davis Square to the Alewife MBTA station and the head of the Minuteman Trail.

The Alewife Linear Park was established in 1985 when the MBTA constructed the Red Line T tunnel between Davis Square and Alewife under an abandoned railroad right-of-way. Since then Somerville cyclists have extended the route past Davis Square and have begun development of a continuous rail-trail toward Lechmere and the Charles River Esplanade paths. Like the SCP, the Alewife Linear Park offers a glimpse of architectural development as you cut across Cambridge toward Fresh Pond. By providing a convenient means of accessing the T by bike, the linear park itself has aided in the revitalization of this stretch of real estate.

The linear park path continues due west past Massachusetts Avenue before winding south at the Russell Field athletic complex. Turn right at the fork at Jerry's Pond, also known as Jerry's Pit. A disused clay pit that became a neighborhood swimming hole after filling with water, Jerry's Pond is an homage to Cambridge's industrial past. You'll follow the signs to Alewife MBTA station, turning right just after the Alewife Brook Parkway overpass toward the Minuteman Commuter Bikeway. Follow the Alewife Linear Park left, past the pond and across the Alewife Station Access Road to the Fitchburg Cutoff, a 0.8-mile railtrail link in the proposed 104-mile Massachusetts Central Rail Trail between Northampton and Boston. Follow the cutoff to Blanchard Road and turn left, and then left again at Concord Avenue, where the Fresh Pond parkland will come into view.

Bike Shop

Bike Boom is a full-service used bike shop in Davis Square specializing in restorations and up-cycled parts. The shop is located at 389 Highland Ave., Somerville; (617) 627-9801; www.bikeboom.net.

The 155-acre Fresh Pond Reservoir is a shallow kettle-hole lake formed by retreating glaciers more than 15,000 years ago. The pond became Cambridge's water supply in 1852, and the city was granted eminent domain over the pond and surrounding land in the 1880s to protect its waters from industrial pollution. In addition to supplying drinking water for the city, the reservation land is among the most popular in Cambridge for its lakefront views and wooded paths. Enter the park's trail loop a couple blocks up Concord Avenue, across from Smith Place. On your immediate right inside the park is the small Blacks Nook pond, which has a small walking loop and preservation area. Continue to the main Fresh Pond loop and turn right, where you'll pass the private Fresh Pond golf course and country club on the reservoir's western edge. Continuing on, the path skirts past the much smaller Lily Pond at the westernmost point of Fresh Pond.

The Somerville Community Path links Somerville to Cambridge. When completed, it will connect the MBTA Red Line to the Green Line.

You'll round the southern tip of Fresh Pond and enter Kingsley Park. This was the site of the Fresh Pond Hotel from 1796 to 1892, when it was relocated to nearby Lakeview Avenue. Follow the paved loop around the park, then turn left to ride past the Cambridge Water Department treatment facility. You are now passing through Tudor Park, named for Boston's "Ice King" Frederic Tudor, who harvested ice from Fresh Pond in the mid-1800s. Tudor's and other ice-harvesting outfits reportedly shipped Fresh Pond ice, which was prized for its purity, as far as Cuba, Europe, and even China.

Follow the shore line north and then west, exiting the Fresh Pond loop through Lusitania Field. Turn right out of the reservation to ride along Concord Avenue once again, crossing at Wheeler Street and continuing right along the bike path parallel to Alewife Brook Parkway. Continue over the overpass and turn into Alewife Station, then follow the path to the right of the bus terminal to the back of the building, where you'll find the Alewife Linear Park path once again for the return leg of the ride.

Turn right under the overpass and continue to Russell Field, where you'll take a left and ride back past the athletic complex. Follow the Somerville Community Path back past Massachusetts Avenue and to Davis Square, where you'll walk your bike southeast across the square and along the MBTA

15

Busway to where the bike path resumes. Ride along the path back to Cedar Street, where you began.

MILES AND DIRECTIONS

0.0 From the end of the Somerville Community Path at Cedar Street, ride west.

0.5 Walk your bike along the MBTA Busway to College Avenue and straight across Davis Square and Holland Street past the opposite Davis Station entrance, where you can remount and continue riding.

1.0 Cross Massachusetts Avenue.

1.6 Turn right past Russell Field.

1.7 Turn right after the overpass toward the Minuteman Commuter Bikeway.

1.8 Cross to the Fitchburg Cutoff Bike Path.

2.6 Turn left onto Blanchard Road.

3.0 Turn left onto Concord Avenue.

3.4 Turn right into the Fresh Pond reservation.

3.5 Turn right onto the Fresh Pond loop.

4.7 Turn left into Kingsley Park.

5.0 Keep left to rejoin the Fresh Pond loop.

5.6 Turn right out of the park.

5.7 Cross Concord Avenue to the opposite bike lane and turn right, curving toward the Alewife Parkway overpass.

6.1 After the overpass, follow the sidewalk left and then across Cambridge Park Drive to Alewife Station. Stay right of the station to rejoin the Alewife Linear Park, and turn right under the overpass.

6.4 Turn left at Russell Field.

7.4 Walk your bike back across Davis Square to the MBTA Busway, and continue riding past the bike racks.

8.0 Finish at the end of the Somerville Community Path.

Somerville Community Path, Alewife Linear Park, and Fresh Pond

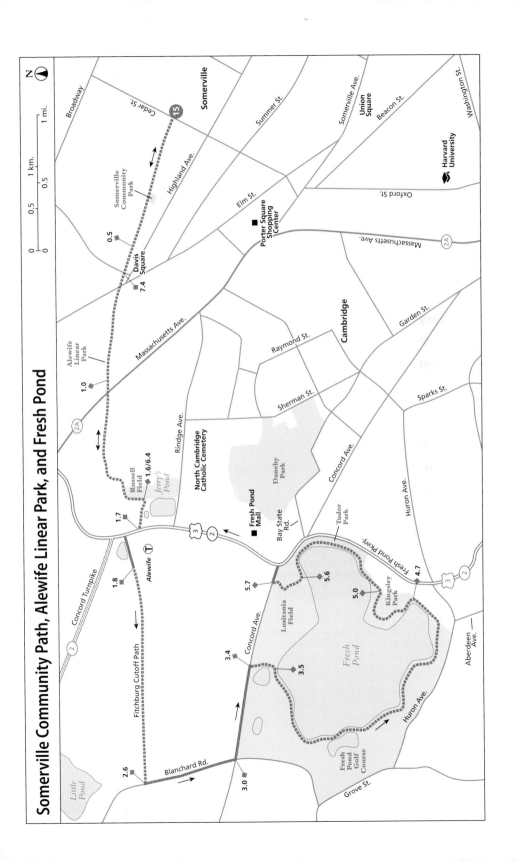

Fresh Pond was once a gem in Frederic Tudor's ice empire, but today is known less for its industry than its preserved woods.

RIDE INFORMATION

Local Events/Attractions
HONK! Street Band Festival: Since 2005 street bands have converged every Columbus Day weekend for a multistage rumpus along the sidewalks, storefronts, and nooks of Davis Square. www.honkfest.org

Museum of Bad Art: This collection of cringe-worthy sculptures, paintings, and multimedia messes adorns the basement of the Somerville Theatre in Davis Square. www.museumofbadart.org

Restrooms
Mile 1.6 and 6.4: Russell Field has public restrooms, as does Alewife Station.

North of Boston

Belmont's Town Hall is a vibrant redbrick structure with sharp turrets (Ride 17).

Looking for adventure outside the metro area? Head north! You can drink in the majestic Walden Pond, Middlesex Fells Reservation, and Horn Pond, or follow the Minuteman Commuter Bikeway to the very beginning of the American Revolution at Lexington Green. Relax along the beaches of Revere, Nahant, and Marblehead, or catch up on ghost stories as you explore Salem. Point your bike north, and in no time you'll see sides of New England history and landscape unlike anything in Boston proper.

Somerville, Medford, and the Mystic River Reservation

Just north of Boston and Cambridge lies the city of Somerville. Fondly known as "Slummerville" until its renaissance in the 1990s, the city is a mishmash of wildly diverse neighborhoods that boasts one of the highest artist densities per capita of any metropolitan area in the country. This ride explores some of Somerville's vibrant city squares, the Tufts University campus at its center, and the Mystic River and Alewife Brook that make up the city's borders.

Start: Prospect Hill Park, Munroe Street.

Length: 9.8 miles

Approximate riding time: 1.5 hours with stops

Best bike: Road bike or mountain bike

Terrain and trail surface: Paved roads and dirt paths through Somerville and Medford, with occasional sections of uneven pavement

Traffic and hazards: Joggers and dog walkers frequent the Blueback River Herring Route, as well as the Mystic River Reservation path and Alewife Greenway Bike Path. Watch for traffic, in particular along Massachusetts Avenue and Somerville Avenue.

Things to see: Prospect Hill Park, Foss Park, Blessing of the Bay Boathouse, Mystic River, Mystic River Reservation, Tufts University, Dilboy Stadium, Davis Square, Union Square

Maps: USGS: *Boston North* and *Lexington* quads; DeLorme: *Massachusetts Atlas & Gazettee,* p. 41

Getting there: By car: There is metered street parking in Union Square and on Munroe Street along Prospect Hill Park. From downtown Boston, take Monsignor O'Brien Highway across the Charles River and continue north along McGrath Highway. Exit at Washington Street, where you'll turn left to Union Square. Take Somerville Avenue right and turn right again on Stone Avenue, which leads up Prospect Hill to Munroe Street. The park is on your immediate left. **By train:** Take the T Orange Line to Sullivan Square. Bikes are allowed on the Orange Line, except from 7 to 10 a.m. and 4 to 7 p.m. Monday through Friday, and without restriction on weekends. Exit the station onto Washington Street and turn right, crossing under McGrath Highway to Somerville Avenue. Turn right through Union Square, then right again at Stone Avenue, which leads up Prospect Hill to Munroe Street. The park is on your immediate left. GPS coordinates for starting point: N42 22.912' / W71 05.618'

THE RIDE

You'll start at Prospect Hill Park at the base of the Prospect Hill Monument, where the first American "Grand Union" flag was raised on January 1, 1776. The panoramic views from Prospect Hill made it an important strategic location during the Revolutionary War, when the hill became known as the "Citadel." The castle and monument, which were erected in 1902, stand as a testament to colonist soldiers' bravery and strategic cunning during the war for independence from Great Britain.

From the base of the monument, ride west along Munroe Street to Walnut Street and turn right. Continue through the neighborhoods of central Somerville, famous for their triple-decker apartment buildings that harken back to the city's past as an industrial center in need of rapid residential expansion. Cross Broadway into Foss Park, the largest green space in Somerville. Founded in 1876 as Broadway Park, this 15-acre space was renamed in 1921 for Army soldier Saxton Conant Foss, who died in WWI. The park is one of Somerville's summer focal points, particularly for the annual Foss Fest music extravaganza. Turn left at Jacques Street, where you'll find the circular white and blue signs that mark the Blueback River Herring Route, which leads from Foss Park to the Mystic Riverfront. Take a right at Temple Street, and a left onto Memorial Road, then follow the Blueback signs through the Somerville Housing Authority complex, which will lead you to Mystic Avenue.

Cross Mystic Avenue under I-93, where you'll catch your first glimpse of the Mystic River behind the Blessing of the Bay Boathouse. The boathouse is named for the trading ship *Blessing of the Bay,* the second vessel built in the colonies in 1631. Governor John Winthrop oversaw the ship's construction—a historic marker at the intersection of Shore Drive and Governor Winthrop Road just across from the boathouse marks the site of Winthrop's home in

The mural near Blessing of the Bay Boathouse is a reminder of past uses for the riverfront, including as a popular beach.

what is today Somerville's Ten Hills neighborhood. The boathouse is operated by the Boys & Girls Club of Middlesex County and offers canoe and paddle-boat rentals by the hour on weekdays. Take the paved path from the boat-house that follows Shore Drive, and cross the Wellington Bridge into Medford, turning at the second path after the bridge into the Mystic River Reservation.

The reservation is a world apart, its serene and peaceful path separated from its surroundings by thick trees and expanses of tall cattails. Established in 1893 as one of the first nature preserves in Massachusetts, the reservation includes parklands in Medford, Somerville, Arlington, and Chelsea along the banks of the Mystic, whose shores are almost entirely public owned. One of the great urban rivers of New England, the Mystic's name is an anglicized deri-vation of "Missi-Tuk," an Algonquian word meaning "a great river whose waters are driven by waves." Until it was first dammed in 1909, the Mystic River rose and fell with saltwater tides twice a day, powering tidal mills and factories along its banks. More recently, the river was immortalized in the gritty 2003 Oscar-winning film *Mystic River,* a Clint Eastwood adaptation of the novel of the same name by Dennis Lehane.

Follow the reservation path until it emerges at the Mystic Valley Parkway, then turn back toward the river along the grassy lawns of MacDonald Park.

Best Bike Rides Boston

Follow the waterfront down to the small boardwalk over the river, which has a particularly spectacular view of the water, bridge, and city skyline beyond. Ride on toward Mystic Valley Parkway once more, turning left at the fork just before the parkway toward the small wooden tower over the marshland. This tower is an ideal rest stop, as its views of the reservation are without parallel. Exit the reservation via the path along the parkway, which you'll follow across the river to Mystic Avenue.

Cross Mystic Avenue to Harvard Street, which you'll follow southwest until Boston Avenue. Turn right to head into the Tufts University campus, taking a right onto Dearborn Road and then a left on Professors Row, which divides the upper and lower campus. Established in 1852 after Charles Tufts donated 20 acres of land on Medford's Walnut Hill, now College Hill, to the Universalist Church, Tufts University consistently ranks in the top fifty institutes of higher learning in the country and is known worldwide in particular for the Fletcher School for Law and Diplomacy.

Turn right onto the paved path across President's Lawn and carry your bike up the short stairs to Ballou Hall. Turn right and ride past the Goddard Chapel, in which you can find the "Easter Lilies" Tiffany stained-glass window. Continue on to the Tisch Library roof, where you'll find one of the most impressive views of Greater Boston outside the city itself. After seeing the roof, ride across the Green past the statue of the Tufts mascot Jumbo, who pays homage to P. T. Barnum, the circus showman and early benefactor of the university.

Turn right at Packard Avenue and continue along Capen Street, which leads to the Capen Path. Cross Alewife Brook Parkway to join the paved Alewife Greenway Bike Path along Dilboy Field and Dilboy Stadium, both named

Bike Shops

Ace Wheelworks is as much about supporting the local bicycling community as providing high-quality repairs, parts, and equipment. The shop is located at 145 Elm St., Somerville; (617) 776-2100; www.wheelworks.com.

Bike Boom is a full-service used bike shop in Davis Square, specializing in restorations and up-cycled parts. The shop is located at 389 Highland Ave., Somerville; (617) 627-9801; www.bikeboom.net.

Paramount Bicycle Repair has years of experience in overhauls, quick tune-ups, and all adjustments in between. The shop is close to Tufts at 104 Bristol Rd., Somerville; (617) 666-6072; www.paramountbicycle.com.

Park Sales & Services, family-owned since 1952, provides a full range of repairs and bikes to Somerville at great prices. Visit the shop at 510 Somerville Ave., Somerville; (617) 666-3647; www.parksales.com.

The library roof at Tufts overlooks the hills of Somerville toward downtown Boston.

after Army Private George Dilboy, the first Greek-American to be awarded the Medal of Honor in World War I. The stadium is home to the Boston Breakers and the Boston Militia, the city's professional women's soccer and football teams, respectively. Continue alongside Alewife Brook Parkway to Massachusetts Avenue, where you'll turn left.

Follow Massachusetts Avenue until its intersection with the Somerville Community Path at Cameron Avenue. Turn left onto the path, which you'll follow to Seven Hills Park in Davis Square, a cultural hub for neighboring parts of Cambridge and Somerville. Landmarks like the Somerville Theatre and the historic Rosebud Diner draw crowds all year, and each October the HONK! Street Band Festival fills Davis with the clamor of marching bands. Turn right onto Elm Street, taking particular care at Davis Square's infamous six-way intersection. Follow Elm Street to Somerville Avenue, where you'll turn left. Ride past Conway Park, the Market Basket grocery store, and the Milk Row Cemetery to arrive in Union Square at the base of Prospect

> With close to 80,000 residents in just slightly over 4 square miles, the city of Somerville is the most densely populated community in New England.

Hill. Cross the square at Washington Street toward Stone Avenue, which you'll take for the final climb to Prospect Hill Parkway and the Prospect Hill Monument, where you began the ride.

MILES AND DIRECTIONS

0.0 Ride west from Prospect Hill Park along Munroe Street.

0.1 Turn right onto Walnut Street.

0.7 Cross Broadway into Foss Park and continue north.

0.9 Turn left onto Jacques Street, where the Blueback River Herring Route begins.

1.1 Turn right onto Temple Street.

1.3 Turn left at Memorial Road, then follow the Blueback River Herring Route right through the housing complex to Mystic Avenue.

1.4 Cross Mystic Avenue under the I-93 overpass to the Blessing of the Bay Boathouse and continue north along the paved path.

1.8 Cross the Wellington Bridge north into Medford.

2.0 Turn left into the Mystic River Reservation, crossing the wooden footbridge.

2.3 Stay left to loop back into the park, following the shoreline.

2.7 Stay left at all forks as you exit the park, passing the observation tower before riding west along Mystic River Parkway and crossing the river.

3.6 Cross Mystic Avenue and continue along Harvard Street.

4.3 Turn right onto Boston Avenue.

4.4 Turn left at Dearborn Road, then left onto Professors Row.

4.7 Turn right into campus, carry your bike up the steps, and turn right to pass the chapel to the library-roof overlook.

4.9 Cut north to the campus green and turn left past Ballou Hall.

5.0 Turn right onto Packard Avenue, which continues into Capen Street.

5.7 Continue onto the Capen Path, then cross Alewife Brook Parkway to ride south along the paved Alewife Greenway Bike Path that borders Dilboy Field.

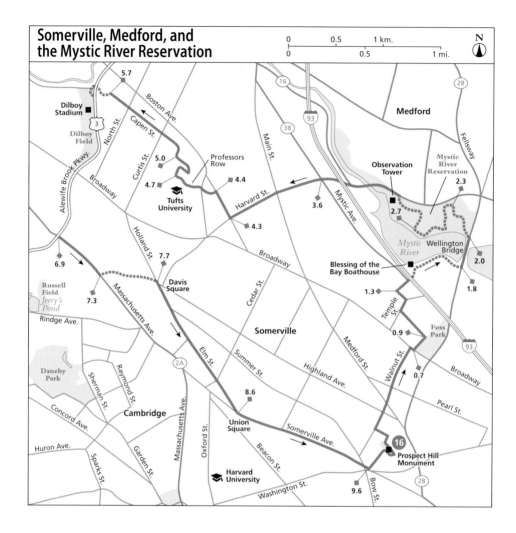

Somerville, Medford, and the Mystic River Reservation

Dilboy Stadium ■

Dilboy Field

5.7

Boston Ave.

Capen St.

North St.

Curtis St.

Broadway

Alewife Brook Pkwy.

5.0

4.7

Tufts University

Professors Row

4.4

Harvard St.

Main St.

Medford

Observation Tower

Mystic River Reservation

2.3

2.7

Fellsway

3.6

Mystic Ave.

4.3

Holland St.

7.7

Davis Square

Broadway

Mystic River

Wellington Bridge

2.0

6.9

Russell Field

Jerry's Pond

7.3

Massachusetts Ave.

Rindge Ave.

Blessing of the Bay Boathouse

1.3

Temple St.

1.8

Cedar St.

Somerville

0.9

Foss Park

93

Danehy Park

Sherman St.

Raymond St.

2A

Elm St.

Summer St.

Highland Ave.

Medford St.

Walnut St.

0.7

Broadway

Concord Ave.

Cambridge

8.6

Pearl St.

Huron Ave.

Sparks St.

Garden St.

Massachusetts Ave.

Oxford St.

Union Square

Somerville Ave.

16

Prospect Hill Monument

Beacon St.

Bow St.

Harvard University

Washington St.

9.6

28

0   0.5   1 km.
0   0.5   1 mi.

N

6.9 Turn left onto Massachusetts Avenue.

7.3 Cross Massachusetts Avenue east onto the Somerville Community Path.

7.7 Turn right onto Elm Street.

8.6 Turn left onto Somerville Avenue.

9.6 Turn left onto Washington Street, then cross Union Square north to Stone Avenue.

9.8 Follow Prospect Hill Parkway to Munroe Street and turn left.

9.9 Arrive back at the starting point at Prospect Hill Park.

RIDE INFORMATION

Local Events/Attractions

New Year's Day Flag-Raising at Prospect Hill Park: Each year the Somerville Historic Preservation Commission marks the anniversary of the raising of the first official flag of the fledgling United States on January 1, 1776, by George Washington. The ceremony includes a reenactment by a George Washington impersonator, demonstrations by the Ancient and Honorable Artillery Company of Massachusetts, and songs from Revolutionary times. www.somerville ma.gov/historic-preservation-commission

What the Fluff Festival: Somerville celebrates its place in history as the birthplace of marshmallow fluff each fall with cooking demonstrations, artwork, and obstacle courses all incorporating the sweetest condiment known to man. www.unionsquaremain.org

SomerStreets: Each summer the city of Somerville hosts a series of community events at its major squares and parks, including Foss Park, Davis Square, and Union Square. www.somervillema.gov

Restrooms

Start/finish: Union Square at the base of Prospect Hill has a number of shops with public restrooms.

Mile 0.7: Foss Park has restrooms and water.

Mile 1.5: The Blessing of the Bay Boathouse has restrooms and water.

Mile 4.8: The Tufts library has public restrooms and water.

Mile 7.7: Davis Square has a number of shops with restrooms.

Mile 9.3: Market Basket grocery store has public restrooms.

17

Walden Pond

Henry David Thoreau's famous retreat to Boston's north continues to draw revelers each summer, who flock to Walden Pond to swim, fish, boat, and picnic. This ride leads from Cambridge Common in Harvard Square through the picturesque towns of Belmont, Lexington, Waltham, Lincoln, and Concord. A number of challenging hills along the wooded route make reaching Walden Pond Reservation that much sweeter. Its serene shores and surrounding woodlands are just as peaceful and contemplative today as they were in more Transcendental times.

Start: Cambridge Common, Massachusetts Avenue, and Garden Street

Length: 27.2 miles

Approximate riding time: 3–3.5 hours with stops

Best bike: Road bike or hybrid

Terrain and trail surface: Paved urban roads and bike lanes

Traffic and hazards: Watch for traffic, particularly at Fresh Pond and close to the highway in Lexington

Things to see: Cambridge Common, Fresh Pond, Belmont, Cambridge Reservoir, Lincoln, deCordova Sculpture Park and Museum, Walden Pond, Walden Pond Beach

Maps: USGS: *Boston North, Boston South, Lexington,* and *Natick* quads. DeLorme: *Massachusetts Atlas & Gazetteer,* pp. 39–41

Getting there: By car: Parking can be tricky around Harvard Square, although you can find street spots. The Harvard Parking Garage is usually a good bet as well. From Boston, take Massachusetts Avenue to Memorial Drive and turn right. Take JFK Street right, then take a left onto Eliot Street, where you'll see the garage on your immediate right. There is also parking at the Charles Hotel. From the garage, take JFK Street north to Massachusetts Avenue and cross left at Harvard Yard to

Cambridge Common. **By train:** Take the T Red Line to Harvard Square. Bikes are allowed on the Red Line, except from 7 to 10 a.m. and 4 to 7 p.m. Monday through Friday, and without restriction on weekends. Exit the station to Church Street and walk your bike north along Massachusetts Avenue to the Cambridge Common. GPS coordinates for starting point: N42 22.538' / W71 07.178'

THE RIDE

You'll start at Cambridge Common, at the intersection of Massachusetts Avenue and Garden Street. Ride along Garden Street past the Common, then stay left at the fork to continue onto Concord Avenue, which you'll follow all the way into Waltham. In a few minutes you'll come to Fresh Pond Parkway, where you'll ride straight through both rotaries to follow Concord Avenue along the pond's northern edge. Take the protected bike lane just after the second rotary, which ends as you cross Blanchard Road into Belmont.

Once an agrarian center, today Belmont is primarily residential, famous for the mansions that have been home to notable residents like Yo-Yo Ma, James Taylor, Mitt Romney, and countless professors from MIT and Harvard. Just past Claypit Pool and Belmont High School, turn right through the tunnel and then left to stay on Concord Avenue. You'll pass the red stone of Belmont Town Hall as you enter the first significant hill of the ride just past Pleasant Street, where you'll climb around the curve into the Belmont Hill neighborhood. As you catch your breath, gape at the incredible properties, each parcel adorned with a stately home and so many trees it's difficult to tell private land from preserves like the Rock Meadow Conservation Area, which you'll pass on the left a few minutes on. Immediately after is the Belmont Country Club to the right, its golf course straddling the line between Belmont and neighboring Lexington. Follow Concord Avenue through this southern segment of Lexington's hills to its terminus at Spring Street.

During Thoreau's time, Walden's ice was shipped as far as India by Frederic Tudor, Boston's "Ice King." Thus Thoreau famously wrote, "The pure Walden water is mingled with the sacred water of the Ganges."

Turn left and ride south briefly along Spring Street, which becomes Smith Street after it enters Waltham. Once known as Watch City for its numerous timepiece factories, today the small city is a center for research and academics,

Cambridge Reservoir is a brief taste of the waterfront views to come at Walden.

home to Brandeis University and Bentley University. Aerosmith rented their "A. Wherehouse" space in Waltham from 1975 into the 1980s, often hosting artists like Boston and Ted Nugent at their complex on Pond Street. You'll ride through the northern edge as you turn right off of Smith Street onto Trapelo Road and cross I-95 into more wooded neighborhood hills.

After another steep climb you'll leave Waltham for the town of Lincoln as you cut between the two halves of Cambridge Reservoir. Completed in the 1890s to address Cambridge's water shortage, the reservoir's "islands" were once natural high points before this area was flooded by damming. Continue along Trapelo toward the center of Lincoln, which was called "Niptown" in colonial times due to its creation from segments carved off from Concord, Weston, and Lexington in 1754. As such, the town is named for Lincolnshire, England, rather than for Honest Abe.

At the end of Trapelo Road in Lincoln Center Historic District, continue straight onto Sandy Pond Road just past the public library, following the signs to the deCordova Sculpture Park and Museum. The museum's modern art and photography collections are small but formidable, crowned with a breathtaking sculpture trail overlooking Flints Pond. Its focus on New England artists since its public opening in 1950 also sets deCordova apart in regional art circles. Turn left just past the museum onto Baker Bridge Road, passing a number of stone-fenced plots as you come to Concord Road and turn right for the final stretch to Walden.

You'll see signs as you cross into Concord for Walden Pond, first for the boat dock and then for the Walden Pond Beach on the left. The reservation, which is a state park as well as a National Historic Landmark, also includes the house owned by Ralph Waldo Emerson on the property where Henry David Thoreau spent his two years, two months, and two days living alone beginning in 1845. Thoreau's time on the wooded shores of this deep kettle-hole pond culminated in his opus, *Walden*, that made the pond famous after it was published in 1854. The book's themes of self-reliance and environmental awareness have made it a standard of college literature surveys today, and thousands come to Walden every year to see a replica of Thoreau's cabin and walk through the woods the scribe himself walked as he wrestled with humanity's place in natural history. The nearby Concord Museum today preserves the sparse bed, chair, and desk from Thoreau's cabin.

Bike Shops

ATA Cycle is Concord's pro bike shop, its master bicycle technicians experienced at fitting seats, wheels, and handlebars to laser precision. The shop is located at 93 Thoreau St., Concord; (978) 369-5960; www.atabike.com.

Quad Bikes is a nonprofit shop run for the Harvard community, but open to the public as well. The shop is located at 51 Shepard St., Cambridge; (617) 496-5955; www.quadbikes.org.

The modern Walden philosopher has a bit more competition to wander the pond's shore and ponder its beauty, which is frequented by bathers and picnickers during the warm-weather months. Walden's beauty and refreshing waters are a fantastic reward for the hilly ride from Cambridge. Those with literary inclinations will also find a number of exhibits that explore Thoreau's life, work, and social experiment on the pond. After you've had your fill, head back south along Concord Road for the return leg.

Follow Concord Road back to Baker Bridge Road and turn left, continuing onto Sandy Pond Road and Trapelo Road through Lincoln and once again across Cambridge Reservoir. Luckily, all those uphills on the way out are now a breeze for the ride back! Cross I-95 and turn left at Smith Street, then right at Concord Avenue to ride into Belmont. Keep left after the Rock Meadow Conservation Area for the last uphill of the ride, which takes you back through the opulence of Belmont Hill. Pass Belmont Town Hall again and turn right through the tunnel and then left to continue on Concord Avenue. Pass once more into Cambridge by Blanchard Road and along the edge of Fresh Pond.

Continue straight through both rotaries to follow Concord Avenue as it meets Garden Street. Ride back to the southern tip of the Cambridge Common, where you began.

MILES AND DIRECTIONS

0.0 From the southern tip of Cambridge Common, ride northwest along Garden Street.

0.3 Keep left at the fork onto Concord Avenue.

1.5 At Fresh Pond Parkway, continue straight through both rotaries to continue along Concord Avenue.

3.3 Turn right onto Concord Avenue, under the overpass, then take your first left.

3.4 Continue straight past Pleasant Street along Concord Avenue as it slopes uphill and curves north.

7.8 Turn left onto Spring Street, which becomes Smith Street.

8.2 Turn right onto Trapelo Road.

10.7 Keep left to stay on Trapelo Road.

11.0 At Lincoln Road, continue straight onto Sandy Pond Road.

11.7 Turn left onto Baker Bridge Road.

12.8 Turn right onto Concord Road.

13.6 Arrive at Walden Pond and turn around.

14.3 Turn left onto Baker Bridge Road.

14.9 Keep right to stay on Baker Bridge Road.

15.5 Turn right onto Sandy Pond Road.

16.1 Continue straight onto Trapelo Road.

18.9 Turn left onto Smith Street, which becomes Spring Street.

19.4 Turn right onto Concord Avenue.

22.6 Keep left to stay on Concord Avenue.

23.8 Turn right under the overpass and then left to stay on Concord Avenue.

Walden Pond

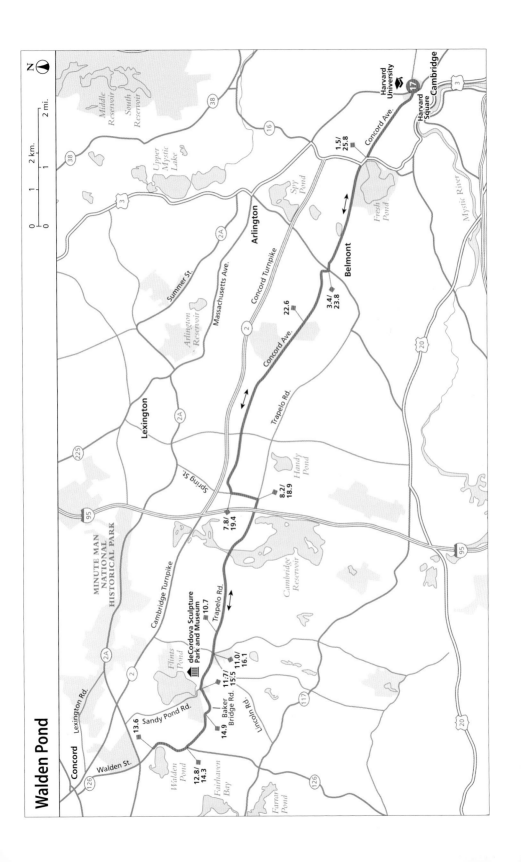

N

0   1   2 km.

0   1   2 mi.

Middle Reservoir

South Reservoir

Upper Mystic Lake

Spy Pond

Fresh Pond

Mystic River

Harvard University

Harvard Square

Cambridge

Concord Ave.

1.5/ 25.8

Belmont

Arlington

Concord Turnpike

3.4/ 23.8

22.6

Concord Ave.

Massachusetts Ave.

Summer St.

Lexington

Arlington Reservoir

Trapelo Rd.

Handy Pond

8.2/ 18.9

Spring St.

7.8/ 19.4

MINUTE MAN NATIONAL HISTORICAL PARK

Cambridge Turnpike

Cambridge Reservoir

deCordova Sculpture Park and Museum   10.7

Trapelo Rd.

Flints Pond

11.0/ 16.1

11.7/ 15.5

Baker Bridge Rd.

14.9

Lincoln Rd.

Sandy Pond Rd.

13.6

Concord

Walden St.

Lexington Rd.

Walden Pond

12.8/ 14.3

Fairhaven Bay

Farrar Pond

25.6 Continue straight through the traffic circle.

25.8 Continue through the traffic circle to stay on Concord Avenue.

27.0 Keep left onto Garden Street.

27.2 Arrive back at Cambridge Common.

RIDE INFORMATION

Local Events/Attractions

deCordova Sculpture Park and Museum: This outdoor sculpture gallery features extensive holdings by New England and Massachusetts artists. www.decordova.org

Walden Pond State Reservation: With its replica of Thoreau's cabin and preserved Walden Woods, this state park allows you to walk the famous Transcendentalist's path to enlightenment. www.walden.org

Restrooms

Start/finish: Harvard Square has a number of shops and restaurants with public restrooms.

Mile 3.3 and 23.8: Belmont has a number of shops and restaurants with public restrooms.

Mile 13.6: Walden Pond Beach has public restrooms.

Lexington, Concord, and the Minute Man National Historical Park

The Minuteman Commuter Bikeway connects Cambridge to the historic towns of Lexington and Concord, where the American Revolution began. Go beyond the Minuteman path to explore revolutionary history along the Battle Road Trail, as well as the literary history of early America once dominated by the literati enclave in Concord. A mix of smooth rail-trail, paved roads, and forest paths with a couple of climbs for good measure, this ride takes you backward in time to the origins of our country.

Start: Alewife T Station

Length: 27.2 miles

Approximate riding time: 3–4 hours with stops

Best bike: Hybrid or mountain bike

Terrain and trail surface: A mix of even rail-trail, paved roads, and dirt trails, with occasional patches of uneven pavement and sandy terrain

Traffic and hazards: Joggers, families with small children, and dog walkers are common sights along the Minuteman Bikeway, particularly closer to Cambridge, Arlington Center, and through Lexington. Watch for uneven and sandy terrain along the Battle Road Trail.

Things to see: Minuteman Commuter Bikeway, Spy Pond, Arlington's Great Meadows, Lexington Depot, Buckman Tavern, Lexington Green, Minute Man National Historical Park, Louisa May Alcott Orchard House, Nathaniel Hawthorne House, Battle Road Trail, Lexington Common

Maps: USGS: *Lexington* and *Concord* quads; DeLorme; *Massachusetts Atlas & Gazetteer*, p 40–41

Getting there: By car: Parking is available at Alewife Station. From Boston, take Massachusetts Avenue north into Cambridge. Turn left onto Alewife Brook Parkway and follow it south to the station. **By train:** Take the T Red Line to Alewife Station. Bikes are allowed on the Red Line, except from 7 to 10 a.m. and 4 to 7 p.m. Monday through Friday, and without restriction on weekends. Follow the signs to the Minuteman Bikeway trailhead on the north side of the station. GPS coordinates for starting point: N42 23.771' / W71 08.454'

THE RIDE

For the first leg of this ride, you'll follow the Minuteman Commuter Bikeway from Alewife to Lexington. Begin at the trailhead behind Alewife Station, next to the Alewife Brook Parkway overpass. Follow the Minuteman signs to head north along the bikeway, passing under the Concord Turnpike overpass, which marks the border between Cambridge and Arlington. A bit farther on you'll pass Spy Pond, where in April 1775 an elderly woman named Mother Batherick took six redcoats prisoner while gathering dandelions along the shore. A few minutes on at Arlington Center, you'll turn right onto Swan Place then turn left briefly along Massachusetts Avenue before turning right onto Mystic Street to rejoin the Minuteman Bikeway. This is the only such drastic break in the path until you reach Lexington.

The path cuts through Arlington's north side, passing Hurd Field at the south end of the Arlington Reservoir and the Great Meadows, a favorite haunt for birders. Just past the Great Meadows, you'll cross into Lexington, world-famous as the site of the "shot heard 'round the world" that sparked the Revolutionary War. Lexington was first settled in 1642 and hosts yearly reenactments of the numerous battles that took place nearby in the colonies' fight for independence from Great Britain. You'll leave the Minuteman Bikeway at Lexington Depot, turning left onto Meriam Street and then right onto Massachusetts Avenue. On your immediate right is Buckman Tavern, where minutemen regulars awaited the British before the Battle of Lexington on April 19, 1775. The tavern's interior is preserved largely as it was in revolutionary days, including its old front door pocked with a British musket ball, according to legend.

Ride past the Minuteman Statue on your left and around Lexington Common, where a monument stands to the colonial soldiers who died in this initial skirmish with the Crown. Turn left at Harrington Road to round the Common and rejoin Massachusetts Avenue, which you'll follow westward through Lexington, past Hastings Park and several neighborhoods. Just after the I-95 overpass, turn right onto Wood Street and then left at Old Massachusetts Avenue to reach the Battle Road Trail on the right at the edge of the Minute Man

National Historical Park. Take the dirt Battle Road Trail as it follows the path British Regulars took between Boston and Concord and back during the April 19, 1775, skirmishes. Along its unpaved route you'll find markers of significant points from that first day of the American Revolution, as well as a number of preserved "witness houses" that were standing at the time of the first clashes.

Follow the markers to wind through the park's deep woods and ride behind the Minute Man Visitor Center, just after which you'll come to the Paul Revere capture site. Here the famed patriot was halted and his horse confiscated, thus ending his midnight ride to warn the countryside of the British advance. After passing through a tunnel under Hanscom Drive, you'll come to the Captain William Smith House, whose namesake owner was not only the captain of the local militia but also the brother of Abigail Adams. The Hartwell Tavern is next, where park rangers in colonial attire offer daily programs, including talks on militia drills and battle formations. Follow the signs right and then left at the "Bloody Angle," where militiamen ambushed British regulars on their retreat from Concord with a volley that killed thirty redcoats. A bit past the Angle you'll cross into Concord.

The Battle Road Trail continues past a handful of more witness houses and through a mix of forest, historic farmland, and lush wetland, practically ever few feet annotated and marked for its particular contribution to the events that led to the birth of the United States. Follow the path to its end at Meriam's Corner, where you'll turn left onto Lexington Road. As you ride into Concord you'll pass a particularly literary pair of historic homes. The first you'll reach is the Wayside, which was home to Louisa May Alcott, the author of *Little Women*, for a time before it was passed to Nathaniel Hawthorne, famous

Bike Shops

ATA Cycle is Concord's pro bike shop, its master bicycle technicians experienced at fitting seats, wheels, and handlebars to laser precision. The shop is located at 93 Thoreau St., Concord; (978) 369-5960; www.atabike.com.

The Bike Stop is conveniently located right along the Minuteman path and carries a full selection of bikes for sale and rent. The Bike Stop is located 43R Dudley St., Arlington; (781)-646-7867; www.abikestop.com.

Quad Cycles, just blocks from the Minuteman path in Arlington Heights, has been offering professional cycling advice and repairs since owner Rustem Gode moved from Cambridge in 2000 to open his own shop. Quad is located at 1043 Massachusetts Ave., Arlington; (781) 648-5222; www. quadcycles.com.

The Minute Man National Historical Park's Battle Road Trail takes you past the witness houses and skirmish sites along this historic way.

for penning *The Scarlet Letter*. Not two minutes on you'll come to Louisa May Alcott's Orchard House, where the author actually wrote her most famous novel at a desk built by her father. Today, both the Orchard House and the Wayside are museums dedicated to the rich literary history of Concord, which also nurtured the talents of Transcendentalists Ralph Waldo Emerson and Henry David Thoreau. Authors' Ridge in nearby Sleepy Hollow Cemetery is the final resting place for Emerson, Thoreau, Hawthorne, and Alcott. The literary weight that Concord once wielded led Henry James to describe it in an 1907 essay as "the biggest little place in America," surpassed only by New York, Boston, and Chicago in cultural importance.

Continuing into the Concord historic district, you'll round the town's Monument Square, an obelisk honoring its Civil War dead. The return leg follows roads parallel to the Battle Road Trail to connect back up with the Minuteman Bikeway. Follow Lexington Road away from the center of Concord, keeping left at its split with the Cambridge Turnpike. Stay right at Meriam's Corner to follow Lexington Road and then North Great Road along the southern edge of the Minute Man National Historical Park. Turn right onto Marrett Road, then left onto Massachusetts Avenue across the I-95 overpass, back through Lexington and around the Lexington Common. Turn left at Meriam

Street to rejoin the Minuteman Bikeway at the Lexington Depot Park, and follow the path right back to Arlington Center.

At Mystic Street you'll exit the trail briefly once again, turning right onto Mystic, then left onto Massachusetts Avenue and right at Swan Place to rejoin the bikeway. Take the bikeway back past Spy Pond to Alewife Station, where you began your ride through our nation's revolutionary origins.

MILES AND DIRECTIONS

0.0 Begin at the Minuteman Commuter Bikeway trailhead, behind Alewife Station, and follow signs north.

0.1 Turn right to continue north along the Minuteman.

0.4 Follow the path to the right.

1.5 Turn right onto Swan Place, then left onto Massachusetts Avenue, and right at Mystic Street to continue on the Minuteman Commuter Bikeway.

6.5 Turn left off of the Minuteman onto Meriam Street, then right onto Massachusetts Avenue, keeping right at Lexington Green.

6.7 Turn left onto Harrington Road, then continue straight onto Massachusetts Avenue.

8.0 Turn right after the I-95 overpass onto Wood Street, then left onto Old Massachusetts Avenue, and immediately right onto the dirt Battle Road Trail.

12.7 Turn left at Meriam's Corner onto Lexington Road.

13.9 Keep right to stay on Lexington Road.

14.2 Turn left to round Monument Square and head back through Concord via Lexington Road.

14.5 Keep left to remain on Lexington Road.

15.5 Keep right to stay on Lexington Road.

16.4 Keep left to stay on Lexington Road and then North Great Road.

18.8 Turn right onto Marrett Road.

18.9 Turn left onto Massachusetts Avenue.

20.6 Keep left at Lexington Green.

Lexington, Concord, and the Minute Man National Historical Park

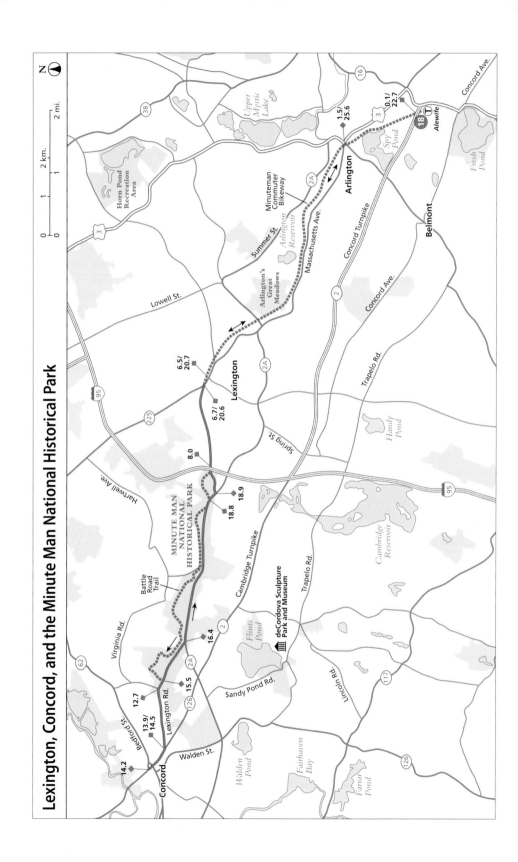

20.7 Turn left onto Meriam Street, and then right onto the Minuteman bikeway.

25.6 Turn right onto Mystic Street, then left onto Massachusetts Avenue, and right onto Swan Place to rejoin the Minuteman.

27.2 Finish at Alewife Station.

RIDE INFORMATION

Local Events/Attractions

Reenactments: There are a number of Revolutionary War reenactment societies that are incredibly active in Lexington and Concord. On Patriots' Day in April, in particular, the historic battlefields along the Minuteman path fill with reenactors and spectators. www.battleroad.org

Minute Man National Historical Park: Costumed reenactors bring history to life throughout this park, particularly around July 4. www.nps.gov/mima

The Old Manse: Just minutes from where the first shots of the Revolution rang out, this historic Georgian clapboard home was, in turns, home to Ralph Waldo Emerson, Henry David Thoreau, and Nathaniel Hawthorne. www.the trustees.org

Restrooms

Start/finish: Alewife Station has restrooms and water fountains.

Mile 1.5 and 25.6: Arlington Center has a number of shops and restaurants with restrooms.

Mile 6.5 and 20.7: The Lexington Visitor Center just off the path from the Lexington Depot has restrooms.

Mile 12.7: The Minute Man National Historical Park has restrooms at Meriam's Corner.

Mile 14.2: The Concord historic district has a number of shops with restrooms.

The Minuteman Commuter Bikeway

Arguably the most popular bike path in the Commonwealth (and one of the most traveled in the country), the Minuteman Commuter Bikeway connects Cambridge to the historic towns just beyond Greater Boston, including Arlington, Lexington, and Bedford. This paved rail-trail makes for a smooth, peaceful ride outside the city along a corridor shaded by trees and lined with the remnants of stone fences that date back to the origins of our country.

Start: Alewife T Station

Length: 20.4 miles

Approximate riding time: 2–2.5 hours with stops

Best bike: Road bike or hybrid

Terrain and trail surface: Paved rail-trail with occasional road crossings

Traffic and hazards: Joggers, families with small children, and dog walkers are common sights along the Minuteman Bikeway, particularly closer to Cambridge, Arlington Center, and through Lexington.

Things to see: Minuteman Commuter Bikeway, Spy Pond, Arlington's Great Meadows, Lexington Depot, Buckman Tavern, Parker Meadow, Tophet Swamp, Bedford Depot Park.

Maps: USGS: *Lexington* and *Concord* quads; DeLorme; *Massachusetts Atlas & Gazetteer,* pp 40–41

Getting there: By car: Parking is available at Alewife Station. From Boston, take Massachusetts Avenue north into Cambridge. Turn left onto Alewife Brook Parkway and follow it south to the station. **By train:** Take the T Red Line to Alewife Station. Bikes are allowed on the Red Line, except from 7 to 10 a.m. and 4 to 7 p.m. Monday through Friday, and without restriction on weekends. Follow the signs to the Minuteman Bikeway trailhead on the north side of the station. GPS coordinates for starting point: N42 23.771' / W71 08.454'

THE RIDE

One of the most celebrated rail-trails in the country, the Minuteman Commuter Bikeway was dedicated in 1992 and designated a White House Millennium Trail in 2000. Its even pavement from Cambridge all the way to Bedford draws thousands of commuters weekly, plus recreational cyclists looking for quick routes out of Greater Boston.

Begin at the trailhead behind Alewife Station, next to the Alewife Brook Parkway overpass. Follow the Minuteman signs to head north along the bikeway, passing under the Concord Turnpike overpass, which marks the border between Arlington and Cambridge. When English colonists first settled here in 1635, they named their new village Menotomy, an Algonquian word meaning "swift running water." Squaw Sachem of the Massachusett tribe sold the land to settlers in exchange for 10 pounds and an agreement that granted her a new woolen coat each year until she died. The town name was changed in April 1867 to honor those buried at Arlington National Cemetery in Virginia.

A bit past the Concord Turnpike overpass you'll come to Spy Pond, where in April 1775 an elderly woman named Mother Batherick took six redcoats prisoner while gathering dandelions along the shore. Mother Batherick reportedly told the captive British soldiers, "If you ever live to get back, you tell King George that an old woman took six of his grenadiers prisoners." Another proud figure connected to Spy Pond was Frederic Tudor, the "Ice King," who made Arlington the center of an international ice business in the nineteenth century, sending the pond's ice as far away as India and

Bike Shops

The Bike Stop is conveniently located right along the Minuteman path, and carries a full selection of bikes for sale and rent. The Bike Stop is located 43R Dudley St., Arlington; (781)-646-7867; www.abikestop.com.

Bikeway Source is just off the end of the bikeway in Bedford, right at the Bedford Depot Park. Its repairs have saved the treads, brakes, and spokes of thousands of cyclists itching to explore beyond the bikeway. Bikeway Source is located at 111 South Rd., Bedford; (781) 275-7799; www.bikewaysource.com.

Quad Cycles, just blocks from the Minuteman path in Arlington Heights, has been offering professional cycling advice and repairs since owner Rustem Gode moved from Cambridge in 2000 to open his own shop. Quad is located at 1043 Massachusetts Ave., Arlington; (781) 648-5222; www.quadcycles.com.

the Caribbean. Today the pond is enjoyed for its recreation and conservation resources.

A few minutes on at Arlington Center, you'll turn right onto Swan Place, then turn left briefly along Massachusetts Avenue, before turning right onto Mystic Street to rejoin the Minuteman Bikeway. (This is the only such drastic break along the entire path until you reach the terminus in Bedford.) At the Mystic Street entrance to the bikeway you'll pass a statue of Samuel Wilson, the meat-packer and native son of Arlington whose wares kept up the strength of American soldiers during the War of 1812. Historians believe Samuel Wilson was the original "Uncle Sam" that gradually morphed into the personification of the US government.

From Mystic Street the path cuts through Arlington's north side, passing Hurd Field at the south end of the Arlington Reservoir and the Great Meadows, a favorite haunt for birders hoping to catch a glimpse of blue herons or numerous other local species. Here you'll cross into Lexington. Famous to elementary schoolchildren across the country as the site of the "shot heard 'round the world" that sparked the Revolutionary War, Lexington was settled in 1642 as part of Cambridge. Today, the town hosts yearly reenactments of the numerous battles that took place nearby in the colonies' fight for independence from Great Britain. Just past the Great Meadows you'll pass Tower Park, one such frequent gathering place for reenactors young and old in colonial infantry garb. Continuing past the Brown Homestead conservation area and Lexington municipal buildings, you'll come to the Lexington Depot, just one of the vestiges of the old railway that you can spot along the Minuteman Bikeway that replaced it.

Crossing Meriam Street, you'll pass behind the Lexington Visitors Center and Buckman Tavern, the headquarters where minutemen awaited the British advance before the Battle of Lexington on April 19, 1775. The tavern's interior has been preserved largely as it was in revolutionary days, including a bullet hole in the old front door that legend holds was made by a British musket ball during the skirmish on Lexington Green.

Continue on through Parker Meadow, Tophet Swamp, and into Bedford. First incorporated in 1729, Bedford boasts the oldest-known flag in the country, which the town's minutemen carried with them as they marched to nearby Concord to face the British. Even today, Bedford's role in American independence is immortalized in the town's seal and emblem. The flag, which is preserved at the Bedford Free Public Library just five minutes from the end of the Minuteman Bikeway, may even have flown at the Old North Bridge in Concord, although this is a point of dispute. The final wooded stretch takes you to Bedford Depot Park, where the Minuteman Bikeway ends. In its heyday

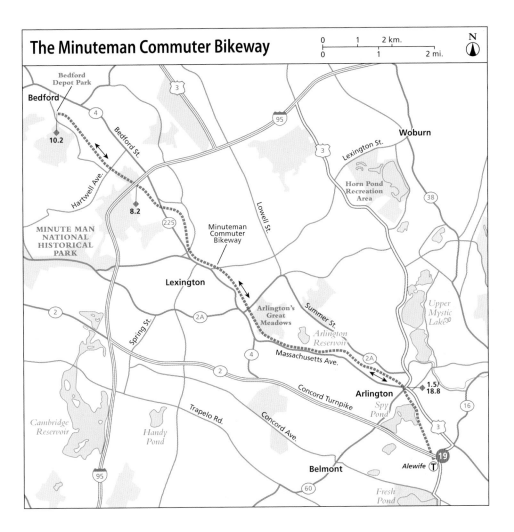

The Minuteman Commuter Bikeway

the depot was a bustling rail hub for the Billerica & Bedford Railroad line and other carriers and ferried hundreds of commuters and untold tons of cargo each day. The vintage Boston & Maine Railroad passenger car now stationed in the park once operated between the depot and Boston, and now stands as an homage to the transportation revolution that spurred industry in this region so many decades ago.

When you're ready to return to Cambridge, follow the Minuteman Bikeway back through Bedford and Lexington to Arlington Center. Turn right at the path's intersection with Mystic Street, then left onto Massachusetts Avenue and right again at Swan Place to rejoin the path. Continue past Spy Pond back to Alewife Station, where the ride began.

MILES AND DIRECTIONS

0.0 Begin at the Minuteman Commuter Bikeway trailhead, behind Alewife Station, and follow signs north.

0.1 Turn right to continue north along the Minuteman.

0.4 Follow the path to the right.

1.5 Turn right onto Swan Place, then left onto Massachusetts Avenue, and right at Mystic Street to continue on the Minuteman Commuter Bikeway.

8.2 Cross the pedestrian footbridge over I-95.

10.2 Arrive at Bedford Depot Park and turn around.

18.8 Turn right onto Mystic Street, then left onto Massachusetts Avenue and right onto Swan Place to rejoin the Minuteman.

20.4 Finish at Alewife Station.

RIDE INFORMATION

Local Events/Attractions
Reenactments: There are a number of Revolutionary War reenactment societies that are incredibly active in Lexington and Concord. On Patriots' Day in April, in particular, the historic battlefields along the Minuteman path fill with reenactors and spectators. www.battleroad.org

Restrooms
Start/finish: Alewife Station has restrooms and water.
Mile 1.5 and Mile 18.8: Arlington Center has a number of shops and restaurants with restrooms.
Mile 6.4 and Mile 14.0: The Lexington Visitors Center just off the path from the Lexington Depot has restrooms.
Mile 10.2: The Bedford Depot Park has restrooms.

Woburn and Horn Pond

The area north of Boston is sprinkled with picturesque ponds and small lakes, their serene calmness so typical of the New England countryside. Nestled squarely between the more oft-traveled Minuteman Trail and Middlesex Fells Reservation, this ride explores three of these oases, following the Mystic River to its two source lakes and continuing through Woburn to Horn Pond. Great for a picnic or a leisurely roll along the shoreline!

Start: Alewife T Station, Cambridge

Length: 14.2 miles

Approximate riding time: 2.5–3 hours with stops

Best bike: Mountain bike or hybrid

Terrain and trail surface: A mix of even paved paths and clear, hard-packed dirt trails, with occasional patches of uneven pavement or rocky terrain

Traffic and hazards: Joggers, skateboarders, and families with small children frequent the Alewife Greenway Bike Path and the paths around these ponds. Watch for traffic along roads.

Things to see: Alewife Greenway Bike Path, Dilboy Stadium, Mystic River, Mystic Lakes, Woburn Pond, Winchester Center Historic District, Spy Pond, Minuteman Commuter Bikeway

Maps: USGS: *Lexington* quad; DeLorme: *Massachusetts Atlas & Gazetteer*, p. 41

Getting there: By car: Parking is available at Alewife Station. From Boston, take Massachusetts Avenue north into Cambridge. Turn left onto Alewife Brook Parkway and follow it south to the station. **By train:** Take the T Red Line to Alewife Station. Bikes are allowed on the Red Line, except from 7 to 10 a.m. and 4 to 7 p.m. Monday through Friday, and without restriction on weekends. Follow the signs to the Minuteman Bikeway trailhead on the north side of the station. GPS coordinates for starting point: N42 23.771' / W71 08.454'

THE RIDE

You'll start at Alewife Station, at the trailhead for the Minuteman Trail on the northeast side of the complex, just behind the bike cages. Follow the Minuteman Trail north out of the station, taking a right onto the Alewife Greenway Bike Path just after the Concord Turnpike overpass. The Turnpike marks the border between Cambridge and the town of Arlington. The path runs alongside Alewife Brook, which flows north from Little Pond in Cambridge to the Mystic River. Major landscaping for the brook was completed in the early 1900s by the Olmsted Brothers, who also spearheaded the Fresh Pond park and whose father, Frederick Law Olmsted, designed Boston's Emerald Necklace as well as Central Park in Manhattan.

At Massachusetts Avenue, cross to the path on the east bank of the waterway, and continue north past St. Paul's Cemetery. The path continues north alongside the Alewife Brook Parkway as it winds past Dilboy Stadium. Named after Army Private George Dilboy, the first Greek-American to be awarded the Medal of Honor in World War I, the stadium is home to the Boston Breakers and the Boston Militia, the city's professional women's soccer and football teams, respectively. At the end of the Dilboy fields you'll curve to the left and cross the Mystic Valley Parkway onto the Mystic River Path.

One of the great urban rivers of New England, the Mystic River flows from the Mystic Lakes to Boston Harbor. Its name is an anglicized derivation of "Missi-Tuk," an Algonquian word meaning "a great river whose waters are driven by waves." Until it was first dammed in 1909, the Mystic River rose and fell with saltwater tides twice a day, powering tidal mills and factories along its banks. More recently, the river was immortalized in the gritty 2003 Oscar-winning film *Mystic River*, a Clint Eastwood adaptation of the novel of the same name by Dennis Lehane. While the river plays a rather dark role in both the book and movie, its banks offer a lush and serene landscape for riding.

Bike Shops

The Bike Stop is conveniently located right along the Minuteman path not far from its split with the Alewife Greenway, and it carries a full selection of bikes for sale and rent. The Bike Stop is located at 43R Dudley St., Arlington; (781)-646-7867; www.abikestop.com.

Quad Cycles, just blocks from the Minuteman path in Arlington Heights, has been offering professional cycling advice and repairs since owner Rustem Gode moved from Cambridge in 2000 to open his own shop. Quad is located at 1043 Massachusetts Ave., Arlington; (781) 648-5222; www.quadcycles.com.

The Alewife Greenway Bike Path splits off from the Minuteman path to curve toward Woburn and onto the Mystic River Path.

Turn right briefly onto Harvard Avenue/River Street and cross immediately into Dugger Park, where the path narrows considerably as it cuts behind the basketball courts and playground.

Passing High Street, you'll come within view of the Lower Mystic Lake. A deep meromictic lake, the Lower Mystic has layers of water that rarely ever mix. This mean that the lake's sediments accumulate into layers that remain undisturbed for thousands of layers, similar to the rings of ancient trees. The bed of the Lower Mystic Lake contains a rich geological history of what the region was like centuries before European settlers established the Massachusetts Bay Colony. You'll pass then to the Upper Mystic Lake, which is fed by the Aberjona River and drains over the Mystic Dam to its lower counterpart. Follow the path past Sandy Beach, a popular beach and swimming spot on the lake's northern shore, as it weaves through a park and connects up to the parkway. Exiting the lakefront, turn left onto Mystic Valley Parkway. Turn right at Bacon Street and then take your first left to rejoin the Mystic Valley Parkway northward.

You're now cutting through the center of Winchester, a charming bedroom-community suburb of Boston. Turn left at Waterfield Road for a detour through the Winchester Center Historic District and town green. At the

In its heyday, Woburn Pond was the posh destination of Boston social cruises via the Middlesex Canal.

end of the green, turn right onto Church Street and follow the traffic circle to Main Street, which you'll follow north past Elliot Park on the shore of Wedge Pond. Turn left at Lake Street and take the Horn Pond Brook Road on the right, which runs behind the Public Works Department building to follow Horn Pond Brook. Continue north through neighborhoods as Horn Pond Brook Road becomes Sylvester Avenue and then Lake Terrace. At Lake Avenue you'll see Horn Pond.

The town of Woburn was first settled at Horn Pond in 1640. A primary source for the Mystic River, Horn Pond was once a popular destination for wealthy Boston residents via cruises along the Middlesex Canal, which ran from the Merrimack River to the port of Boston in the first half of the nineteenth century. Continue north onto Arlington Road, then cross just before Hudson Street onto the shoreline bike path.

Round the water's northern edge, which allows a stunning view of the whole pond. Stay left at the fork to ride between the pond's small northern section and its main body, then continue through the main recreation area to Pond Street to begin your ride back toward Cambridge. Turn right onto Pond Street and follow it to Cambridge Street, where you'll turn left again. After two brief climbs the Mystic Lakes come into view once again Cambridge Street becomes Mystic Street on its wind into Arlington. Turn left at Massachusetts Avenue and then right onto Swan Place, where you'll see the entrance to the Minuteman Commuter Bikeway on your left. This rail-trail will carry you past Spy Pond, back under the Concord Turnpike overpass to Alewife Station.

MILES AND DIRECTIONS

0.0 Follow the Minuteman Trail north out of the station.

0.3 Turn right onto the Alewife Greenway Bike Path just after the Concord Turnpike overpass.

0.8 Turn right briefly onto Massachusetts Avenue, then quickly left back onto the Alewife Greenway Bike Path on the other side of Alewife Brook Parkway and continue north.

1.9 Cross Mystic Valley Parkway and continue west along the Mystic River Path.

2.2 Turn right at Harvard Avenue/River Street across the river, then cross Harvard Avenue to continue along the Mystic River Path behind the basketball courts in Dugger Park.

2.7 Cross High Street to continue along the Mystic River Path, keeping left at the fork.

3.5 Cross Lake Shore Drive to continue along the Mystic River Path.

4.2 Follow the path left past Sandy Beach as it curves through the park.

4.5 Turn left onto Mystic Valley Parkway.

4.8 Turn right onto Bacon Street, then take your first left back onto Mystic Valley Parkway heading north, keeping right at the fork with Lloyd Street.

5.4 Turn left at Waterfield Road.

5.6 Turn right to cut through the green at the Winchester Center Historic District.

5.7 Turn right on Church Street and enter the traffic circle, taking the fifth right onto Main Street.

6.1 Turn left onto Lake Street, then take a quick right at the sign onto Horn Pond Brook Road path, just to the right of the Public Works Department building.

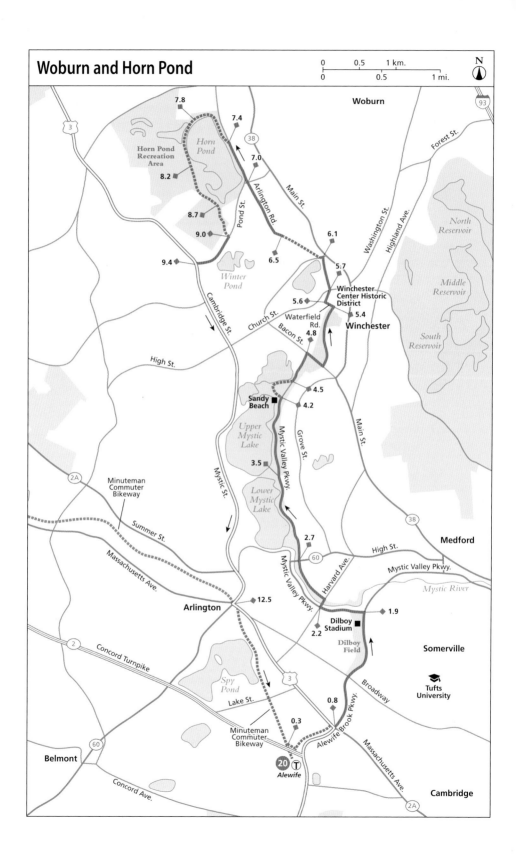

Woburn and Horn Pond

0   0.5   1 km.

0   0.5   1 mi.

N

Woburn

Horn Pond
Recreation
Area

Horn
Pond

North
Reservoir

Middle
Reservoir

South
Reservoir

Winter
Pond

Winchester
Center Historic
District

Winchester

Waterfield
Rd.

Sandy
Beach

Upper
Mystic
Lake

Lower
Mystic
Lake

Minuteman
Commuter
Bikeway

Medford

Arlington

Dilboy
Stadium

Dilboy
Field

Somerville

Tufts
University

Spy
Pond

Minuteman
Commuter
Bikeway

Belmont

Alewife

Cambridge

7.8
7.4
7.0
8.2
8.7
9.0
9.4
6.5
6.1
5.7
5.6
5.4
4.8
4.5
4.2
3.5
2.7
12.5
2.2
1.9
0.8
0.3
20

Street labels: Forest St., Washington St., Highland Ave., Arlington Rd., Main St., Pond St., Cambridge St., Church St., Bacon St., High St., Mystic St., Mystic Valley Pkwy., Grove St., Main St., Summer St., Massachusetts Ave., Concord Turnpike, Harvard Ave., High St., Mystic Valley Pkwy., Mystic River, Broadway, Lake St., Alewife Brook Pkwy., Massachusetts Ave., Concord Ave.

6.5 Exit the path onto Middlesex Street, which turns into Sylvester Avenue and then Lake Terrace as you ride north.

7.0 Cross Lake Avenue onto Arlington Road.

7.4 Cross just before Hudson Street onto the bike path along the pond shore.

7.8 Keep left at the fork to cross between the upper and lower sections of the pond.

8.2 Keep right at the fork.

8.7 Keep right to remain on the path.

9.0 Turn right onto Pond Street.

9.4 Turn left onto Cambridge Street, which becomes Mystic Street after passing Arlington Street.

12.5 Turn left onto Massachusetts Avenue, then a quick right onto Swan Place, where you'll enter the Minuteman Commuter Bikeway.

14.2 Arrive back at the starting point at Alewife Station.

RIDE INFORMATION

Local Events/Attractions
Upper Mystic Lake: Popular for freshwater swimming at Sandy Beach and the Medford Boat Club. www.mass.gov/dcr/parks/metroboston/mystic.htm
Dilboy Stadium: Home to Boston's professional women's soccer and football teams, the Boston Breakers and Boston Militia, Dilboy hosts thrilling games throughout the spring, summer, and fall. www.bostonbreakerssoccer.com and www.bostonmilitia.com

Restrooms
Start/finish: Alewife Station has public restrooms.
Mile 1.7: Dilboy Stadium has public restrooms.
Mile 5.6: The Winchester Center Historic District has a number of shops with restrooms.
Mile 12.5: There are a number of shops at Arlington Center with public restrooms.

Middlesex Fells Reservation

Those looking for an invigorating ride need search no further than Middlesex Fells Reservation, north of Boston. Its craggy hills make the Fells a favorite among mountain bikers hungry for a challenging jaunt through deep woods and meadows. This ride follows the Fells Mountain Bike Loop and unpaved fire roads to explore the reservation's western half. Preserved as a wild oasis against urban and suburban sprawl, the Fells beckon with an alluring alternative to more manicured bike paths nearby.

Start: Lower Sheep Fold Parking Lot, Stoneham

Length: 6.3 miles

Approximate riding time: 1.5–2 hours with stops

Best bike: Mountain bike

Terrain and trail surface: Steep and rocky bike paths with patches of sandy trail

Traffic and hazards: Watch for rocks and logs along the path, as well as hikers and horseback riders.

Things to see: Middlesex Fells Reservation, Sheep Fold, Railroad Trestle Trail, Bear Hill, Wright Tower, North Reservoir, South Reservoir, Panther Cave, Silver Mine Path

Maps: USGS: *Framingham* and *Boston North* quads; DeLorme: *Massachusetts Atlas & Gazetteer,* pp. 29, 41

Getting there: By car: From Boston, take I-93N toward Concord, New Hampshire, then take exit 33 to merge onto MA 28N/Fellsway W. Follow the signs to the Middlesex Fells Reservation and park in the Lower Sheep Fold Parking Lot. **By train:** Take the Orange Line or commuter rail to Malden Center Station. Bikes are allowed on the Orange Line, except from 7 to 10 a.m. and 4 to 7 p.m. Monday through Friday, and without restriction on weekends. Check the commuter rail timetable for bike details. Exit the station onto Pleasant Street, and ride west to the Fellsway W and turn right. Follow signs north to the Middlesex Fells Reservation's Lower Sheep Fold Parking Lot. GPS coordinates for starting point: N42 27.162'/W71 06.352'

THE RIDE

You'll start the ride at the Lower Sheep Fold Parking Lot, located on the east edge of the reservation's principal area to the west of I-93. In total, the Middlesex Fells Reservation comprises more than 2,500 acres of parkland, including a number of lakes, ponds, and reservoirs. The word "fells" comes from the Saxon term for rocky, hilly land, an apt description that fits the reservation perfectly. This area was first explored by Governor John Winthrop of the Massachusetts Bay Colony in 1632 and was the site of periodic mining and timber harvesting before its designation as preservation land in 1894. Charles Eliot, a protege of famed landscape architect Frederick Law Olmsted who also designed initial plans for the Esplanade and oversaw the development of Fresh Pond in Cambridge, was a vocal advocate for the nationwide preservation of land, comparing his work to libraries' efforts to preserve important books and museums to maintain works of art. His efforts centered around the Middlesex Fells in particular, and he oversaw planning the reservation's boundaries and much of its landscaping to emphasize natural features of beauty and distinction.

> ## Bike Shops
>
> **City Cycle** carries a full selection of new bicycles, and its staff is experienced at making top-notch repairs in a pinch. The shop is located at 286 Main St., Stoneham; (781) 438-0358; www.citycyclein.com.
> **JRA Cycles** has bikes and parts for every need, including the mountain bikes needed for this ride. The shop is located at 229 Salem St., Medford; (781) 391-3636; www.jracycles.com.

From the eastern edge of the lower parking lot, follow the dirt path east and turn left onto the Mountain Bike Loop, which you'll follow for most of the ride. In case you lose your way, look for signs or trees emblazoned with green rectangles, the symbol for the mountain bike loop. Right away you'll be plunged into deep woods along trails that intersperse gravel, hard-packed earth, and sandy stretches for a ride of variety. Keep a sharp eye for changes in terrain or obstacles in the path such as fallen branches, which can be particularly common in the fall or after storms.

Keep left at the fork with Railroad Trestle Trail to continue along the Mountain Bike Loop up Bear Hill. At the top of the hill lies a stone tower, near the spot where the Middlesex Fells Association was founded in 1880 with a goal of saving the Fells from development. William Flagg and Elizur Wright, a naturalist and a mathematician, respectively, founded the association as part of a nationwide movement to preserve land near major cities in order to promote healthy interactions with nature for urban dwellers. While both figures died before the protected Fells became a reality, the astounding beauty of the preservation even today stands as an enduring testament to their dogged determination and passion for conserving public lands for future generations.

Keep left at the trail's fork up to Wright Tower, which was constructed in 1937 under the auspices of the Works Project Administration. Continue along the Mountain Bike Loop through an invigorating and rocky downslope that takes you to the park's northernmost edge. Take a left to follow the loop west, allowing the green rectangles on periodic trees to guide you around the northern tip of the North Reservoir. Take care not to stray too close to the water's edge, which is restricted to public access. The Mountain Bike Loop skirts the restricted boundary as it reaches the reservation's western edge and proceeds south and then southwest. While the challenging terrain requires focus, be sure to take in the reservation's more than 800 species of plant life as you ride. If you're lucky, you may spot an osprey, deer, turtle, or any number of animals that make their homes in the Fells.

Take the Mountain Bike Loop south along the restricted area surrounding Long Pond, then curve west at the southern tip of South Reservoir, where the bike path emerges from the woods briefly at South Border Road. At the loop's intersection with the Cross Fells Trail, signified by blue sign blazes, and the Middle Road dirt fire path, take a right and head farther south, following signs to Panther Cave.

Curving around the Panther Cave rock outcropping, take a left at the sign for Red Cross Path and head back north. Stay right at the fork to continue along Silver Mine Path back to the Mountain Bike Loop, which snakes north back to Lower Sheep Fold Parking Lot, where the ride began.

MILES AND DIRECTIONS

0.0 From the Lower Sheep Fold Parking Lot, follow the dirt trail east and turn left onto the Mountain Bike Loop.

0.3 Keep left at the fork with Railroad Trestle Trail to continue along the Mountain Bike Loop.

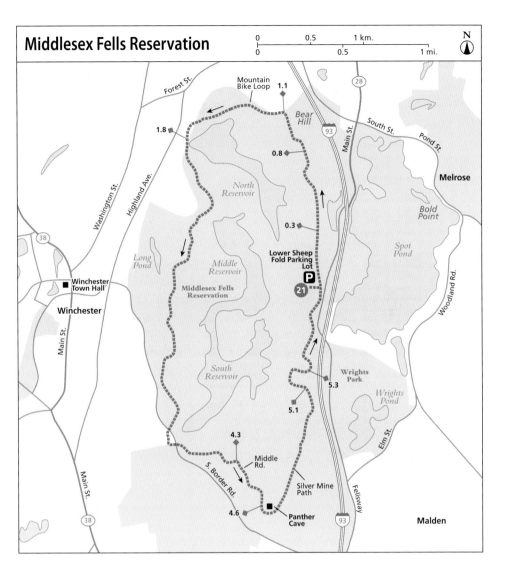

Middlesex Fells Reservation

0   0.5   1 km.

0   0.5   1 mi.

0.8   Keep left at the trail's fork up to Bear Hill.

1.1   Take a left to follow the loop west.

1.8   Continue south along the Mountain Bike Loop.

4.3   At the loop's intersection with the Cross Fells Trail, turn right onto the Middle Road dirt fire path.

4.6   Curve left around the Panther Cave rock outcropping onto the Red Cross Path.

5.1   Stay right at the fork to continue along Silver Mine Path.

The Mountain Bike Loop explores the outer boundary of Middlesex Fells.

5.3 Merge back to the Mountain Bike Loop.

6.3 Turn left back to Lower Sheep Fold Parking Lot.

RIDE INFORMATION

Local Events/Attractions

Guided Fells hikes: Park rangers and docents from the Friends of the Middlesex Fells Reservation offer year-round guided walks and hikes that focus on the natural history of the park and its cultural history. www.fells.org

Restrooms

There are no public restrooms in the Middlesex Fells Reservation.

Northern Strand Community Trail to Lynn Woods

The Minuteman Commuter Bikeway may be Boston's best-known rail-trail, but it's by no means the only game in town. Across the Commonwealth, bike advocates tirelessly refashion former railroad passages into dedicated bike paths. Opened in 2012, the Northern Strand Community Trail runs from Everett to Lynn, passing through Malden, Revere, and Saugus along the way. This ride along an official link in the East Coast Greenway offers the rare chance of not only riding from dense suburb to picturesque woodlands, but also of watching biking history unfold as the trail continues to stretch to the sea.

Start: Northern Strand Community Trail, Prescott Street and Tremont Street in Everett.

Length: 21.6 miles

Approximate riding time: 2.5–3 hours with stops

Best bike: Hybrid or mountain bike

Terrain and trail surface: A mix of dirt trail, gravel path, and paved road

Traffic and hazards: Hikers and dog walkers frequent the rail-trail and Lynn Woods. Watch for patches of loose dirt, sand, or uneven pavement, particularly in Lynn Woods.

Things to see: Northern Strand Community Trail, Bell Rock Cemetery, Saugus, Breed's Pond, Pine Grove Cemetery, Lynn Woods Reservation, Stone Tower.

Maps: USGS: *Boston North* and *Lynn* quads; DeLorme: *Massachusetts Atlas & Gazetteer,* pp. 29, 41

Getting there: By car: From Boston, take the Charlestown Bridge across to Charlestown and continue along New Rutherford Avenue to Sullivan Square. At the traffic circle, take the third exit to continue across to Everett via Broadway. At the traffic circle, take the third exit again onto Main Street, then turn left at Prescott Street. The ride start is at the intersection of Prescott Street and Tremont Street. **By train:** Take the Orange Line or commuter rail to Malden Center station. Bikes are allowed on the Orange Line, except from 7 to 10 a.m. and 4 to 7 p.m. Monday through Friday, and without restriction on weekends. Check the commuter rail timetable for bike details. Exit the station left onto Centre Street, then take a right onto Main Street. Turn right at Prescott Street and begin the ride at the intersection with Tremont Street. GPS coordinates for starting point: N42 24.611′ / W71 04.024′

THE RIDE

You'll start at the southern end of the Northern Strand Community Trail in Everett, just across the Mystic River from Somerville. Established in 1870 after seceding from neighboring Malden, Everett has secured its place in US history as being the last city to have a bicameral legislature: Until 2011, Everett was governed by a mayor along with a seven-member board of aldermen and a "common council" with eighteen representatives. The city is named for Edward Everett, the one-term Whig governor of Massachusetts, longtime Congressman, and famous orator whose two-hour speech at Gettysburg in 1863 immediately preceded Abraham Lincoln's two-minute address.

Malden High School, which you pass twice along this ride, has one of the oldest and most storied football rivalries in the country: Its Thanksgiving Day scrimmages with Medford High School date back to 1889, when Medford won 4–0.

Head north along the Northern Strand Community Trail, which was officially incorporated into the plans for the East Coast Greenway in 2007. Under development since 1991, the East Coast Greenway is an ambitious long-distance urban trail project that will connect traffic-free routes along the East Coast into a seamless route 3,000 miles long, from Calais on the tip of Maine down to Florida's Key West. Using the momentum of the East Coast Greenway designation, bike advocates with Bike to the Sea have propelled their twenty-year effort to establish a car-free trail between Everett to the beaches in Revere, Lynn, and Nahant. This ride explores the trails completed to date, which connect Everett to Lynn.

Within a few minutes you'll cross from Everett into Malden, then pass the historic Bell Rock Cemetery on your right. Incorporated in 1649, Malden was the first town to petition the colonial government to declare independence from the British crown. The trail curves northeast just past the cemetery, crossing Main Street and Ferry Street before skirting Malden High School.

Carefully cross Eastern Avenue to continue east along the Northern Strand to its interruption at Beach Street, which marks the boundary between Malden and Revere. Once called North Chelsea, the city changed its name in 1871 in honor of Paul Revere. Turn right at Beach Street and then left onto Lynn Street to ride north through Revere through this break in the trail. Pass beneath Bennett Highway onto Salem Street, and turn left back onto the Northern Strand Community Trail where it resumes just past the Salem Street Park.

As you ride along the tree-covered trail, you'll pass from Revere into Saugus. Historically recognized as the birthplace of industry in colonial America, Saugus was first settled by Europeans in 1629. You'll cut north into the town's center before curving east yet again, riding due south of the famed Saugus Iron Works that were the first powerful iron forges in the New World and among the most advanced anywhere in the world when constructed in 1646. The reconstructed site includes the seven massive waterwheels that powered the forge, blast furnace, and mill machinery at the iron works. While the Saugus Iron Works ceased operations in approximately 1670, its metallurgists and apprentices dispersed throughout the New World along with the knowledge and skills gained at this impressive forge. As such, Saugus played a critical role in shaping America's fledgling economy. You'll exit Saugus as you pass the Saugus River and come to the current end of the Northern Strand Community Trail in Lynn, at Lincoln Avenue.

Bike Shops

Hollywood Bike Shop is tucked away on a back street in Lynn, but its lifelong mechanic-owner does quality repairs at cut rates. The shop is located at 83 River St., Lynn; (781) 595-2991. **North Shore Cycle** has the largest selection of bikes and parts on the North Shore and the tune-up experience to match. The shop is located at 251 Western Ave., Lynn; (781) 581-2700; www.nscycles.com.

Like Saugus, Lynn was among the first places settled by Europeans. The town also developed its own specialized industry from the start, opening the first leather tannery in colonial America. The town quickly became a center of shoemaking, the dominance of that industry reflected today in the boot that crown's the city's seal. The boots that shod the Continental army were

Breed's Pond is one of three lakes in Lynn Woods.

made in Lynn tanneries. Turn left onto Boston Street, then make a quick left at Winnepurkit Avenue and stay right at the fork with Holyoke Street. Continue northeast to Myrtle Street and turn left, continuing straight past Walnut Street onto Dungeon Avenue and then Parkland Avenue past the southern shore of Breed's Pond and Pine Grove Cemetery. Make another left at Lynnfield Street and ride past Sluice Pond and the St. Mary Cemetery, keeping left at the fork onto Great Woods Road that leads into Lynn Woods.

At 2,200 acres, Lynn Woods Reservation is among the largest municipal parks in the United States, and accounts for nearly a fifth of the city's area. The reservation holds three active reservoirs: Breed's Pond, which you already passed on Parkland Avenue, plus Birch Pond and Walden Pond, not to be confused with Thoreau's Walden to the northwest of Boston. Ride straight on Great Woods Road, past the entrance to the municipal golf course, and follow the dirt and gravel path uphill into the wooded reservation. You'll pass below Walden Pond before keeping left at the fork to head uphill once again to Stone Tower, built atop the highest point in all of Lynn, at Burrill Hill. The 48-foot-tall field tower was erected in 1936 as part of the Works Progress Administration investment in public parks, and served as a wildfire lookout deck for many decades. The tower is open for visitors to take in the breathtaking views of Lynn's waterfront and the Boston skyline from this ideal vantage point.

Best Bike Rides Boston

Riding downhill from the tower, you'll pass Long Swamp on your right before taking a left onto the dirt Dungeon Road, which curves downhill once more to briefly jog along the western shore of Breed's Pond.

Turn left a bit after the pond to exit the reservation and begin the ride back to Everett. Follow Pennybrook Road to Walnut Street and turn left, then take a right onto Myrtle Street and another right at Holyoke Street. Keep left at Winnepurkit Avenue and then right at Boston Street, where you'll find the trailhead of the Northern Strand once again. Follow the bike path back through Saugus, Revere, and Malden and to where you began the ride in Everett.

MILES AND DIRECTIONS

0.0 Begin at the intersection of Tremont Street and Prescott Street, and ride north along the Northern Strand Community Trail.

1.4 Cross Eastern Avenue to continue along the Northern Strand Community Trail.

3.4 Exit the Northern Strand Community Trail and turn right onto Beach Street, then left onto Lynn Street.

3.8 Pass under the overpass onto Salem Street.

4.3 Turn left to rejoin the Northern Strand Community Trail just past the Salem Street Park.

7.1 Exit the Northern Strand Community Trail and turn left onto Boston Street.

7.3 Turn left onto Winnepurkit Avenue, then stay right at the fork with Holyoke Street.

8.0 Turn left onto Myrtle Street.

8.1 Continue straight onto Dungeon Avenue past Walnut Street.

9.6 Turn left onto Lynnfield Street.

10.3 Turn left onto Great Woods Road and continue straight through the parking lot onto the dirt path.

10.7 Keep left at the fork to follow Great Woods Road.

10.9 Take the middle path to continue uphill.

11.2 Continue past Stone Tower.

11.7 Turn left onto Dungeon Road.

Northern Strand Community Trail to Lynn Woods

12.5 Turn left onto Pennybrook Road.

13.1 Turn left onto Walnut Street.

13.5 Turn right onto Myrtle Street.

13.6 Turn right onto Holyoke Street.

14.3 Turn left onto Winnepurkit Avenue, then stay right onto Boston Street.

14.6 Turn right to rejoin the Northern Strand Community Trail.

17.3 Exit the trail and turn right onto Salem Street.

18.2 Turn right onto Beach Street, then left to rejoin the rail-trail.

21.6 Finish at the intersection of Tremont Street and Prescott Street.

Stone Tower was erected under the auspices of the Works Progress Administration in 1936.

RIDE INFORMATION

Local Events/Attractions

Saugus Iron Works: See how industry in the young United States took root in this first iron foundry in the colonies. www.nps.gov/sair

Restrooms

Start/finish: Main Street in Everett has a number of shops and restaurants with restrooms and water.

Mile 1.4 and 20.2: Malden Centre has a number of shops and restaurants.

Mile 7.1 and 14.6: There are a number of shops and restaurants along Lincoln Street.

Lynn and Marblehead

Lynn and Marblehead are two favorite destinations along the North Shore, their beaches, coastline, and small-town charm a perennial draw for Bostonians. This ride follows the main drag of the Lynn Shore to the Marblehead Rail-Trail, around the jaw-dropping Marblehead Neck and up to the tip of Marblehead at Fort Sewall. From popular sandy beaches to more secluded lighthouses and yachts by the score, you'll take in all the best parts of the North Shore life!

Start: Lynn Heritage State Park, Lynn

Length: 19.7 miles

Approximate riding time: 2.5–3 hours with stops

Best bike: Hybrid or mountain bike

Terrain and trail surface: A mix of paved urban roads and hard-packed dirt and gravel rail-trail, with occasional patches of uneven pavement or rocky terrain

Traffic and hazards: Watch for traffic along roads, particularly on the Lynnway and along Lynn Shore Drive. Joggers, hikers, dog walkers, and families with small children frequent the Marblehead Rail-Trail.

Things to see: Lynn Heritage State Park, Woodbury's Point, Deer Cove, Red Rock Park, King's Beach, Marblehead Rail-Trail, Marblehead Neck, Lady Cove, Devereaux Beach, Marblehead Light Tower, Fort Sewall.

Maps: USGS: *Lynn, Marblehead North,* and *Marblehead South* quads; DeLorme: *Massachusetts Atlas & Gazetteer,* pp. 29–30, 41–42

Getting there: By car: From Boston, take MA 1A N to North Shore Road, which you'll follow north onto the Lynnway. There is parking available at Lynn Heritage State Park. **By train:** Take the commuter rail to Lynn on the Newburyport/Rockport line. Check the commuter rail timetable for bike rack availability. Exit the station and ride south along Market Street. Turn left onto the Lynnway and then right into Lynn Heritage State Park. GPS coordinates for starting point: N42 27.566' / W70 56.622'

THE RIDE

Start at the Lynn Heritage State Park, along the Lynnway. One of the smaller cities of Massachusetts, Lynn was first settled by Europeans in 1629. The boot in the city's seal is an homage to the leather tanning and shoemaking industry for which the city was once renowned. The boots worn by the Continental army during the Revolutionary War were manufactured by cobblers from Lynn, and the city remains a minor industrial center today. The grassy waterfront park looks out onto Broad Sound of Massachusetts Bay, your view of Boston obstructed by Winthrop and Deer Island.

Turn right onto the Lynnway out of the park and continue to the rotary, where you'll take the second right onto Lynn Shore Drive. The long beachfront on your right extends nearly 4 miles in total from Nahant Beach in the south all the way to Swampscott. You'll pass the Woodbury's Point promontory and Deer Cove before coming to the grassy oval at Red Rock Park on your right, which is particularly popular for the tide pools that form along its crags. Past Red Rock is King's Beach, another stretch of sandy oceanfront to ride along as you pass from Lynn into Swampscott at Eastern Avenue.

Bike Shops

Hollywood Bike Shop is tucked away on a back street in Lynn, but its lifelong mechanic-owner does quality repairs at cut rates. The shop is located at 83 River St., Lynn; (781) 595-2991.

Marblehead Cycle offers tune-ups, repairs, and group rides around the area. The shop is located at 25 Bessom St., Marblehead; (781) 631-1570; www.marbleheadcycle.com.

North Shore Cycle has the largest selection of bikes and parts on the North Shore and the tune-up experience to match. The shop is located at 251 Western Ave., Lynn; (781) 581-2700; www.nscycles.com.

The beach town of Swampscott broke off from Lynn in 1852, its name an anglicization of a Naumkeag word, "M'squompskut," which means "land of the red rock." Follow Humphrey Street right along the Swampscott shoreline and past Phillips Park, keeping left at the fork with Atlantic Avenue to stay on Humphrey Street. Ride through the residential neighborhood to Beach Bluff Avenue and turn right, where you'll find the beginning of the Marblehead Rail-Trail on the left, across the street from Manton Road. Take this short paved section past the house and across the street to the main unpaved trail. This Y-shaped rail-trail follows abandoned railroad right-of-ways from the Eastern Railroad Company—you're riding along the Southwest Trail toward Marblehead. The Marblehead Rail-Trail is part of the East Coast Greenway, an ambitious long-distance urban trail project under development since 1991: when

King's Beach along Lynn Shore fills up quickly on hot summer days.

completed, the ECG will connects traffic-free routes along the East Coast into a seamless trail 3,000 miles long from Calais on the tip of Maine down to Florida's Key West. The beginning segment of the rail-trail can be rocky, but as you pass the Ware Pond Conservation Area and Rockaway Avenue, the gravel evens out considerably into a smooth ride.

The first British settlers arrived in the Marblehead area in the early 1600s to escape the strict Puritan rule in Salem, and they lived in peace with the Naumkeag tribe of the Algonquin Nation until a smallpox epidemic wiped out the Naumkeags from 1615 to 1619. The town was granted formal independence from Salem in 1648 and has been known as Marvell Head, Marble Harbour, and Foy throughout the years. Today, the town is known for its beach mansions, yacht clubs, and quaint waterfront district, as well as for its beaches. Follow the rail-trail to Pleasant Street and turn right, then right again at Ocean Avenue to cross over to Marblehead Neck via the sandbar between Lady Cove's hundreds of moored boats to the left, and the ever-popular Devereaux Beach to the right.

The Marblehead Neck, in particular, holds spectacular summer homes and oceanside mansions, as well as the Marblehead Wildlife Sanctuary. Follow Ocean Avenue as it curves along the southern edge of the Neck and then north, passing Castle Rock Park on the right, once a lookout for pirate and enemy ships with its incredible vantage of the Atlantic horizon. Follow Ocean Avenue right to Follett Street and turn left to the northern point of the Neck at Chandler Hovey Park, also known as Lighthouse Point. The park and its lighthouse once belonged to the federal government, but were bought by a Neck resident in 1948 and donated for the town's enjoyment. The Marblehead Light Tower overlooks this serene park with unrivaled views north across Salem Sound and west across Lady Cove to the Marblehead mainland. Follow Nahant Street back to Ocean Avenue and turn right, staying right to ride along Harbor Avenue down the Neck's western shore. Take Ocean Avenue back across the Neck to the mainland and turn right onto Atlantic Avenue toward the center of Marblehead.

Pass Seaside Park and continue to Washington Street, where you'll turn right. Follow Washington Street to Franklin Street, riding through Marblehead's charming shopping district and historic neighborhoods, where you'll pass the Marblehead Museum and the former Jeremiah Lee mansion. Turn right on Franklin, following Selman Street right at the one-way sign and then turning left onto Front Street to arrive at Fort Sewall on Marblehead Harbor. This historic fort on the promontory was first established in 1644 as Gale's Head, further fortified in 1742 to defend against the French, and then enlarged during the Revolutionary War and War of 1812 to protect the coastal towns from British frigates. The fort has since been designated a National Historic Landmark, its underground barracks and stockade remaining to this day. From the park's easternmost tip, you can look northeast to Crowninshield Island, a 5-acre outcropping and nature preserve accessible by foot only at low tide.

When you've taken in the seascapes in every direction, follow Front Street back to Franklin Street along the one-way, and turn left at Washington Street. Take Washington Street back to Essex Street and turn right, then take a left at Memorial Park onto Pleasant Street. Ride along Pleasant Street past the Marblehead Veterans Middle School to rejoin the Marblehead Rail-Trail just before Mohawk Road. Follow the rail-trail back to Beach Bluff Avenue and turn right, then left onto Humphrey Street, which you'll ride back into Swampscott to Lynn Shore Drive. Pass King's Beach and Red Rock Park once again as you head into the rotary, taking your first exit onto the Lynnway. Cross via the pedestrian ramp into Lynn Heritage State Park, where you began the ride.

MILES AND DIRECTIONS

0.0 Begin at Lynn Heritage State Park, and turn right onto the Lynnway.

0.4 Enter the rotary and take the second exit onto Lynn Shore Drive.

3.1 Turn left to remain on Humphrey Street.

3.8 Turn right onto Beach Bluff Avenue.

3.9 Turn left onto the Marblehead Rail-Trail.

Lynn and Marblehead

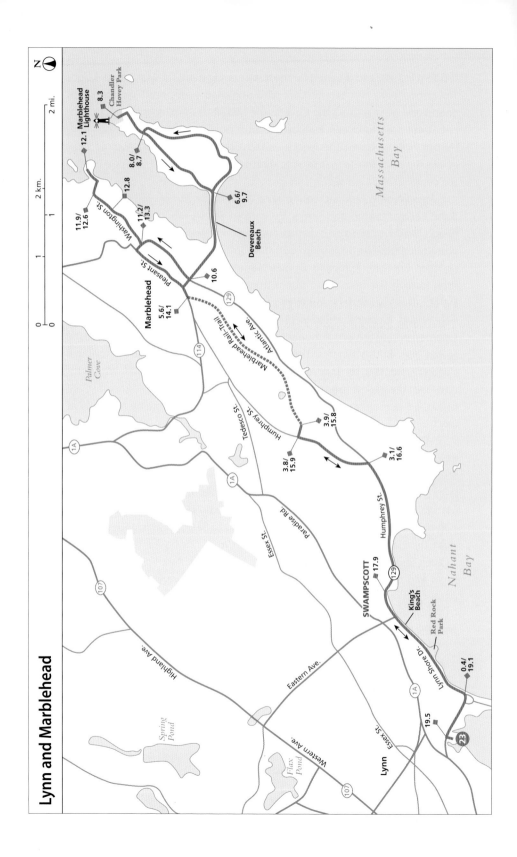

N

Marblehead Lighthouse 12.1
8.3 Chandler Hovey Park

8.0/ 8.7

12.8

11.2/ 13.3

Washington St.

11.9/ 12.6

6.6/ 9.7

Devereaux Beach

Marblehead

Pleasant St.

5.6/ 14.1

10.6

129

Palmer Cove

Marblehead Rail Trail

Atlantic Ave.

114

Tedesco St.

Humphrey St.

3.9/ 15.8

3.8/ 15.9

3.1/ 16.6

Paradise Rd.

1A

1A

Essex St.

Highland Ave.

107

Spring Pond

Massachusetts Bay

Humphrey St.

SWAMPSCOTT 17.9

129

King's Beach

Red Rock Park

Nahant Bay

Lynn Shore Dr.

Eastern Ave.

Western Ave.

1A

0.4/ 19.1

19.5

23

Lynn

Essex St.

107

Flax Pond

0   1   2 km.

0   1   2 mi.

5.6 Turn right onto Pleasant Street, then right again onto Ocean Avenue.

6.6 Stay right to remain on Ocean Avenue.

8.0 Turn right to stay on Ocean Avenue.

8.3 Turn left onto Follett Street, which you'll follow into Chandler Hovey Park.

8.4 Turn right onto Kimball Street.

8.6 Turn left onto Nahant Street.

8.7 Turn right onto Ocean Avenue.

8.8 Keep left onto Harbor Avenue.

9.7 Continue onto Ocean Avenue.

10.6 Turn right onto Atlantic Avenue.

11.2 Turn right onto Washington Street.

11.9 Turn right onto Franklin Street.

12.0 Turn left onto Front Street.

12.1 Turn right into Fort Sewall and turn around.

12.5 Turn right onto Franklin Street.

12.6 Turn left onto Washington Street.

12.8 Keep right around Market Square to continue on Washington Street.

13.3 Turn right onto Essex Street.

13.4 Turn left onto Pleasant Street.

14.1 Turn left onto the Marblehead Rail-Trail.

15.8 Turn right onto Beach Bluff Avenue.

15.9 Turn left onto Humphrey Street.

16.6 Turn right onto Humphrey Street.

17.9 Keep left to stay on Humphrey Street.

19.1 Enter the rotary and take the first exit onto the Lynnway.

19.5 Take the pedestrian bridge over the Lynnway.

19.7 Finish at Lynn Heritage State Park.

The Marblehead Light Tower at Chandler Hovey Park overlooks Lady Cove.

RIDE INFORMATION

Local Events/Attractions

Fort Sewall: Not only is this fort an ideal location to take in Marblehead Harbor, it also explores the town's maritime and military history with its preserved bunkers and artillery walls. www.marblehead.org

Marblehead Neck Wildlife Sanctuary: This conservation land, which is maintained by the Massachusetts Audubon Society, is a haven for migratory birds in the middle of the Marblehead Neck. www.massaudubon.org

Restrooms

Start/finish: There are restrooms at Lynn Heritage State Park.

Mile 1.0 to 3.1: There are a number of shops and restaurants along Lynn Shore Drive and Humphrey Street with restrooms and water.

Mile 6.4 and 9.9: There are restrooms at Devereaux Beach.

Mile 12.1: Fort Sewall has restroom facilities.

Mile 13.3: There are a number of shops and restaurants at Washington Street and Essex Street with restrooms and water.

Revere Beach to Nahant

Too many Bostonians forget just how close the Hub is to prime beaches and oceanfront retreats. This ride follows the coast beginning at Revere Beach, a quick subway ride from downtown, past Lynn and around to the tiny beach town of Nahant. Savor the saltwater breezes and stunning oceanside views as you hug shore to an oft-forgotten treasure just north of the city.

Start: Revere Beach, Revere Beach Boulevard and Beach Street, Revere

Length: 19.0 miles

Approximate riding time: 2.5–3 hours with stops

Best bike: Road bike or hybrid

Terrain and trail surface: Well-paved roads, with brief stretches of gravel and dirt path

Traffic and hazards: Joggers, skateboarders, families with small children, and dog walkers frequent the beaches and paths along this ride. Be mindful of traffic along roads, particularly at rotaries and overpasses.

Things to see: Revere Beach, Lynn Heritage State Park, Nahant Beach, Bailey's Hill Park, Kelley Greens at Nahant, Nahant Harbor, Lodge Park, Northeastern University Marine Science Center, Forty Steps Beach.

Maps: USGS: *Lynn* quad; DeLorme: *Massachusetts Atlas & Gazetteer*, pp. 41–42

Getting there: By car: From Boston, take MA 1A N to Winthrop Road and exit left. Follow Winthrop Road as it curves north, taking the second exit out of the rotary onto Revere Beach Boulevard. You can find both metered and free parking along Revere Beach Boulevard, including near the ride start at Beach Street and Revere Beach Boulevard. **By train:** Take the Blue Line to the Revere station. Bikes are allowed on the Blue

Line, except from 7 to 9 a.m. inbound and 4 to 6 p.m. outbound Monday through Friday, and without restriction on weekends. Exit the station onto Beach Street and turn right to the start of the ride at the gazebo. GPS coordinates for starting point: N42 24.497' / W70 59.473'

THE RIDE

You'll start at Revere Beach, just a few minutes from downtown on the Blue Line of the T. From the gazebo at Beach Street and Revere Beach Boulevard, ride north along the shore. Revere Beach is another of Boston's firsts: the first public beach in the United States, established in 1896. After the state legislature created the Revere Beach Reservation in 1895, they commissioned Charles Eliot, a protege of Frederick Law Olmsted who also designed Manhattan's Central Park, to oversee the creation of the beachfront preserve. Eliot's first task was to the shift the narrow gauge railroad track, which once followed right along the beachfront. By the 1920s, Revere Beach had become a popular vacation and day-trip destination on par with Coney Island, complete with decadent ballrooms, carnival rides, and roller coasters. The Cyclone wooden roller coaster, which opened in 1925, was the tallest such ride in the world until 1964.

Bike Shops

Hollywood Bike Shop is tucked away on a back street in Lynn, but its lifelong mechanic-owner does quality repairs at cut rates. The shop is located at 83 River St., Lynn; (781) 595-2991.

North Shore Cycle has the largest selection of bikes and parts on the North Shore and the tune-up experience to match. The shop is located at 251 Western Ave., Lynn; (781) 581-2700; www.nscycles.com.

The area enjoyed its heyday through the end of the 1960s, but fell on hard times through the '70s and '80s. The Cyclone was destroyed by fire in 1969 after decades of battering from sea storms, and the once opulent dance halls slowly shut down or were turned into honky-tonk bars. Beginning in the late 1980s, city and state development authorities poured intense revitalization energy and funds into Revere Beach and reopened it in 1992. In 1996, Revere Beach was designated a National Historic Landmark.

Follow the beach northeast along Revere Beach Boulevard. Each July, in addition to the typical revelers drawn here to swim and tan, the beach hosts the New England Sand Sculpting Festival. Its entrants are unfathomably

The cliffs at Bailey's Hill Park offer incredible views of the city and Atlantic Ocean.

skilled at creating intricate works of art from the sand beneath their feet as they compete for cash and renown. On your left you'll also pass the original Kelly's Roast Beef, which opened in 1951 and today is known across New England as much for its lobster rolls as its namesake sandwiches. As the beach comes to an end, continue straight through the small rotary onto Lynnway.

Follow the Lynnway through the Point of Pines neighborhood, keeping left at the fork with Rice Avenue to cross over into Lynn via the General Edwards Bridge. One of the smaller cities of Massachusetts, Lynn was first settled by Europeans in 1629. The boot in the city's seal is an homage to the tanning and shoemaking industry for which the city was once famous. The boots worn by the Continental army during the Revolutionary War were manufactured by Lynn's leatherworkers and cobblers. The city remains a minor industrial center today. Take the Lynnway past the strip of auto dealerships and around the curve between North Shore Community College and Lynn Heritage State Park. Continue to the rotary, where you'll take the first exit right onto Nahant Road.

The Nahant area was first settled by Europeans in 1630 when Thomas Dexter bought the peninsula from Poquanum, the Sachem of Nahant, for a suit of clothes. It was long used as grazing grounds for the cattle and goats of Lynn residents, until its transformation into a resort town at the turn of the nineteenth century. By 1817, a daily steamboat ran from Boston to Nahant, and by the 1850s the town had one of the most massive hotel complexes on the Atlantic Coast. It wasn't until the end of the 1800s that the town transformed itself again into its current residential state.

Take Nahant Road past the Little Nahant Island on the left, keeping right at the fork to continue along Castle Road as it slopes uphill. At the intersection with Gardner Road, ride straight onto Colby Way for the downhill slope. Take a left on Bass Point Road and enter Bailey's Hill Park. The paved path to the immediate right just inside the park leads to stunning views of Lewis Cove and Nahant Harbor atop Bailey's Hill, although you'll have to walk the final stretch without your bike.

Continue to follow the shoreline via the gravel path from Bass Point Road to Willow Road, which runs along the Kelley Greens at the Nahant golf course and country club. Follow Willow Road past the golf course and along Dorothy Cove until it curves into Cliff Street. Take Vernon Street to the right and then turn left at Swallow Cave Road to come to the Northeastern University Marine Science Center and Lodge Park.

The Marine Science Center is built on the site of the Nahant Hotel, which occupied the land from 1823 until it burned down in 1861. Once a popular summer residence for Boston high society, the property was bought by John Lodge, father of famed Massachusetts senator Henry Cabot Lodge and namesake of the current park. During WWII this land housed a number of fortifications to protect Boston from attack, including a magnetic loop station to detect submarines. Northeastern University established the Marine Science Center in 1967. Enter the park and follow signs along Nahant Road to Lodge Park. This oblong stretch of lawn on the very tip of Nahant affords some of the most breathtaking views along the Massachusetts shore, with ocean as far as you can see in almost every direction. Rest a spell on one of the park's many benches, then retrace your steps back out of the park for the return leg back to Revere Beach.

The residential town of Nahant is the smallest municipality by area in the Commonwealth, at a mere 1.0 square mile.

Continue along Nahant Road through the center of town, past the Nahant Town Hall and Nahant Country Club and Greenlawn Cemetery, where the causeway back to Lynn will come back into view. Cross back to the rotary, taking the second exit onto the Lynnway that will pass by North Shore Community College and across General Edwards Bridge back into Revere. Exit North Shore Road just after the bridge and continue along Lynnway through Point of Pines back to Revere Beach Boulevard. When the street becomes one-way about two-thirds down the beach, turn right onto Revere Street and then left at Ocean Avenue. Continue past the Wonderland T stop and turn left at Beach Street to rejoin the beach, where you began the ride.

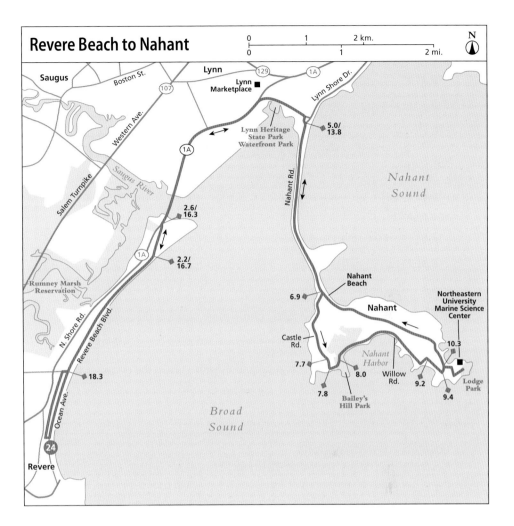

Revere Beach to Nahant

0   1   2 km.
0   1   2 mi.

N

Saugus

Boston St.

Lynn

Lynn
Marketplace

Lynn Shore Dr.

107

129

1A

Western Ave.

Lynn Heritage
State Park
Waterfront Park

5.0/
13.8

Salem Turnpike

Saugus River

1A

Nahant Rd.

Nahant
Sound

2.6/
16.3

1A

2.2/
16.7

Rumney Marsh
Reservation

Nahant
Beach

6.9

Northeastern
University
Marine Science
Center

Nahant

N. Shore Rd.

Revere Beach Blvd.

Castle
Rd.

7.7

Nahant
Harbor

10.3

18.3

Willow
Rd.

9.2

8.0

7.8

Bailey's
Hill Park

Lodge
Park

9.4

Ocean Ave.

Broad
Sound

24

Revere

MILES AND DIRECTIONS

0.0   From the gazebo at Beach Street and Revere Beach Boulevard, head north along Revere Beach, keeping the water to your right.

2.2   Continue through the rotary onto the Lynnway.

2.6   Take the ramp onto the General Edwards Bridge.

5.0   Enter the rotary and take the first exit onto Nahant Road.

6.9   Stay right onto Castle Road.

7.7   At the intersection with Gardner Road, ride straight onto Colby Way.

7.8 Turn left on Bass Point Road and enter Bailey's Hill Park.

8.0 Follow the gravel path to Willow Road, where you'll continue right.

9.2 Turn right onto Vernon Street.

9.4 Turn left onto Swallow Cave Road and enter the Northeastern University Marine Science Center, where you'll follow signs along the paved path to Lodge Park.

10.3 Exit the Northeastern University Marine Science Center complex and turn right onto Nahant Road.

13.8 Enter the rotary and take the second exit onto the Lynnway.

16.3 Keep right after the General Edwards Bridge onto North Shore Road.

16.5 Keep right onto the Lynnway.

16.7 Continue through the rotary onto Revere Beach Boulevard.

18.3 Turn right onto Revere Street and then left onto Ocean Avenue.

19.0 Turn left onto Beach Street back to the ride start at the ramada along Revere Beach Boulevard.

RIDE INFORMATION

Local Events/Attractions

Revere Beach Sand Sculpting Festival: This unique artistic competition draws hundreds of thousands of visitors to Revere each summer to see incredible creations carved out of the beach. www.reverebeach.com

Restrooms

Start/finish: There are restrooms and water along Revere Beach Boulevard, both along the beach and at the many shops and storefronts.
Mile 6.4 and 12.4: There are a number of shops and restaurants at Nahant Beach with restrooms and water.
Mile 9.5: The Northeastern University Marine Science Center has restrooms.

25

Salem

The fabled city of Salem is famous, of course, for its less-than-charitable colonial track record when it came to hysterical public burnings. In addition to unearthing some of Salem's rich history, not all of it witch-centric, this ride also explores a number of the city's coastline retreats and ocean vistas. Whether you're seeking colonial sites or seaside views, Salem has both!

Start: Salem Common

Length: 10.1 miles

Approximate riding time: 2.5–3 hours with stops

Best bike: Mountain bike or hybrid

Terrain and trail surface: A mix of even paved paths and clear, hard-packed dirt trails, with occasional patches of uneven pavement or rocky terrain

Traffic and hazards: Joggers, skateboarders, families with small children, dog walkers, and geese frequent the trails along the waterfront. Watch for traffic along Washington Street, Jefferson Avenue, and Highland Avenue in particular.

Things to see: Salem Common, Salem Willows Park, Winter Island, Palmer Cove, Forest River Park, Gallows Hill Park, Salem Witch Museum.

Maps: USGS: *Salem* and *Marblehead North* quads; DeLorme: *Massachusetts Atlas & Gazetteer,* pp. 29–30

Getting there: By car: From Boston, take US 1 N across the Tobin Memorial Bridge. Take the MA 60 exit toward Malden/Revere to MA 107N/Salem Turnpike, which you'll follow onto Essex Street to downtown Salem. Street parking is available, or garage parking is available at the Museum Place Mall. **By train:** Take the commuter rail to Salem, checking the timetable for bike rack availability. Exit the station onto Bridge Street, which you'll follow to Winter Street before turning right to the Salem Common. GPS coordinates for starting point: N42 31.425' / W70 53.370'

THE RIDE

Start at Salem Common, in the heart of the city's historic downtown. Like the larger Boston Common, this 9-acre park's history began with city's founding, in this case in 1626. Initially it was used for common pastureland and to host military drills for the town militia. The Salem Common is recognized as the birthplace of the National Guard: In 1636, the first muster of multicommunity militia took place on these grounds when the North, South, and East Regiments of the Massachusetts Bay Colony were established. The neighborhoods surrounding the Salem Common are filled with historic homes.

From the gazebo at the center of the Common, take the center path northeast out of the park, and continue onto Briggs Street. Turn left at Webb Street, then take a right onto the beach bike path opposite Andrew Street. Savor your first seaside view, this time of Collins Cove. Continue along the waterfront path until it terminates at Szetala Lane, which you'll take left and continue along as it turns into Memorial Drive and Restaurant Row. Take a small loop through Salem Willows Park, its grassy small hills one of many ideal spots for beachfront picnics along this ride.

Turn right onto Fort Avenue and continue until you reach Winter Island Road, where you'll turn left and ride past the Winter Island Yacht Club to Waikiki Beach. Winter Island was the site of Fort Pickering, established in 1644 as a naval outpost. Keeping left as you ride toward the waterline, you'll see the Fort Pickering Light, a lighthouse that has guided ships in Salem Sound since 1871.

Take Winter Island Road back to Fort Avenue, and turn left. Take another left at Essex Street to ride through the Salem Common neighborhood once again until you reach Hawthorne Boulevard, where you turn left. Continue onto Congress Street until you reach the Palmer Cove Playground, where you'll ride along the water for a few blocks before turning right onto Leach Street. Follow

Salem Witch Trials

Between 1692 and 1693, more than 200 people were accused of practicing witchcraft during the Salem witch trials. The dark history of these trials began in early 1692, when several young girls in the Salem colony began throwing fits and tantrums, which, under pressure from local magistrates, they blamed on three women—a slave, a homeless beggar, and an elderly matron. After the frenzy of accusations and executions subsided, a total of twenty people were put to death for witchcraft: nineteen by the gallows and one by stoning. The colony later declared the trials unlawful and officially restored the good names of all put to death.

The Salem Common is the birthplace of the National Guard, since it was one of the first mustering points for town militia.

the green bike sign to turn left at Summit Avenue and left again at Clinton Avenue, which takes you to Forest River Park. Home to living-history museum Salem Pioneer Village 1630, the park provides another hilly vantage point for taking in Palmer Cove. Take a loop around the park then follow the green bike sign to turn left onto West Avenue.

Continue onto Loring Avenue past Salem State University, then turn right onto Jefferson Avenue for the only real climb of the ride. Turn left onto Wilson Street, right onto Highland Avenue and then left onto Proctor Street, which will take you to Gallows Hill Park. Popular legend places the hangings of close to twenty accused witches between 1692 and 1693 near this site. Take Pope Street to Boston Street and turn left, then take a right onto Bridge Street.

Bike Shops

Salem Cycle is the closest shop to the Salem Common. It is located at 72 Washington St., Salem; (978) 741-2222; www.salemcycle.com.
The Urbane Cyclist specializes in city and hybrid bikes. The shop is located at 144 Washington St., Salem; (978) 594-5174; www.the urbanecyclist.com.

The water on your right is the North River. Turn left at Flint Street and then ride into the Salem Dog Park, which runs alongside the North River. Exit the dog park and turn right onto North Street, continuing until Essex Street, where you'll turn left back toward the Salem Common Historic District. Ride along Essex Street until the Peabody Essex Museum, which was founded in

1799 as a "cabinet of natural and artificial curiosities" by the East India Marine Society, an organization of Salem captains who had sailed beyond either the Cape of Good Hope on the southern tip of Africa or Cape Horn at the southern tip of South America. Today, the Peabody Essex Museum contains diverse collections of international art, architecture, and culture that rival many in Boston's Museum of Fine Arts or the museums of Manhattan.

Turn left at New Liberty Street and then right onto Brown Street. Follow Brown Street past the Salem Witch Museum and the statue of Salem founder Roger Conant to the Salem Common, where you began the ride.

MILES AND DIRECTIONS

0.0 Ride northeast along the center path from the gazebo at the center of the Common, and continue onto Briggs Street.

0.3 Turn left at Webb Street, then take a right onto the beach bike path opposite Andrew Street.

0.6 Turn left onto Szetela Lane, which becomes Memorial Drive.

1.2 Keep left at the split to ride through Salem Willows Park, then turn right onto Fort Avenue.

1.7 Turn left onto Winter Island Road and stay right.

2.1 Keep left to ride toward the water, then loop back toward Fort Avenue.

2.7 Turn left onto Fort Avenue.

3.2 Keep right to stay on Fort Avenue.

3.4 Turn left on Essex Street.

3.9 Turn left at Hawthorne Boulevard, and continue onto Congress Street

4.4 Continue past Leavitt Street to Palmer Cove Playground.

4.6 Turn right on Leach Street.

4.8 Turn left at Summit Avenue.

5.1 Turn left at Clifton Avenue, then keep right to curve into Forest River Park.

5.3 Turn left into Forest River Park and follow the loop.

5.8 Turn left onto West Avenue.

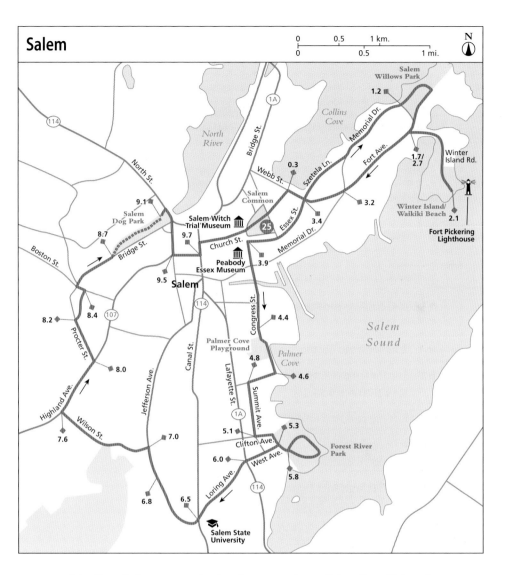

Salem

6.0   Cross Lafayette onto Loring Avenue and pass Salem State University.

6.5   Turn right onto Jefferson Avenue.

6.8   Stay left at the fork to continue along Jefferson Avenue.

7.0   Turn left onto Wilson Street.

7.6   Turn right onto Highland Avenue.

8.0   Turn left onto Proctor Street.

8.2   Take Pope Street right.

Fort Pickering Light has guided ships around Winter Island since 1871.

8.4 Turn left onto Boston Street, then right onto Bridge Street.

8.7 Turn left onto Flint Street then right into the Salem Dog Park just after the train tracks.

9.1 Exit the park and follow the road up to North Street, where you'll turn right and cross the river.

9.5 Turn left onto Essex Street.

9.7 Turn left onto Washington Street then right onto Church Street, which becomes Brown Street.

10.1 Return to the starting point at Salem Common.

RIDE INFORMATION

Local Events/Attractions
Salem Witch Museum chronicles the Salem Witch Trials of 1692 in all their grit. The museum's Halloween party is legendary. Find the museum at 19½ North Washington Sq., Salem; (978) 744-1692; www.salemwitchmuseum.com.

Restrooms
Start/finish: There are a number of shops around the Salem Common with restrooms.
Mile 2.0: Winter Island Park has public restrooms.

Salem to Gloucester

The North Shore coastline blends forest, cliffs, and beachfront with that captivating beauty so distinct to New England. This ride from Salem to the fishing village of Gloucester follows the shoreline through the coastal towns of Beverly and Manchester. Perfect for a day trip to explore some of the most charming and peaceful stretches of the North Shore!

Start: Salem Common, Salem

Length: 31.4 miles

Approximate riding time: 3–3.5 hours with stops

Best bike: Road bike or hybrid

Terrain and trail surface: Even paved paths, with occasional patches of uneven pavement or rocky terrain

Traffic and hazards: Watch for traffic, particularly at traffic circles and bridges.

Things to see: Salem Common, Beverly Harbor, Fish Flake Hill Historic District, Mackerel Cove, Prides Crossing, Beverly Farms, Manchester-by-the-Sea, Magnolia, Gloucester Fisherman's Memorial.

Maps: USGS: *Salem, Marblehead North,* and *Gloucester* quads; DeLorme: *Massachusetts Atlas & Gazetteer,* pp. 30–31, 42

Getting there: By car: From Boston, take US 1N across the Tobin Memorial Bridge. Take the MA 60 exit toward Malden/Revere to MA 107N/Salem Turnpike, which you'll follow onto Essex Street to downtown Salem. Street parking is available, or you can find garage parking at the Museum Place Mall. **By train:** Take the commuter rail to Salem. See the timetable for availability of bike racks. Exit the station onto Bridge Street, which you'll follow to Winter Street, and turn right to the Salem Common. GPS coordinates for starting point: N42 31.416' / W70 53.361'

THE RIDE

Start at Salem Common, in the heart of the city's historic downtown. Like the larger Boston Common, this 9-acre park has a history tracing back to the city's founding, in this case in 1626. At that time, it was used for common pasture-land and to host military drills for the town militia. The Salem Common is thus considered the birthplace of the National Guard: In 1636, the first muster of multicommunity militia took place on these grounds when the North, South, and East Regiments of the Massachusetts Bay Colony were established.

From the gazebo at the center of the Common, take the path northwest, past the wooden arch that is a replica of the historic gates that once adorned the Common. Exit the park onto North Washington Square and turn right, then take the first left onto Winter Street. Take Bridge Street right and follow it across the Veterans Memorial Bridge, which connects Salem to Beverly. To your left is the convergence of the Danvers, Bass, and Waters Rivers; to the right their waters mingle into the ocean in Beverly Harbor and Salem Sound. Cross the bridge into Beverly and take your first right onto Water Street, which curves left into Lothrop Street to follow the town's shoreline.

Incorporated as a separate town from Salem in 1668 and designated a city in 1894, Beverly has a number of historical claims to distinction. In 1787, the first cotton mill in the Americas was constructed at the Beverly Cotton Manufactory. The city also vies with several other communities, including nearby Marblehead, to be known as the birthplace of the US Navy, since one of the first schooners commissioned by George Washington sailed from Beverly Harbor in September 1775. Whether its birthplace claim is legitimate or not, Beverly's history attests to its strong ties to the sea. Following Lothrop Street, you'll pass the Fish Flake Hill Historic District, a National Historic Site filled with historic homes and buildings from the city's fishery heyday. The district takes its name from the drying tables, or "flakes," that once filled fish-drying yards along the harbor until the late nineteenth century, when maritime ventures yielded to industry as the city's primary economic driver.

Follow Lothrop Street along the picturesque Mackerel Cove, its sandy beach a popular draw during the summers. Since the early twentieth century the city has become something of a resort town, in its early days drawing such figures as President William Howard Taft and Supreme Court Justice Oliver Wendell Holmes Jr., who took up summer residence on the Beverly coast. Turn right at Hale Street and ride through the lawn-filled suburbs, curving right to stay on Hale Street and pass Endicott College. In short succession you'll ride through the historic neighborhoods of Prides Crossing and Beverly Farms, where you'll see the remaining summer mansions built for business magnates at the turn of the twentieth century. Beverly Hills in California is named for

Beverly Farms. Keep right at West Street and follow the curve, then continue straight onto Hale Street once again.

You'll ride now across the town boundary into Manchester-by-the-Sea, also known simply as Manchester. This adorable town was founded as Jeffery's Creek, then incorporated as Manchester in 1645. To distinguish the town from the larger Manchester, New Hampshire, railroad conductors and summer residents began calling it Manchester-by-the-Sea, a name formally adopted by a narrow town vote in 1990. Continuing along Hale Street and then Bridge Street, you'll come to the Manchester town center and turn right onto Summer Street. Like Beverly and much of the North Shore, Manchester today is a summer haven for Bostonians, its seaside estates and beaches famous across New England. Day-trippers frequent Manchester's Singing Beach, named for its sand, which squeaks underfoot.

Summer Street curves away from the coast for a stretch as you leave Manchester-by-the-Sea and press along Cape Ann toward Gloucester. Just past the Coolidge Reservation, take a right at Raymond Street to dip past

Bike Shops

Big Mike's Bikes is Gloucester's only full-service bike shop and sells new and used bikes in addition to servicing all manner of repairs and tune-ups. The shop is located at 50 Maplewood Ave., Gloucester; (978) 222-3737; www.bigmikesbikes.org.

Browns of Beverly Bicycles has been family owned and operated since 1947. The shop is located at 278 Cabot St., Beverly; (978) 922-0376; www.brownsofbeverlybicycles.com.

Centraal Cycle is among the more green shops close to Boston, emphasizing environmentally friendly products and practices in line with its top-notch customer service philosophy. The shop is located at 237 Cabot St., Beverly; (978) 922-2400; www.centraalcycle.com.

Retrogression in Beverly specializes in fixed-gear and single-speed bikes, but does repairs on all types of cycles. The shop is located at 3 Front St., Beverly; (978) 969-0066.

Salem Cycle is the closest shop to the Salem Common. It is located at 72 Washington St., Salem; (978) 741-2222; www.salemcycle.com.

Seaside Cycle in Manchester puts top emphasis on comfort and safety, and its tune-ups are backed by a professional staff of top-shelf mechanics. The shop is located at 23 Elm St., Manchester-by-the-Sea; (978) 526-1200; www.seasidecycle.com.

The Urbane Cyclist specializes in city and hybrid bikes. The shop is located at 144 Washington St., Salem; (978) 594-5174; www.theurbane cyclist.com.

Clark Pond into Gloucester's Magnolia village. Follow Shore Road around the Magnolia coastline to take in its shallow cove and large island just offshore. Take Shore Road to Hesperus Avenue and turn right for the final wooded stretch. Take a right at Western Avenue, which will take you past Stage Fort Park and Washington Cemetery, across the bridge to your destination at the Fisherman's Memorial in the center of Gloucester's shore.

Gloucester predates both Salem and Boston by at least five years, although the original settlement was short-lived due to harsh conditions. Fishermen began to dominate the economy beginning in the mid-1700s, and Gloucester remains a fishery center today. The oxidized copper statue before you memorializes the hundreds of fishermen lost at sea from Gloucester over the past 300 years. A number of festivals, such as the Saint Peter's Fiesta each June, celebrate the city's fishing history.

When you're ready to head back, take Western Avenue west, away from Gloucester. Follow Western Avenue to Summer Street and across the town line in Manchester. In the center of Manchester, turn right at Washington Street and then left at Union Street, keeping left to stay on Bridge Street. Continue onto Hale Street into Beverly Farms, then stay straight onto West Street and turn left once more onto Hale Street. Pass Endicott College and turn left to stay on Hale Street, then take a left onto Lothrop Street back past Independence Park.

Turn right at Stone Street and then left at Cabot Street to cross the bridge back into Salem. Take a left just after the bridge onto Bridge Street, then left again at Winter Street to reach the Salem Common, where you began.

MILES AND DIRECTIONS

0.0 Ride northwest along the path from the gazebo at the center of the Common to turn right onto North Washington Square, then first left onto Winter Street.

0.2 Turn right onto Bridge Street.

0.9 Continue across the Veterans Memorial Bridge.

1.4 Turn right just off the bridge onto Water Street, which curves into Lothrop Street.

2.5 Curve right onto Hale Street.

3.5 Keep right to stay on Hale Street.

4.8 Keep right to stay on Hale Street.

Salem to Gloucester

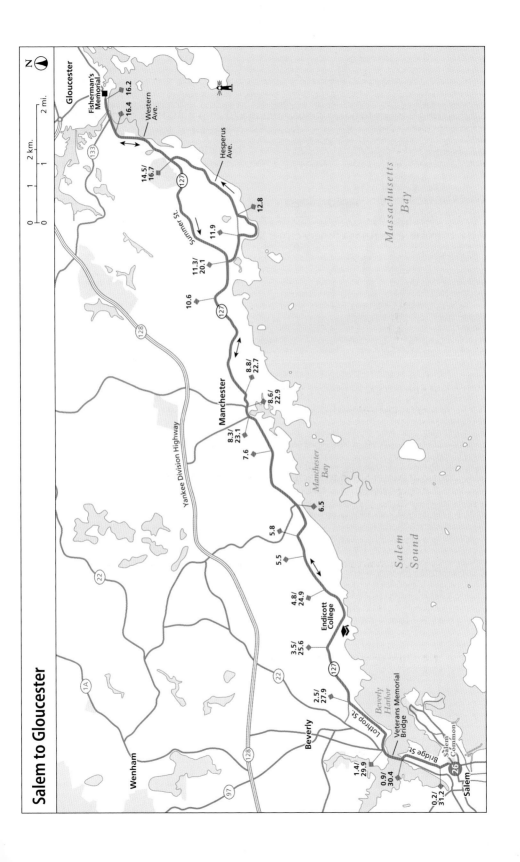

Gloucester's Magnolia village is an idyllic seaside escape.

5.5 Keep right to stay on Hale Street.

5.8 Turn right to continue on West Street.

6.5 Keep right to stay on Hale Street, which becomes Bridge Street.

7.6 Keep left to stay on Bridge Street.

8.3 Turn right onto Central Street.

8.6 Turn right onto Beach Street, then left onto Summer Street.

8.8 Keep right to stay on Summer Street.

10.6 Keep right to stay on Summer Street.

11.3 Turn right onto Raymond Street.

11.9 Turn right onto Shore Road.

12.8 Turn right onto Hesperus Avenue.

14.5 Turn right onto Western Avenue.

16.2 Arrive at the Gloucester Fisherman's Memorial statue and turn around.

16.4 Stay straight to continue on Western Avenue.

16.7 Keep left to stay on Western Avenue.

20.1 Turn right onto Summer Street.

22.7 Turn right onto Washington Street, then left onto Union Street.

22.9 Turn left onto Central Street.

23.1 Keep left to continue onto Bridge Street.

24.9 Keep left to stay on Hale Street.

25.6 Turn left to stay on Hale Street.

27.9 Turn left to stay on Hale Street.

28.9 Turn left onto Lothrop Street.

29.6 Turn right onto Stone Street.

29.9 Turn left onto Cabot Street and cross the bridge back into Salem.

30.4 Take the first left after the bridge onto Bridge Street.

31. 2 Turn left onto Winter Street.

31.4 Arrive back at the Salem Common.

RIDE INFORMATION

Local Events/Attractions
Salem Witch Museum: Learn about the Salem Witch Trials of 1692 in all their grit, or stop by for the museum's legendary Halloween party. More information is available at (978) 744-1692 or www.salemwitchmuseum.com.

Festival By the Sea: Celebrate the local art, food, and culture of Cape Ann at this annual festival in Manchester-by-the-Sea each August. www.capeann chamber.com

St. Peter's Fiesta: Gloucester's biggest festival honors the patron saint of fishermen with five days of boat races, parades, and the infamous Greasy Pole competition. www.stpetersfiesta.org

Restrooms
Start/finish: There are a number of shops around the Salem Common with restrooms.

Mile 5.8 and 25.6: There are lots of shops and restaurants at Beverly Farms.

Mile 16.2: Western Avenue in Gloucester has many shops and restaurants.

Gloucester to Rockport

About an hour north of Boston lies Cape Ann, the summer-vacation mecca known for its prime beachfronts and picturesque coastal retreats. This ride traces the cape from Gloucester to Rockport and back around, passing fishing villages, farm country, and marshes along the way. With plenty of history and unrivaled views of the ocean, this ride has a bit of everything to coax any cyclist out of the city.

Start: Fisherman's Memorial, Gloucester

Length: 19.7 miles

Approximate riding time: 2–3 hours with stops

Best bike: Road bike or hybrid

Terrain and trail surface: Paved roads

Traffic and hazards: Watch for patches of uneven or sandy pavement, particularly along the shoreline.

Things to see: Fisherman's Memorial, Niles Beach, Good Harbor Beach, Delmater Sanctuary, Rockport, Halibut Point State Park, Goose Cove, Annisquam River.

Maps: USGS: *Gloucester* and *Rockport* quads; DeLorme: *Massachusetts Atlas & Gazetteer*, pp. 30–31

Getting there: By car: From Boston, take I-93N to exit 27, turning onto US 1N via the Tobin Bridge. Take MA 128 N toward Waltham and Gloucester. Exit at Washington Street in Gloucester, turning right onto Washington Street, then right again onto Centennial Avenue, finally turning left onto Western Avenue, which you'll follow to the Fisherman's Memorial. Parking is available in a lot at the beach where Western Avenue curves north. **By train:** Take the commuter rail to Gloucester via the Newburyport/Rockport line. Check the commuter rail timetable for bike details. Exit the station left onto Washington Street, then take a left at Middle Street and a right onto Western Avenue, which you'll follow to the Fisherman's Memorial. GPS coordinates for starting point: N42 36.603' / W70 40.226'

Gloucester's Western Avenue is the picture of patriotic fanfare every July 4th.

THE RIDE

You'll start at the Fisherman's Memorial on Gloucester's Western Avenue. Gloucester predates both Salem and Boston by at least five years, its settlement the result of an expedition of the Dorchester Company from England. Although the original settlement was short-lived due to harsh conditions and more fertile soil near modern Salem, the area was slowly populated with loggers and farmers until fishermen began to dominate the economy beginning in the mid-1700s.

The burgeoning fishing economy drew immigrants from Italy and Portugal in the nineteenth century, and their influence is still felt today in the many festivals celebrated throughout the year. During Saint Peter's Fiesta, which honors the patron saint of fishermen at the end of June, relatives of fishermen past and present parade through the streets, attend an open-air Mass in St. Peter's Square, and watch the seine boat races in the harbor. One of the culminating events of the festival is the Greasy Pole, a contest in which a 45-foot telephone pole (an approximation of a ship's mast) with a red flag nailed to its end is attached to a platform at Pavilion Beach. Brave contestants try to walk the heavily greased pole to grab the flag, with the vast majority slipping into the water below, not infrequently injuring themselves in the process. The victorious few are paraded around town once they swim back to shore. This celebration of Gloucester's fishing history draws revelers from across New

England each summer. Gloucester remains a fishery center today, and the oxidized copper statue at the start of the ride memorializes the hundreds of fishermen lost at sea from Gloucester over the past 300 years.

From the memorial, ride east along Western Avenue, keeping the beach-front on your right. After the street curves left, turn right and follow Rogers Street to East Main Street, where you'll turn right toward East Gloucester. This neighborhood of Gloucester holds the greatest concentration of the city's art-ists, including the Rocky Neck Art Colony, the oldest such working art colony in the country. Continue onto Eastern Point Boulevard to Niles Beach and turn left onto Farrington Avenue, following the curve into Atlantic Road on the eastern coast of East Gloucester.

Bike Shop

Big Mike's Bikes is Gloucester's only full-service bike shop and sells new and used bikes in addition to offering all manner of repairs and tune-ups. The shop is located at 50 Maplewood Ave., Gloucester; (978) 222-3737; www.bigmikesbikes.org.

A number of small beaches dot the roadside as you come to Good Har-bor Beach, a mix of marsh and ocean-front where Atlantic Road curves into Thatcher Road. Here the road contin-ues through coastal forest, including Delmater Sanctuary on the left as you near Rockport. While the road is never more than a few hundred feet from the sea, dense trees and farmhouses block it from view as you continue onto South Street and then Mt. Pleasant Street through the center of Rockport.

Once largely an uninhabited part of Gloucester and used primarily for timber harvesting, Rockport was incorporated as a separate town in 1840. Since then it has developed into a summer resort, surrounded as it is on three sides by the Atlantic. Much of the town shuts down during the winter months, but in fine weather the visitors flock here in droves for its beaches, seafood, lighthouses, and handicraft workshops. Take Mt. Pleasant Street to Main Street and turn left, then keep right at Beach Street to ride past the town's two principal beachfronts. Merge onto Granite Street to continue north to the northernmost tip of Cape Ann at Halibut Point State Park. Closed to bikes, unfortunately, the park is worth an excursion on foot if you need a rest for the return leg to Gloucester along the cape's western shore.

As you round the cape's tip and head south back into Gloucester, you'll stay much more within view of the ocean, as you gaze out at Ipswich Bay. Keep right onto Langsford Street at the Seaside Cemetery, then follow Wash-ington Street south into the Annisquam neighborhood of Gloucester, named for the river you'll come to at Lobster Cove. After crossing the water with Goose Cove to your left, you'll ride downhill through additional stretches of beautiful neighborhoods, crossing the Annisquam River once again past Rey-nard Street before rounding the marshy Mill Pond.

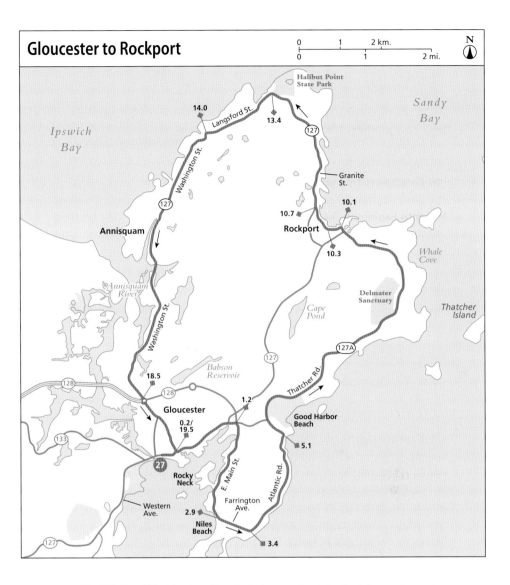

You'll follow Washington Street all the way back to the Gloucester waterfront, taking care at the rotary with MA 128 and following signs south to Gloucester. A bit past the Gloucester commuter rail station, you'll take Middle Street right back to Western Avenue and Fisherman's Memorial, where you began the ride.

MILES AND DIRECTIONS

0.0   Begin at the Gloucester Fisherman's Memorial, and ride east along Western Avenue with traffic, keeping the waterfront to your right.

0.2   Turn right onto Rogers Street.

1.2 Turn right onto East Main Street, which becomes Eastern Point Road.

2.9 Turn left onto Farrington Avenue.

3.4 Turn left onto Atlantic Road.

5.1 Keep left to continue onto Thatcher Road, which becomes South, then Pleasant Street.

10.1 Turn left onto Main Street.

10.3 Keep right onto Beach Street.

10.7 Turn right onto Granite Street.

13.4 Stay right onto Langsford Street.

14.0 Turn left onto Washington Street.

18.5 Enter the rotary and take the second exit to continue along Washington Street.

19.5 Turn left onto Middle Street.

19.6 Turn right onto Western Avenue.

19.7 End at Gloucester Fisherman's Memorial.

RIDE INFORMATION

Local Events/Attractions
St. Peter's Fiesta: Gloucester's biggest festival honors the patron saint of fishermen with five days of boat races, parades, and the infamous Greasy Pole competition. www.stpetersfiesta.org

Gloucester Schooner Festival: This celebration of sailing and ocean-going vessels culminates in the Mayor's Race, a fixture of the Gloucester Harbor since 1985. www.gloucesterschoonerfestival.net

Rockport Tree Lighting: Santa arrives by lobster boat to Rockport's Bearskin Neck each December, followed by the lighting of the town's tree right on the waterfront. www.rockportusa.com

Restrooms
Start/finish: Western Avenue has a number of shops and restaurants with restrooms and water.

Mile 9.5 to 10.1: The Rockport shopping district has a number of shops and restaurants with restrooms and water.

South of Boston

Nickerson Beach boasts beautiful cliffs with views of Boston Harbor (Ride 29).

The landscapes and towns south of Boston are as breathtaking as they are wildly different. Head due south from Boston's South End to explore the Blue Hills Reservation and its thousands of hilly acres surrounding the pristine Houghton's Pond. Follow the South Shore coastline from Scituate to Hull and take in the vast Massachusetts Bay and outer reaches of Boston Harbor. Colonial fortresses, historic estates, stunning vistas, and coastal views await you.

South End to Blue Hills

This ride into the serenity of the Blue Hills Reservation is a straight shot from the city, taking you from the South End, through Roxbury and Mattapan, into the quiet suburbs of Milton. Traveling south from the heart of the city, you'll see some of the most breathtaking natural vistas in New England, including the reservation's wooded hills and the beachfront along Houghton's Pond. If a wooded retreat is what you seek, head to the hills!

Start: Massachusetts Avenue and Washington Street, South End, Boston

Length: 20.6 miles

Approximate riding time: 2.5–3 hours with stop

Best bike: Road bike or hybrid

Terrain and trail surface: Well-paved urban roads and bike lanes, with dirt path within Blue Hills Reservation

Traffic and hazards: Watch for traffic along Washington Street and Blue Hill Avenue, particularly at traffic circles and major intersections.

Things to see: South End, Roxbury, Twelfth Baptist Church, Dudley Square, Franklin Park Zoo, Franklin Park, Mattapan, Milton, Blue Hills Reservation, Houghton's Pond, Brookwood Farm, Prowse Farm

Maps: USGS: *Boston South* and *Blue Hills* quads; DeLorme: *Massachusetts Atlas & Gazetteer,* pp. 41, 53

Getting there: By car: Parking can be very limited in the South End. There is street parking along Massachusetts Avenue and side streets, or else park in the Stanhope Garage. Take Massachusetts Avenue to the South End, turning right onto Harrison Street. The garage is immediately on your right, off of Northampton. Exiting the garage, ride back to Massachusetts Avenue and turn left, then make a left at Washington Street. **By train:** Take the Silver Line or the 1, 8, 10, 15, 170, or CT1 bus to Washington Street at Massachusetts Avenue. Bikes are allowed on all buses with bike racks, without restriction. GPS coordinates for starting point: N42 20.185′ / W71 04.625′

THE RIDE

You'll start at Massachusetts Avenue and Washington Street, in Boston's South End. This area was once tidal marsh and was filled from the 1830s to the 1870s with gravel from Needham and submerged timbers. The architecture in the South End attests to its development in the mid-nineteenth century. In vogue during that era, the many red-bricked brownstones with a mixture of renaissance revival and European-inspired facades are today considered a hallmark of classic Bostonian architecture. By many estimates, the South End holds the most Victorian brownstones of any area in New England.

Pass Ramsay Park and Melnea Cass Boulevard into Roxbury, one of the first towns founded in the Massachusetts Bay Colony. Roxbury was its own municipality until its annexation to Boston in 1868 and later received the influx of African Americans from the South in the 1940s and 1950s. The neighborhood was the training ground for such notable civil rights leaders as Malcolm X and Martin Luther King Jr. Today, the neighborhood is also home to a diverse immigrant community drawing from Latin America and the Caribbean, and is touted by City Hall as the "heart of black culture" in Boston.

Follow Washington Street to Dudley Street and turn left, then take the first right onto Warren Street. Just past Moreland Street, you'll see Twelfth Baptist Church on your left. Established in 1840, this landmark of the civil rights struggle hosted such visiting preachers as the prominent abolitionists William Lloyd Garrison and Frederick Douglass. Civil rights leaders like Martin Luther King Jr. also established deep roots in the Twelfth Baptist community. A bit farther on, past Warren Gardens and Martin Luther King Boulevard, you'll come to Boston Latin Academy on your right. A public exam school, Boston Latin is both the first public school ever established in the United States as well as the oldest existing school, having been established in 1635. It is consistently rated among the top high schools in the country. Turn right onto Blue Hill Avenue to ride past Franklin Park Zoo and Franklin Park into Mattapan.

Bike Shops

Community Bicycle Supply in the South End has been family owned and operated for nearly forty years and carries an extensive collection of bikes, apparel, and parts. The shop is located at 496 Tremont St., Boston; (617) 542-8623.

Dave's Bike Infirmary was established in 1974 and offers a wide array of repair classes in addition to equipment, tune-ups, and mechanic services. The shop is located at 440 Granite Ave., Milton; (617) 696-6123; www.daves-bike.com.

Blue Hills Parkway is a straight shot to the Blue Hills Reservation from Milton.

This neighborhood was officially part of neighboring Dorchester until the Boston Redevelopment Authority gave it its own zip code in the 1960s. A Jewish bastion until the 1970s, Mattapan is today largely populated with Caribbean immigrants. Coming up on the left is the stunning Mattapan Branch of the Boston Public Library, which opened in 2009. You'll shortly pass through South Mattapan and cross the Neponset River that runs from Westwood to the south all the way to the Quincy Shore in the east.

Here you'll cross into Milton. Keep left at the fork to ride along Blue Hills Parkway. Milton separated from Dorchester in 1662 and has resisted annexation for years. The town was an early industrial site in the Massachusetts Bay Colony, home to some of the first gristmills, sawmills, and paper mills in the New World. The chocolate factory established at the old gristmill in 1764 was also the first chocolate factory in New England. Today, Milton is known as one of the most Irish towns in the country: More than a third of residents cite Irish heritage as their principal ancestry. Pass the Popes Pond woods and continue past Canton Avenue onto Unquity Road, named after the Neponset tribe word meaning "Lower Falls," which they used for the lands surrounding Milton. Stay left at Harland Street and pass the Harland Street Conservation Area on your left, riding through one last suburban stretch before reaching Hillside Street, where you'll turn right.

Hillside Street will take you into the chain of twenty-two hills known as the Blue Hills Reservation. Named by early European settlers for the hills' bluish hue when seen from a distance, the reservation in fact gets its trademark color from the abundance of a silicate mineral called riebeckite. Historians believe that "Massachusetts," which in the Algonquian family of languages translates to "people who live near the great hill," refers to the Blue Hills and the Great Blue Hill, the tallest point in modern Norfolk County at over 635 feet, which lies on the northwestern edge of the reservation. The 7,000-acre Blue Hills Reservation is perfect for skiing, swimming, horseback riding, rock climbing, and biking along its miles and miles of trails. Follow Hillside Street past the historic park headquarters on your right, its main building built in 1904, eleven years after the Metropolitan Parks Commission purchased the Blue Hills Reservation lands for public recreation. The park headquarters building is one of sixteen historic structures within the reservation on the National Register of Historic Places. After the parks commission established the reservation, Frederick Law Olmsted's protege Charles Eliot designed the parkways leading into and out of the park, including Unquity Road and Hillside Street.

Turn left at the parking lot for Houghton's Pond and ride through the park to the pond's shore, your destination. A favorite summertime swimming spot, the beaches at Houghton's Pond are just one of the natural gems you'll find in the Blue Hills. As deep as 42 feet in some places, this kettle hole pond was formed by receding glaciers approximately 10,000 years ago. Take in the impressive diversity of flora and fauna around the pond: Its all-around serene beauty lends the whole area a tranquil air.

When you're ready to head back toward Boston, ride back to Hillside Street and turn left. Ride past Brookwood Farm, a combination of historic farm and modern community growing center, then the 55-acre Prowse Farm, an odd mix of medical device company headquarters and historical preserve. At the corner of this property once stood the Doty Tavern, where in 1774 a gathering of rebellious colonists drew up the Suffolk Resolves, a precursor of the Declaration of Independence. Take a right onto Washington Street and continue north back toward Milton, passing Curry College. Follow Blue Hill Avenue all the way back to Mattapan and into Roxbury, turning left onto Warren Street. Take Warren Street past Dudley Square and onto Washington Street, which runs back to the ride's start at Massachusetts Avenue.

MILES AND DIRECTIONS

0.0 Begin at the intersection of Massachusetts Avenue and Washington Street, and ride southwest along Washington Street.

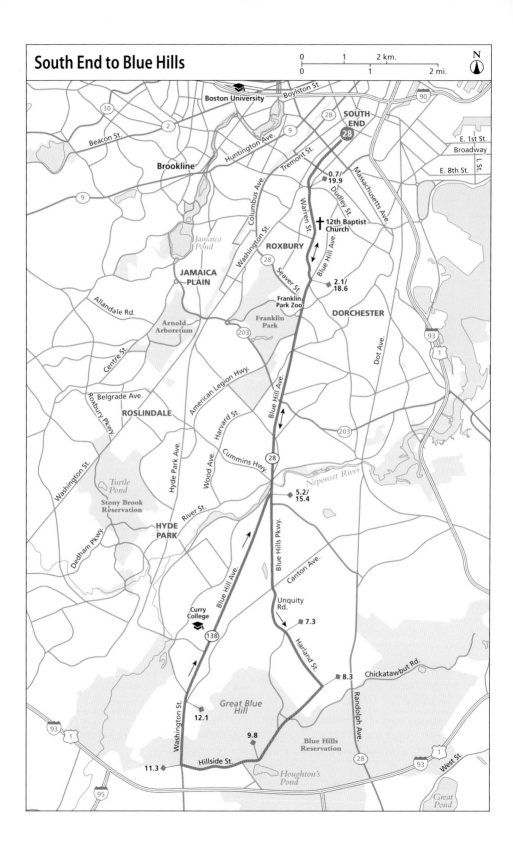

South End to Blue Hills

0   1   2 km.

0   1   2 mi.

N

90

Boston University

Boylston St.

30

2

SOUTH
END

28

E. 1st St.

Broadway

Beacon St.

9

Huntington Ave.

28

Tremont St.

Massachusetts Ave.

E. 8th St.

L St.

Brookline

Columbus Ave.

9

Washington St.

Warren St.

0.7/
19.9

Dudley St.

12th Baptist
Church

ROXBURY

28

Seaver St.

Blue Hill Ave.

**JAMAICA
PLAIN**

*Jamaica
Pond*

2.1/
18.6

Allandale Rd.

Franklin
Park Zoo

DORCHESTER

**Arnold
Arboretum**

203

**Franklin
Park**

Dot Ave.

93

Centre St.

1

Belgrade Ave.

Roxbury Pkwy.

American Legion Hwy.

Harvard St.

Blue Hill Ave.

203

ROSLINDALE

Hyde Park Ave.

Wood Ave.

Cummins Hwy.

28

Neponset River

Washington St.

*Turtle
Pond*

River St.

5.2/
15.4

**Stony Brook
Reservation**

**HYDE
PARK**

Blue Hills Pkwy.

Dedham Pkwy.

Canton Ave.

Blue Hill Ave.

Curry
College

138

Unquity
Rd.

7.3

Harland St.

8.3

Chickatawbut Rd.

Randolph Ave.

93

1

Washington St.

*Great Blue
Hill*

12.1

9.8

**Blue Hills
Reservation**

28

93

West St.

11.3

Hillside St.

*Houghton's
Pond*

95

*Great
Pond*

0.5 Keep right to continue along Washington Street.

0.7 Turn left onto Dudley Street, then right onto Warren Street.

2.1 Turn right onto Blue Hill Avenue.

5.2 Keep left onto Blue Hills Parkway.

6.6 Continue straight onto Unquity Road.

7.3 Keep left onto Harland Street.

8.3 Turn right onto Hillside Street.

9.8 Turn left into the Blue Hills Reservation parking lot and follow the signs to Houghton's Pond.

10.1 Turn left out of the parking lot back onto Hillside Street.

11.3 Turn right onto Washington Street.

12.1 Stay left to continue on Blue Hill Avenue.

15.4 Turn left at the intersection to continue on Blue Hill Avenue.

18.6 Turn left onto Warren Street.

19.9 Keep left to stay on Warren Street through Dudley Square.

20.1 Continue straight onto Washington Street.

20.6 Arrive back at the intersection of Massachusetts Avenue and Washington Street.

RIDE INFORMATION

Local Events/Attractions

Roxbury International Film Festival: Originally the Dudley Film Festival when established in 1999, this festival of independent film puts Boston on the cinematic map each year. www.roxburyinternationalfilmfestival.org

Franklin Park Kite and Bike Festival: A yearly tradition in Roxbury with roots back to 1969, this celebration allows revelers to explore the park's skies and bike paths the weekend after Mother's Day. www.franklinparkcoalition.org

Blue Hills Weather Observatory: This historic weather station hosts weekend guided tours at the top of Great Blue Hill. www.bluehill.org

Houghton's Pond: Open for swimming every day during July and August. www.mass.gov/dcr

Houghton's Pond has a cordoned swimming area and modern bathhouse at its beach.

Prowse Farm: Crowned with an equestrian track, this historic park also hosts a number of concerts throughout the year, including the Life is Good Festival each summer. www.prowsefarm.org

Restrooms

Start/finish: A number of shops and restaurants along Massachusetts Avenue, as well as many in Roxbury and Mattapan, have restrooms and water.
Mile 9.8: Houghton's Pond has public restrooms at the bathhouse.

Castle Island to Nickerson Beach

For colonial Bostonians, the Old Harbor was not only a refreshing vista, but the anchor of their way of life and connection to the rest of the world. This ride rounds the harbor from the fortified Castle Island in Dorchester, around UMass Boston's seaside campus, and across to the cliffs of Quincy's secluded Nickerson Beach, following the shoreline for extended views of the harbor and its numerous islets. With hefty doses of sea breezes and beachfront, this ride is the perfect seaside escape from landlocked doldrums.

Start: Head Island Causeway, Castle Island

Length: 19.4 miles

Approximate riding time: 2–2.5 hours with stops

Best bike: Road bike or hybrid

Terrain and trail surface: Well-paved urban roads and bike paths

Traffic and hazards: Joggers, skateboarders, families with small children, and dog walkers frequent the beaches and paths along this ride. Be careful of traffic along roads, particularly at rotaries and overpasses.

Things to see: Pleasure Bay, Castle Island, L Street Beach, M Street Beach, Carson Beach, Savin Hill Beach, Tenean Beach, UMass Boston, John F. Kennedy Presidential Library, Vietnam War Memorial, Savin Hill, Neponset Trail, Nickerson Beach, Squantum Marshes

Maps: USGS: *Boston South* quad; DeLorme: *Massachusetts Atlas & Gazetteer*, p. 41

Getting there: By car: There is parking at Castle Island at the end of William J. Day Boulevard. From downtown, take Summer Street east across Fort Point into South Boston and turn left onto East Broadway. Take a left onto William J. Day Boulevard, and follow it to the lot at Castle Island. **By train:** Take the T Red Line to JFK/UMass. Bikes are allowed on the Red Line, except from 7 to 10 a.m. and 4 to 7 p.m. Monday through

Friday and without restriction on weekends. Exit the station onto Columbia Road and turn right, carefully crossing the traffic circle to William J. Day Boulevard, which you'll follow along the harbor to Castle Island. GPS coordinates for starting point: N42 19.831' / W71 00.913'

THE RIDE

You'll start on the Head Island Causeway, which encloses Pleasure Bay and connects to Castle Island. No longer a true island due to extensive landfill, Castle Island is home to Fort Independence, the oldest continuously fortified site built by the English in the United States. This site has hosted battlements since the mid-1600s, although its current pentagon-shaped fort was completed in the mid-1800s and fell out of use after the Civil War. The park has one of the most exquisite sunrise vantage points of anywhere in the city.

Ride west along the causeway path, continuing alongside William J. Day Boulevard. These are the popular L and M Street Beaches, united by the Curley Community Center, which Mayor James Curley completed in 1931 as a recreation spot for the working class of South Boston and Dorchester. Follow the path past the bathhouses across from Joe Moakley Park, then continue south along William J. Day Boulevard and around the southern shore of Carson Beach.

> Frederick Law Olmsted envisioned connecting Castle Island to the Emerald Necklace. His proposed parkway, to be called "the Dorchesterway," never materialized.

Follow the waterline through Dorchester Shores Reservation and Old Harbor Park, where the path veers away from the shore briefly toward the University of Massachusetts, Boston campus. Turn left onto the gravel path of the Harborwalk to the John F. Kennedy Presidential Library. The glass-and-steel museum, which is the only official national memorial to JFK, was originally slated to be built in Harvard, but was completed on the harbor in 1979. In addition to preserving and exhibiting the letters and papers of the thirty-fifth President, the JFK Library is also the curator of Nobel Laureate Ernest Hemingway's repository. From the library's boardwalk there is a fantastic view across the harbor to Thompson Island, one of the larger bodies in the Boston Harbor Islands system.

Continue along the water's edge and around the university campus. Established in 1964 in the midst of the civil rights movement and intense social upheaval, UMass Boston moved to its current location on Dorchester's

Tenean Beach is tucked away within view of the colorful Boston Gas tanks.

Columbia Point in 1974. The only public university in Boston, it recently opened a residential campus for its historically commuting-only students.

Round the peninsula to ride along William T. Morrissey Boulevard. You'll pass the somber Vietnam War Memorial, dedicated in 2008, as you enter the Savin Hill neighborhood and Savin Hill Beach, an area settled by Puritans just a few months before Boston was founded. Originally called Rock Hill and later Old Hill, the area came to its present name by the invention of a local hotelier in 1819, who took the name from the red juniper, or Savin, a type of tree that grew abundantly nearby. After crossing Savin Hill Cove, carefully cross Morrissey Boulevard onto the sidewalk under the I-93 overpass, then stay left and ride along Freeport Street. Continue onto Tenean Street and then turn left onto Conley Street.

Follow Conley Street to Tenean Beach along the Neponset River. Ride along the Neponset Trail by the water, exiting the beachfront to take a left on Tenean Street and continue onto Water Street. Water Street curves right into Taylor Street, where the Neponset Trail resumes. Turn right just after the overpass to exit the park onto Hancock Street. Ride on the sidewalk over the bridge spanning the Neponset River as you cross into the city of Quincy.

Nicknamed the "City of Presidents," Quincy is the birthplace of John Adams and his son John Quincy Adams, the second and sixth presidents, as well as of John Hancock, whose bold signature on the Declaration of Independence is so famous. Incorporated after the Revolution in 1792, the city is named for Colonel John Quincy, grandfather of Abigail Adams, for whom John Quincy Adams was named.

Turn left at Kendall Street, left again briefly onto Newbury Avenue and then right on Botolph Street. Take a left onto East Squantum Street, which you'll follow past the Moswetuset Hummock. In 1621, Plymouth Colony commander Myles Standish and Tisquantum, also called Squanto, a Patuxet guide, visited Chief Chickatawbut at this spot, which was the seat of the Massachusett tribe. Just past the hummock is Squantum Marsh, once a fertile mollusk-harvesting ground for the tribe. After colonization and the expansion of Boston into the eighteenth century, the Squantum neighborhood of Quincy became a resort destination for city dwellers. Past the marshes, stay left onto Dorchester Street and follow the shore to Nickerson Beach, a smaller beach with spectacular views across the harbor. The dirt path just off of Moon Island Road leads to Squaw Rock, its cliffs a tranquil place to take in downtown and the harbor islands, including Moon Island and Long Island just across the causeway, which are not open to the public.

When you're ready to head back, retrace your route along to East Squantum Street, turning right onto Victory Road to cut through Quincy's Marina Bay. Follow the rotary to Seaport Drive, then turn left onto Commander Shea Boulevard back toward Quincy. Turn left just before the road curves and follow Quincy Shore Drive to the ramps up to the bridge bike lane. Take the bridge back across the Neponset River into Boston and ride briefly along Neponset Avenue before taking Redfield Street right. Turn left to follow Water Street back to Tenean Beach. Riding north, you're facing the iconic and colorful mural on the Boston Gas tanks across the water. Exit the park via Conley Street and turn right onto Tenean Street, continuing to Freeport Street. Merge onto William T. Morrissey Boulevard and cross back across Savin Hill Cove, where the Harborwalk path begins parallel to the street.

Bike Shops

Ashmont Cycles opened its doors in 2011 and has already attracted a loyal following in Dorchester for its competitive pricing, quality repairs, and weekly guided rides around Milton, Stoughton, and Quincy. The shop is located at 551 Talbot Ave., Dorchester; (617) 282-6552; www.ashmontcycles.com.

MyBike styles itself as an "untraditional" bike shop because of its concierge "house calls," electric bike offerings, and other add-ons to typical services you'd expect from a full-service bike shop. MyBike is located at 391 West Broadway, South Boston; (617) 202-9720; www.mybike.com.

Follow the Harborwalk path around the UMass Boston peninsula and back to Carson Beach. Follow the water around Pleasure Bay to the Head Island Causeway, where you began the ride.

MILES AND DIRECTIONS

0.0 From the gazebo on the Head Island Causeway, ride west around Pleasure Bay to William J. Day Boulevard.

0.4 Turn left to follow the Harborwalk that runs alongside William J. Day Boulevard.

2.1 Follow the Harborwalk left.

3.0 Turn left and follow the dirt path along the shoreline toward the JFK Presidential Library on Columbia Point.

4.4 Follow the Harborwalk left along William T. Morrissey Boulevard.

5.2 Carefully cross William T. Morrissey Boulevard and ride under the overpass, turning left onto Freeport Street.

5.8 Turn left onto Tenean Street.

5.9 Turn left onto Conley Street.

6.0 Ride along Tenean Beach via the Neponset Trail.

6.4 Ride straight along Water Street.

6.5 Turn right onto Taylor Street, and continue onto the Neponset Trail.

6.8 Turn right just after the overpass to exit the park onto Hancock Street.

6.9 Turn right to ride on the sidewalk over the bridge into Quincy.

7.7 Turn left onto Kendall Street, left again briefly onto Newbury Avenue and then right on Botolph Street.

8.1 Turn left onto East Squantum Street.

8.4 Keep right to stay on East Squantum Street.

9.3 Keep left onto Dorchester Street.

9.8 Arrive at Nickerson Beach and walk your bike to the cliffs at Squaw Rock, where you'll turn around.

10.4 Keep right onto East Squantum Street.

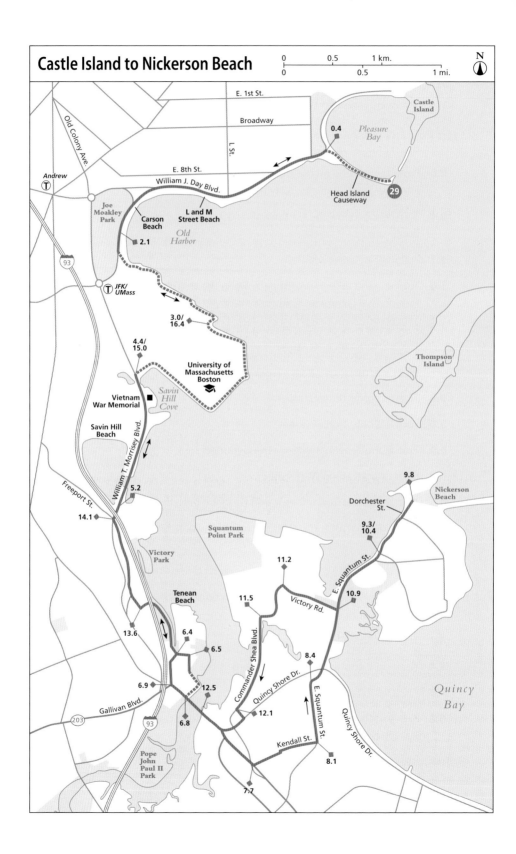

Castle Island to Nickerson Beach

0   0.5   1 km.
0   0.5   1 mi.

N

E. 1st St.

Broadway

Castle Island

Pleasure Bay

0.4

L St.

Andrew T

E. 8th St.

William J. Day Blvd.

Head Island Causeway

29

Old Colony Ave.

Joe Moakley Park

Carson Beach

L and M Street Beach

Old Harbor

2.1

93

JFK/ UMass T

3.0/ 16.4

University of Massachusetts Boston

Thompson Island

4.4/ 15.0

Vietnam War Memorial

Savin Hill Cove

Savin Hill Beach

William T. Morrisey Blvd.

9.8

Nickerson Beach

Freeport St.

5.2

Dorchester St.

9.3/ 10.4

14.1

Squantum Point Park

E. Squantum St.

Victory Park

11.2

10.9

Tenean Beach

11.5

Victory Rd.

13.6

6.4

6.5

Commander Shea Blvd.

Quincy Shore Dr.

8.4

E. Squantum St.

Quincy Bay

6.9

12.5

12.1

Gallivan Blvd.

203

93

6.8

Kendall St.

Quincy Shore Dr.

Pope John Paul II Park

7.7

8.1

10.9 Turn right onto Victory Road.

11.2 Take the second exit out of the traffic circle onto Seaport Drive.

11.5 Turn left onto Commander Shea Boulevard.

12.1 Turn left and follow Quincy Shore Drive right to the ramps up to the bridge bike lane.

12.5 Cross the bridge across the Neponset River into Boston.

12.9 Turn right onto Redfield Street.

13.0 Turn left onto Water Street back past Tenean Beach.

13.5 Turn right onto Tenean Street.

13.6 Turn right onto Freeport Street.

14.1 Merge onto William T. Morrissey Boulevard.

15.0 Turn right onto the Harborwalk path at UMass.

16.4 Turn right to continue along the Harborwalk.

19.4 Arrive back at the Head Island Causeway ramada.

RIDE INFORMATION

Local Events/Attractions

Guided tours of Castle Island: The Castle Island Association sponsors free hour-long guided tours of Fort Independence every Saturday and Sunday from noon to 3:30 p.m. from Memorial Day through Columbus Day. www.boston fortindependence.com

Twilight Skyline Viewing: For an unguided tour of the Boston skyline, visit Fort Independence's upper level, which is open to the public every Thursday evening in June, July, and August from 7 p.m. until dusk. www.bostonfort independence.com

Boston Harborfest: Join the Independence Day celebrations that take place in and along Boston Harbor during the week of July 4th. www.bostonharbor fest.com

Restrooms

Start/finish: Castle Island has restrooms and water.
Mile 1.0 and 18.3: Curley Community Center has restrooms and water.
Mile 2.0 and 17.4: Old Harbor bathhouse has restrooms and water.
Mile 3.7 and 15.7: UMass Boston has public restrooms and water.

Blue Hills Reservation

The 7,000-acre Blue Hills Reservation, which lies less than 20 miles south of Boston, offers breathtaking views, challenging climbs, and refreshing forest vistas. The reservation's varied landscape will take you through thick forest, marsh, and meadow landscapes just minutes apart, and past ponds, bogs, reservoirs, and even swampland in rapid succession. So close to the city but a world apart, the Blue Hills are a favorite retreat for urban dwellers who feel briefly drawn to a wilder setting.

Start: Blue Hills Reservation visitor center, Houghton's Pond, Milton

Length: 14.9 miles

Approximate riding time: 2–2.5 hours with stops

Best bike: Road bike, mountain bike, or hybrid

Terrain and trail surface: A mix of paved roads and clear, hard-packed dirt trails, with occasional patches of uneven pavement or rocky terrain and a handful of steep climbs

Traffic and hazards: Watch for cars, particularly outside the reservation.

Things to see: Blue Hills Reservation, Houghton's Pond, Park Headquarters, Chickatawbut Observation Tower, Great Pond, Massasoit College, Prowse Farm, Brookwood Farm

Maps: USGS: *Blue Hills* quad; DeLorme: *Massachusetts Atlas & Gazetteer,* pp. 41, 53

Getting there: By car: Parking is available at Houghton's Pond. From Boston, take I-93S to exit 3. Follow Blue Hill River Road to Hillside Street and take a right. Houghton's Pond will be on your right. The visitor center is within sight of the parking lot, on the shore of the pond. **By train:** Take the Franklin commuter rail line to Readville. Check the schedule for bike details. Take Neponset Valley Parkway east to Blue Hill Avenue and turn right, then take a left onto Hillside Street until the Houghton's Pond parking lot. GPS coordinates for starting point: N42 12.521' / W71 05.777'

Named by early European settlers for the hills' bluish hue from a distance, which comes from the abundance of a silicate mineral called riebeckite, the Blue Hills' chain of twenty-two summits beckons thousands of nature seekers out of Boston's urban wild each year and into the reservation's natural beauty, where they enjoy skiing, swimming, horseback riding, rock climbing, and, of course, biking.

Begin at the Blue Hills Reservation visitor center on the shore of Houghton's Pond. A favorite summertime swimming destination, the beaches at Houghton's Pond are just one of the natural gems you'll find in the Blue Hills. As deep as 42 feet in some places, the kettle hole pond was formed by receding glaciers approximately 10,000 years ago. The Massachusett people, from whom the Massachusetts Bay Colony derived its name, fished the pond and hunted the surrounding lands when settlers arrived. In the Algonquian family of languages, "Massachusetts" translates to "people who live near the great hill," which historians believe

Bike Shop

Dave's Bike Infirmary was established in 1974 and offers a wide array of repair classes in addition to equipment, tune-ups, and mechanic services. The shop is located at 440 Granite Ave., Milton; (617) 696-6123; www.daves-bike.com.

refers to the Blue Hills and the Great Blue Hill, the tallest point in modern Norfolk County at over 635 feet, which lies on the northwestern edge of the reservation.

Ride southeast from the visitor center along the pond's shore past the bathhouse, keeping left at the fork on the eastern edge of the lake. After a brief unpaved section of the trail, you'll reach the first steep climb of the ride as the path becomes paved once again and curves back into the forest. This incline is a brief taste of the challenging (and fulfilling) ride before you. Turn right onto the gravel path halfway down the other side, and turn right onto Hillside Street.

Immediately on your left you'll pass the historic park headquarters. The building was built in 1904, eleven years after the Metropolitan Parks Commission purchased the Blue Hills Reservation lands for public recreation. The park headquarters is one of sixteen historic structures within the reservation on the National Register of Historic Places. Continue onto Chickatawbut Road, named for Chief Chickatawbut of the Massachusett people, who met with Plymouth Colony commander Myles Standish and Tisquantum, popularly known as Squanto, in 1621.

The Blue Hills landscape includes marshy areas in addition to its ponds and woods.

Continuing along Chickatawbut Road past Randolph Avenue, you'll come to the second considerable climb. You're rewarded at the top with a stunning view of the Boston skyline through a clearing on the left side of the road, just opposite the footpath that leads to the Chickatawbut Observation Tower. The tower was built by the Civilian Conservation Corps in 1933, one of many improvements to the reservation funded by FDR's New Deal investment in public works and infrastructure projects. Savor the downhill the last mile out of the reservation as you wind past the Blue Hills Reservoir and the Quincy Cemetery before taking a right onto Granite Street.

Follow this brief stretch of thoroughfare to West Street, where you'll turn right into a charming New England neighborhood. Continue past the Blue Hills Cemetery through another forest-lined corridor along the reservation's southeast edge. As the trees recede you'll be able to view Great Pond, which supplies water to the town of Randolph. In typical New England fashion, West Street becomes Pond Street, which turns into Reed Street, Canton Street, and finally Randolph Street as you pass through the residential neighborhoods of Randolph and Canton. After passing Massasoit College at Blue Hills, turn right onto Turnpike Street, paying attention to increased traffic.

After Turnpike Street turns into Washington Street at Ponkapoag Golf Club, you'll face the final climb of the ride. A short sprint past the I-93 on-off ramps brings you to Hillside Street, where you'll turn right into the Blue Hills Reservation. On your right is the 55-acre Prowse Farm, an odd mix of medical device company headquarters and historical preserve. At the corner of this property once stood the Doty Tavern, where in 1774 a gathering of rebellious colonists drew up the Suffolk Resolves, which shaped the Declaration of Independence. Just a bit farther along Blue Hill River Road lies the picturesque Brookwood Farm, a combination of historic farm and modern community growing center that raises organic produce on 4 acres of the larger parcel.

Continuing along Hillside Street past its intersection with Blue Hill Road, turn at the sign for Houghton's Pond and take the path toward the visitor center, where you began the ride.

MILES AND DIRECTIONS

0.0 From the visitor center, take the path east along Houghton's Pond.

0.3 Stay left at the fork and climb the hill.

0.8 Turn right onto the gravel path.

1.0 Turn right onto Hillside Street, keeping right at both forks to continue onto Chickatawbut Road.

2.6 Continue on Chickatawbut Road through Randolph Avenue, passing the Chickatawbut Observation Tower and lookout point at the top of the hill.

4.2 Stay right at the fork to continue on Chickatawbut Road.

4.7 Turn right onto Granite Street.

5.9 Turn right onto West Street.

6.9 Stay left at the fork to continue on West Street, which becomes Pond Street.

8.6 Continue straight past North Main Street onto Reed Street, which becomes Canton Street past MA 24 and finally Randolph Street as you pass Massasoit College.

11.7 Turn right onto Turnpike Street, which becomes Washington Street.

13.6 Turn right onto Blue Hill River Road, which becomes Hillside Street.

14.8 Turn right into the Houghton's Pond parking lot.

14.9 Arrive back at the visitor center.

Blue Hills Reservation

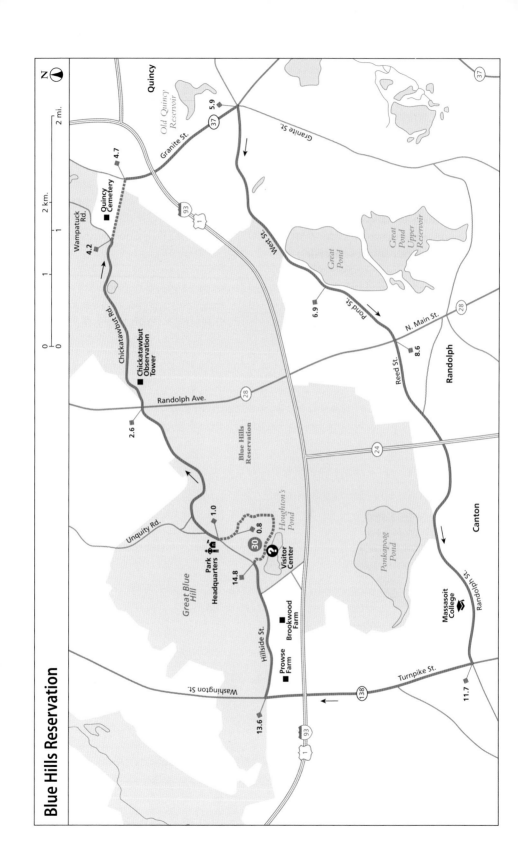

RIDE INFORMATION

Local Events/Attractions

Blue Hill Observatory and Science Center: At the summit of Great Blue Hill, this National Historic Landmark is a regional center for weather research. www.bluehill.org/observatory

Houghton's Pond: Open for swimming July and August, seven days a week. www.mass.gov/dcr

Prowse Farm: Crowned with an equestrian track, this historic park also hosts a number of concerts throughout the year, including the Life is Good Festival each summer. www.prowsefarm.org

Restrooms

Start/finish: The Blue Hills Reservation visitor center has restrooms and water.

Mile 5.0 to 5.9: Granite Street passes a number of shopping centers and restaurants with public restrooms.

Quincy to Nut Island

The "City of Presidents," Quincy is but a brief T ride from downtown. Its meandering coastline and views of the Boston skyline across the harbor draw cyclists of all levels to the Quincy Shore. This ride is a quick loop from Quincy Center out to the breathtaking Nut Island that juts into Quincy Bay, then north up Quincy Shore Drive and back down through Quincy via Newport Avenue. Along the way, you'll hit that sweet spot combination of history and beachfront that makes Quincy so unique.

Start: Quincy Center Station, Hancock Street, Quincy

Length: 13.4 miles

Approximate riding time: 1.5–2 hours with stops

Best bike: Road bike, mountain bike, or hybrid

Terrain and trail surface: Paved urban roads and bike paths

Traffic and hazards: Watch for traffic, particularly along Quincy Shore Drive and Newport Avenue.

Things to see: Quincy Center, United First Parish Church, Mount Wollaston Cemetery, Hough's Neck, Nut Island, Quincy Shore, Wollaston Beach, Adams National Historical Park

Maps: USGS: *Boston South* and *Hull* quads. DeLorme: *Massachusetts Atlas & Gazetteer,* pp. 41–42, 53

Getting there: By car: From Boston, follow I-93 S toward Quincy and take exit 12 to cross the bridge into Quincy. Turn right onto Newport Avenue and park along Hancock Street or at the Galleria at Presidents Place on Hancock Street. **By train:** Take the Red Line or commuter rail to Quincy Center Station. Bikes are allowed on the Red Line, except from 7 to 10 a.m. and 4 to 7 p.m. Monday through Friday, and without restriction on weekends. Check the commuter rail timetable for bike details. GPS coordinates for starting point: N42 15.082′ / W71 00.230′

THE RIDE

You'll start the ride at Quincy Center, just next to the Quincy Center station on the Red Line. You're in nearly the precise geographic center of Quincy, which is nicknamed the "City of Presidents" as the birthplace of John Adams and his son John Quincy Adams, the second and sixth presidents, as well as of John Hancock. Incorporated after the Revolution in 1792, the city is named for Colonel John Quincy, grandfather of Abigail Adams, for whom John Quincy Adams, in turn, was also named. A shipbuilding center throughout its history due to its long shoreline, Quincy was also the site of the first commercial railroad in the country and its first iron furnace. Once considered a streetcar suburb of Boston, Quincy has grown into a city in its own right since the middle of last century, and boasts a significant immigrant population, particularly from Asia.

From Quincy Center, ride southeast along Hancock Street and curve left around United First Parish Church. Often called "church of the Presidents," it was attended by both John Adams and John Quincy Adams and their wives, Abigail Adams and Louisa Catherine Adams, all four of whom are buried beneath the church in the Adams crypt. Inside the church is the Adams family pew, which is marked with a plaque. The current church structure, which is on the National Register of Historic Places, was completed in 1828 through financing by President John Adams, and the structure's granite, save the pillars, comes from a quarry on Adams family land. While the original bell was cast by Paul Revere, it was replaced when it was not loud enough to serve as a fire alarm to the surrounding neighborhoods. Each year, the White House sends wreaths to lay on the presidents' tombs on their birthdays: for John Adams on October 30 and for John Quincy on July 11.

Ride straight past the church onto Coddington Street, which you'll follow past Quincy High School and Faxon Field on your left. Cross the Southern

Bike Shops

Anderson Bicycle prides itself on expertise and more than forty years of repair experience from its certified technicians and bicycle engineers. The shop is located at 380 Washington St., Quincy; (617) 769-9669; www.andersonbicycle.com.
Boston Bike Guy offers reasonable tune-ups and a solid selection of new and used bikes. The shop is located at 1450 Hancock St., Quincy; (617) 773-0717; www.bostonbikeguy.com.
Country Ski and Sport is a full-service bike shop located at 161 Quincy Ave., Quincy; (617) 773-3993; www.countryski.com.

Part of the Boston Harbor Islands, Nut Island overlooks Quincy Harbor.

Artery onto Sea Street as you pass the historic Mount Wollaston Cemetery, on your left. Founded in 1855 after the Hancock Cemetery in the center of Quincy had been filled nearly to capacity, it is located just west of Quincy's founding spot at Mount Wollaston hillside. The cemetery takes inspiration from such famous cemeteries near Boston as Mount Auburn Cemetery in Cambridge and Forest Hills Cemetery in Jamaica Plain. Notable burials include many members of the Adams line, including John Adams's son, grandsons, and great-grandsons. The cemetery also features a number of ornate granite monuments to fallen soldiers, firemen, and policemen of Quincy.

Continue along Sea Street through the Merrymount and Adams Shore neighborhoods of east Quincy and then out to Hough's Neck. Known as "the Neck" and its residents as "Neckers," the peninsula is also known around the world as a hub for flounder fishing. Follow Sea Street to Sea Avenue and mount the hill to Nut Island. Once a true island in Boston Harbor, today Nut Island is part of the Boston Harbor Islands National Recreation Area. Connected to Deer Island across the bay via a 5-mile deep-bore sewage treatment tunnel, Nut Island is also the site of a treatment plant that once made this area incredibly unpopular to visit. Improvements to the plant and surrounding land have turned this into one of the prime sites for viewing downtown Boston and the whole Quincy Bay, as well as other islands in Boston Harbor.

Follow the bike path to the right and ride counterclockwise around the treatment plant to the tip of Nut Island. Once you've rounded the island, exit

Best Bike Rides Boston

the park onto Island Avenue. Turn right at Sea Street and then take successive rights again at Bay View Avenue, Winthrop Street, and Manet Avenue to follow the coastline. Merge back onto Sea Street as you exit Hough's Neck, then turn right onto Quincy Shore Drive to continue exploring the coast.

Within minutes, the vast Quincy Bay will come back into view, and you'll have another clear sightline of Boston Harbor. Ride on either the street or sidewalk bike path as you head north along the stone seawall to Wollaston Beach, the largest beach along Boston Harbor. Wollaston is known across the country as one of the environmental victories for water quality, due to Quincy's successful lawsuit in 1982 against the Commonwealth for discharging waste into its coastal waters. The beach and its water have since been rehabilitated as part of the wider cleanup of Massachusetts Bay. During the summers the more than 2 miles of Wollaston's sandy waterfront are filled with sunbathers and beachgoers.

> Stone Library, John Quincy Adams's presidential library at Adams National Historical Park, contains nearly 14,000 volumes in twelve languages. The president, an avid reader, built the library entirely out of stone in 1870 so as to be fireproof.

Follow Quincy Shore Drive to the end of the coastline at East Squantum Street, where you'll turn left to cut through North Quincy for the final leg back toward Quincy Center. Take another left just past Hancock Street and the North Quincy T station onto Newport Avenue. On your right you'll come to Adams National Historical Park, the birthplace of both John and John Quincy Adams, and their painstakingly preserved family estate. The grounds include Peacefield, the family's historic home which housed four generations of the Adams clan. Keep left past the park onto Adams Street, which merges into Hancock Street. Follow Hancock Street to Quincy Center, where the ride began.

MILES AND DIRECTIONS

0.0 From Quincy Center Station, turn right onto Hancock Street and ride east.

0.1 Keep left at the fork just past the church and continue straight onto Coddington Street.

0.5 Continue straight onto Sea Street past Southern Artery.

2.5 Keep right to continue along Sea Street.

2.9 Keep left to continue along Sea Street.

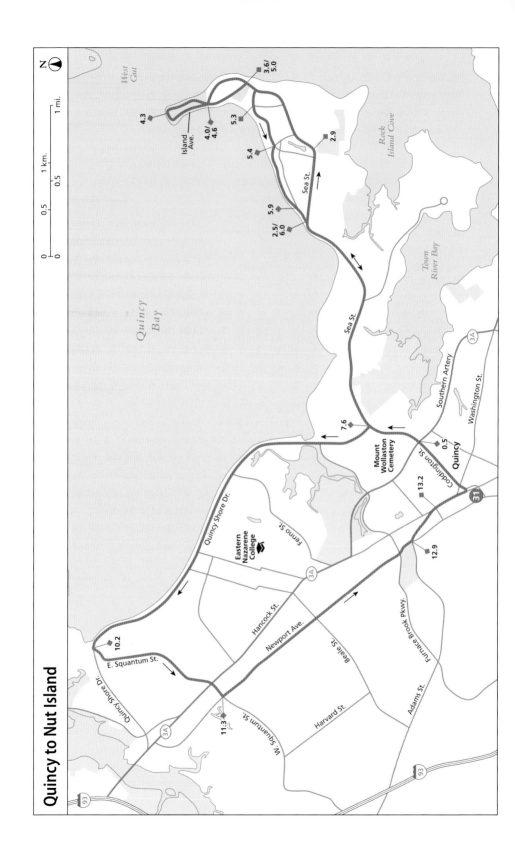

Quincy to Nut Island

West Gut

Quincy Bay

Rock Island Cove

Town River Bay

Island Ave.

Sea St.

Sea St.

Quincy Shore Dr.

Quincy Shore Dr.

Eastern Nazarene College

Fenno St.

Mount Wollaston Cemetery

Coddington St.

Quincy

Southern Artery

Washington St.

3A

3A

3A

Hancock St.

Newport Ave.

Beale St.

Harvard St.

W. Squantum St.

E. Squantum St.

Furnace Brook Pkwy.

Adams St.

93

93

3A

N

0   0.5   1 km.

0   0.5   1 mi.

3.6/5.0

4.3

4.0/4.6

5.3

5.4

2.9

5.9

2.5/6.0

7.6

10.2

11.3

13.2

12.9

0.5

31

3.6 Keep right to continue along Sea Street to Sea Avenue.

4.0 Turn right into the Nut Island Reservation.

4.3 Round the tip of Nut Island onto Island Avenue.

4.6 Keep right out of the park on Island Avenue.

5.0 Turn right onto Sea Street, then turn right onto Bay View Avenue.

5.3 Turn right onto Winthrop Street.

5.4 Turn right onto Manet Avenue.

5.9 Turn right onto Babcock Street.

6.0 Merge back onto Sea Street.

7.6 Turn right onto Quincy Shore Drive.

10.2 Turn left onto East Squantum Street.

11.3 Turn left onto Newport Avenue.

12.9 Keep left onto Adams Street.

13.2 Merges into Hancock Street.

13.4 Arrive back at Quincy Center Station.

RIDE INFORMATION

Local Events/Attractions
Quincy August Moon Festival: For nearly thirty years, this cultural event has drawn thousands to Hancock Street for food and performances celebrating Quincy's growing Asian population. www.quincyasianresources.org

Presidential Wreath Laying Ceremony: The Church of the Presidents in Quincy Center hosts two wreath-laying ceremonies on the birthdays of John Adams and John Quincy Adams, on October 30 and July 11, respectively. www.ufpc.org

Adams National Historical Park: Explore the birthplace of two presidents and the family home built up over generations. www.nps.gov/adam

Restrooms
Start/finish: Quincy Center has a number of shops and restaurants with restrooms.

Mile 8.7: Wollaston Beach has restrooms.

32

Braintree, Weymouth, and World's End

Just at the end of the Red Line past Quincy lies a world apart from Boston, where the small-town streets are lined with trees, historic homes, and coastline. This ride will take you through the hills of Braintree and the small city of Weymouth to the breathtaking World's End conservation area on a peninsula in coastal Hingham. Whether you want take in the city from the far side of Boston Harbor or escape urban life entirely for a while among the trees and marshes, this ride will bring you to the end of the world and back again.

Start: Braintree Station, Braintree

Length: 21.9 miles

Approximate riding time: 3–3.5 hours with stops

Best bike: Road bike, hybrid or mountain bike

Terrain and trail surface: Well-paved roads and bike lanes, with a dirt and gravel path around World's End.

Traffic and hazards: Watch for traffic along roads, particularly at curves and rotaries. Hikers, joggers, and dog walkers frequent the trails of World's End.

Things to see: Braintree, Weymouth, Abigail Adams State Park, Bathing Beach, World's End Reservation

Maps: USGS: *Hull, Nantasket Beach, Cohasset,* and *Weymouth* quads; DeLorme: *Massachusetts Atlas & Gazetteer,* pp. 53–55

Getting there: By car: From Boston, take I-93S toward Quincy, exiting at 7 to merge onto MA 3S. Take exit 17 to Braintree and exit the traffic circle at the first right onto Union Street. Braintree Station is on the left. **By train:** Take the Red Line or commuter rail to Braintree Station. Bikes are allowed on the Red Line, except from 7 to 10 a.m. and 4 to 7 p.m. Monday through Friday, and without restriction on weekends. Check the commuter rail timetable for bike details. GPS coordinates for starting point: N42 12.405' / W71 00.066'

THE RIDE

You'll start at Braintree Station, at the end of the MBTA Red Line in Braintree. Legally a city under Massachusetts law, having elected its first mayor in 2008, the town of Braintree was incorporated in 1640, making it among the oldest in the Commonwealth. The town once included all the land from nearby Quincy, Randolph, and Holbrook. Although Quincy styles itself "City of Presidents," all three of John Quincy, John Quincy Adams, and famous statesman John Hancock were born before Braintree was subdivided.

Braintree is also famous around the world as the site of the 1920 murders that led to the execution of Ferdinando Nicola Sacco and Bartolomeo Venzetti. The Sacco and Venzetti trial is today held up as the epitome of a biased prosecution based more on political profiling than ironclad evidence. In 1977, on the fiftieth anniversary of the pair's execution, Massachusetts governor Michael Dukakis declared the trial a miscarriage of justice due to the prosecutor's bully tactic of forcing both defendants to outline their anarchist beliefs in court.

From Braintree Station, turn left onto Ivory Street and then right at Union Street. Take care as you enter the rotary, exiting at the second right to continue along Union Street. You'll roll past a mix of historic and contemporary homes as you come to the edge of Braintree at Weymouth Landing. Take a left onto Quincy Avenue, then first right onto the F.L. Wright Connector to Commercial Street, where you'll take a left and continue through Weymouth.

The city of Weymouth has its origins in 1622, when the failed colony of Wessagusset was founded with sixty men from London. After a little over a year, mismanagement of supplies led to frequent pilfering from the nearby Massachusett tribe, which in turn generated conflicts between colonists and Native Americans. It would take several more false starts before Weymouth was officially incorporated as part of the Massachusetts Bay Colony in 1630, and by 1635 it had stabilized with the city's current boundaries.

Bike Shop

The Bicycle Link has been serving the South Shore as a full-service shop since 1987. The shop is located at 230 Washington St., Weymouth; (781) 337-7125; www.thebicyclelink.com.

Follow Commercial Street briefly along the waterfront at Fore River and through a stretch of neighborhoods, then take a left at Church Street, which becomes Green Street. A couple blocks up you'll see signs for Weymouth's other historical claim as the birthplace of Abigail Adams. The house where Abigail was born and married John Adams lies just north of the ride route, at

The World's End trails were originally intended to be carriage roads under Frederick Law Olmsted's designs for a suburb.

North Street and Norton Street by Weymouth's Old North Cemetery. Abigail lived in Weymouth from her birth in 1744 until her wedding in 1764, when the future first couple moved to Braintree. Following Green Street as it curves left and then turning right on Bridge Street, you'll pass Abigail Adams State Park just before crossing the bridge into Hingham.

Incorporated in 1635, Hingham has its own presidential connections to rival Quincy and Braintree's. Abraham Lincoln's ancestor Samuel Lincoln came to Hingham at fifteen years old to join his older brother, Thomas, a weaver. Beside Honest Abe, Samuel Lincoln's descendents would include a slew of prominent political figures, including one governor of Maine and a father-son pair of Massachusetts governors. During World War II, Eleanor Roosevelt's book *This Is America* thrust Hingham into the national spotlight as the ideal of Americana. The first lady began her book project a month after the Pearl Harbor bombing to raise the country's spirits and focus its energy on supporting the war effort. Mrs. Roosevelt crowned Hingham's Main Street "the most beautiful Main Street in America."

Following Lincoln Street, you'll pass the Hingham shipyards, which produced destroyers and other steel warships at record speed to supply the Allies navy. Today a commercial marina and boardwalk, the shipyard once hosted the tallest single-story building in New England, a 1,000-foot steel mill that was torn down in 2006. Keep left at the fork with Broad Cove Road, which skirts a stretch of wetlands before curving right around its namesake cove. You'll pass Bathing Beach on the left and a number of wharfs as you follow Summer Street through the rotary. Ride up a minor hill and take a left at Martins Lane, which you'll follow as it winds all the way to World's End.

A preservation and conservation area today part of the Boston Harbor Islands string of parks, World's End has had several near misses at historic developments. After purchasing the peninsula in the 1850s and developing a vast farming estate and mansion that includes many of the homes you'll pass on your way to the park, owner John Brewer asked famous landscape architect Frederick Law Olmsted to design a residential subdivision of 163 plots. In 1889 Olmsted began building the carriage roads that today circle the reservation and also planting trees to line them, but the development stalled and plots were never cleared. Fifty years later, World's End was shortlisted as the site of a permanent United Nations headquarters, which had been established in 1945 at the close of World War II. When New York's Lake Success was chosen, World's End was then briefly considered to hold a nuclear power plant in 1965. The Trustees of Reservations, a New England preservation coalition, purchased the land in 1967 to develop the fantastic public park it is today.

Entrance to the park is free for cyclists and hikers. Just past the gate, turn right onto the gravel path that circles the reservation. This is Weir River Road, one of Olmsted's carriage paths. Stay on this main path as it cuts through the forest and marshes, which are often foggy on morning rides. Turn right at the T with Barnes Road and ride along the base of the hillside fields cleared in preparation for Olmsted's development. The trees lining the road were planted for the subdivision as well. Continue across the narrow neck to the final stretch of the peninsula and keep right. Across the Weir River inlet to your right is the Hull peninsula and Nantasket Beach. In just a few moments you'll come to the tip of World's End, where you'll be able to spy the outlying Boston Harbor Islands and minor peninsulas around Hingham Bay. A popular spot for picnickers and true to its name, the edge of World's End feels so remote from urban life, with Boston's skyline just visible across the water.

When you're ready for the return leg, continue around the tip of the peninsula and follow the gravel carriage path right around the hummocks and back across the neck toward the park gate. Take Martins Lane back to Summer Street and turn right, riding back past the rotary and along the waterfront before turning left onto North Street. Stay left at South Street to ride through one of Hingham's quaint strips of storefronts. Follow South Street to Fort Hill Street and turn left to continue south back into Weymouth, where the street turns into Commercial Street. Take Broad Street right to Washington Street and turn right again, riding back to Weymouth Landing on the city's boundary with Braintree.

Turn left onto Commercial Street once again and ride back through Braintree, taking care at the rotary. Turn left at Ivory Street to arrive back at Braintree Station, where the ride began.

MILES AND DIRECTIONS

0.0 From Braintree Station, turn left onto Ivory Street.

0.2 Turn right onto Union Street.

0.3 Take the second exit out of the rotary onto Union Street.

2.2 Turn left onto onto Quincy Avenue, then first right onto the F. L. Wright Connector.

2.3 Turn left onto Commercial Street.

3.5 Keep left at Church Street.

4.4 Turn left onto Green Street.

5.0 Turn right onto Bridge Street.

6.9 Keep left onto Broad Cove Road.

7.9 Keep left onto Otis Street.

8.3 Take the second exit out of the rotary onto Summer Street.

8.8 Turn left onto Martins Lane.

9.5 Enter the World's End Reservation and take the first right through the parking lot.

10.2 Turn right onto the carriage road.

10.5 Continue straight across the neck and keep right to round the tip of World's End.

11.4 Keep right to return to the entrance to World's End and exit onto Martins Lane.

13.5 Turn right onto Summer Street.

13.9 Continue straight through the traffic circle.

14.1 Turn left onto North Street.

14.4 Stay left at South Street.

15.4 Turn left onto Fort Hill Street.

Braintree, Weymouth, and World's End

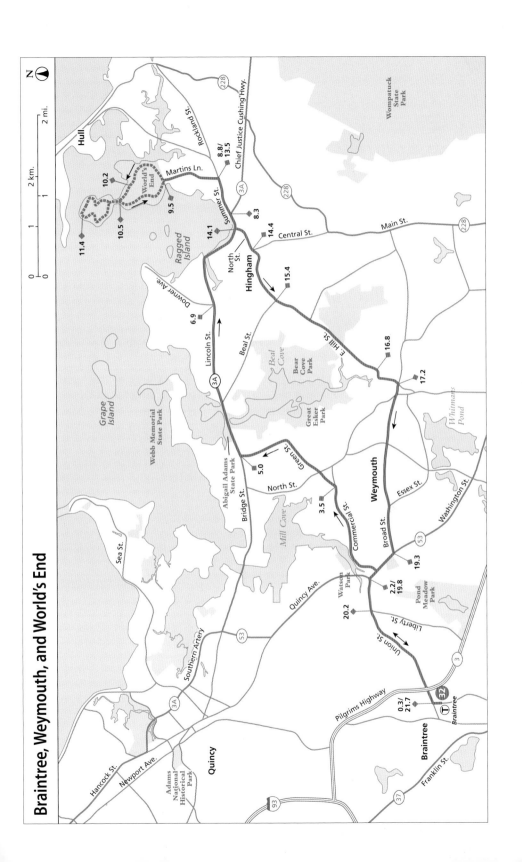

0   1   2 mi.

0   1   2 km.

Hull

World's End

Martins Ln.

10.2

11.4

10.5

9.5

8.8/
13.5

Rockland St.

Chief Justice Cushing Hwy.

228

Summer St.

14.1

8.3

Ragged
Island

Downer Ave.

6.9

North
St.

Central St.

14.4

Hingham

15.4

Main St.

228

228

3A

Beal St.

E. Hill St.

16.8

17.2

Lincoln St.

3A

Grape
Island

Webb Memorial
State Park

Beal
Cove

Bear
Cove
Park

Great
Esker
Park

Whitmans
Pond

Wompatuck
State
Park

Abigail Adams
State Park

Bridge St.

Green St.

5.0

North St.

Mill Cove

3.5

Commercial St.

Broad St.

Weymouth

Essex St.

Washington St.

53

19.3

2.2/
19.8

Pond
Meadow
Park

20.2

Watson
Park

Liberty St.

Union St.

Quincy Ave.

Sea St.

Southern Artery

53

Hancock St.

Newport Ave.

Adams
National
Historical
Park

Quincy

3A

93

Pilgrims Highway

0.3/
21.7

32

T   Braintree

Braintree

Franklin St.

37

3

16.8 Keep right onto Commercial Street.

17.2 Turn right onto Broad Street.

19.3 Turn right onto Washington Street.

19.8 Turn left onto Commercial Street.

20.2 Stay left onto Union Street.

21.3 Enter the traffic circle and take the second exit onto Union Street.

21.7 Turn left onto Ivory Street.

21.9 Finish at Braintree Station.

RIDE INFORMATION

Local Events/Attractions
Independence Day: Hingham goes all-out for July 4th, with a legendary patriotic road race and parade. www.hingham-ma.com

World's End Summer Solstice: Come for the annual celebration of the longest day of the year with waterfront musical performances. www.thetrustees.org

Old Ship Church: The oldest church in continuous use in the United States, this seventeenth-century Puritan meetinghouse was erected in 1681 and offers daily tours. www.oldshipchurch.org

Restrooms
Start/finish: Braintree Station has restrooms and water.

Mile 2.2 and 19.8: There are a number of shops and restaurants with public restrooms and water in Weymouth Landing.

Mile 7.9 and 14.1: Hingham has a number of shops and restaurants along the route.

Scituate to Hull

The South Shore is a captivating mix of rocky coastline and sandy beaches, its coastal towns a fascinating mix of working-class residential stretches, luxury mansions, and quaint beach getaways. This ride follows the Atlantic from Scituate around Cohasset Cover to the northernmost point of Hull peninsula. Savor the incomparable ocean views and bring your appetite for some of the freshest seafood of your life!

Start: Museum Beach, Scituate

Length: 31.7 miles

Approximate riding time: 3–3.5 hours with stops

Best bike: Road bike or hybrid

Terrain and trail surface: Well-paved roads

Traffic and hazards: Watch for traffic, particularly along curves and traffic circles near Hull and along Nantasket Beach.

Things to see: Museum Beach, Old Scituate Lighthouse, Cohasset Harbor, Straits Pond, Nantasket Beach, Spinnaker Island, Pemberton Point, Fort Andrews.

Maps: USGS: *Hull, Nantasket Beach, Cohasset,* and *Scituate* quads; DeLorme: *Massachusetts Atlas & Gazetteer,* pp. 42, 54–55

Getting there: By car: From Boston, take I-93S to MA 3S, and exit onto MA 123E to the traffic circle in front of Scituate Town Hall. Follow Driftway, and then Kent Street and Front Street through the Scituate waterfront. Turn right onto Jericho Road to Museum Beach at Bay Ridge Road. **By train:** Take the commuter rail to Scituate on the Greenbush line. Check the commuter rail timetable for bike details. Exit the station left onto Driftway and continue onto Kent Street then Front Street through Scituate. Turn right onto Jericho Road to Museum Beach at Bay Ridge Road. GPS coordinates for starting point: N42 12.287' / W70 43.461'

THE RIDE

You'll start at Museum Beach along the shore of Scituate, halfway between Plymouth and Boston along the South Shore. Settled in 1630 and incorporated in 1636, Scituate has long been a fishing village. Follow Jericho Road northeast along the waterfront, keeping the ocean to your right before turning right along Lighthouse Road around to the Old Scituate Lighthouse, which was built in 1810. During the War of 1812, Rebecca and Abigail Bates, teenage daughters of the lighthouse keeper, rebuffed two boats full of British soldiers by banging a drum and playing a fife. The sisters have been knighted the Lighthouse Army of Two for their heroics. Continue along Lighthouse Road, keeping straight onto Turner Road and then Oceanside Drive to pass the rows of beach bungalows for which Scituate is known. Curve left onto First Avenue, then turn right onto Hatherly Road to continue north.

Pass Musquashcut Pond on your right before turning left onto Gannett Road. Take your first right to follow Indian Trail through a wooded neighborhood, turning left onto Otis Avenue and then right at Border Street to cross the town line into Cohasset.

Named for an Algonquian word meaning "long rocky place," Cohasset lives up to the description for its wandering shore dotted with cliffs and boulders. It became a separate town from neighboring Hingham in 1770. Like Brookline, Cohasset is an unconnected island of Norfolk County, as Hull and Hingham voted at the beginning of the nineteenth century to join Plymouth County. Take Border Street around Cohasset Harbor, keeping right at Summer Street and turning right again onto Margin Street. Stay left at the fork to continue along Atlantic Avenue through a residential stretch, across a neck with the Cohasset Inner Harbor to your left and the Atlantic to your right. Here the iconic rocky shoreline really begins as you continue north along Atlantic Avenue and then Jerusalem Road to the Cohasset town line with Hull.

Stay right at the fork onto Summit Avenue, then left at the next fork to continue along Atlantic Avenue once again past Straits Pond. One of the smallest towns in the Commonwealth, Hull's peninsula, with its distinctive layout, has been the summer home of such figures as President Calvin Coolidge and the Kennedys. This area was originally a series of islands connected by sandbars.

> ### Bike Shop
>
> **Cohasset Cycle Sports** has been offering neighborly advice, repairs, and equipment to the South Shore for more than twenty-five years. The shop is located at 754 Chief Justice Cushing Highway/MA 3A, Cohasset; (781) 383-0707; www.cohassetcycle.com.

At a number of necks along the South Shore, you can have water to both sides, such as this one with the Atlantic Ocean before you and Cohasset Inner Harbor to your back.

Europeans first settled here in 1621 with a trading post for exchange with the Wampanoags, who called the area "Nantasket," meaning "low-tide place." The town was officially incorporated in 1644. Follow Atlantic Avenue as it meanders briefly away from the coast, turning right onto Nantasket Avenue toward the town's prime beaches.

The uninterrupted ocean view to your right is the vast Massachusetts Bay, and you'll have intermittent views of the protected Hull Bay to your left. The lengthy beach stretching before you is Nantasket Beach, one of the busiest each summer in all of Massachusetts. The beach is known for its sandy tide pools at low tide, for which tourists once took steamboats three times a day from Boston's pier. The beach also once held an outpost of the Massachusetts Humane Society, its lifesaving crew a matter of legend throughout the 1800s for rescuing an estimated 1,000 people from shipwrecks.

Many of the boardwalk restaurants and shops are open only during the summer months, when tourists pour into Hull in droves for sun and revelry. Keep left to remain on Nantasket Avenue, continuing past Monument Square into the working-class neighborhood of the alphabet streets. Hull's year-round residents primarily live in these grid neighborhoods at the northern end of the peninsula. Keep right to stay on Nantasket Avenue to Hull's northernmost tip, then curve left toward the eastern point.

Peddocks Island

The now abandoned Fort Andrews on Peddocks Island once housed about a hundred soldiers. The fort was erected in 1897 to protect the southern reaches of Boston Harbor. Ferries run daily between Hull and Peddocks Island, one of the largest in the Boston Harbor Islands chain. In addition to the abandoned fort and other historic structures, the island is one of the few around the harbor that are still home to active, private residences.

Stay left onto Spring Street to pass Spinnaker Island, formerly known as Little Hog Island during its days as a military artillery fort during World War II. Today the island holds a condominium complex. Stay left onto Main Street as you pass the US Coast Guard outpost and several boat docks along Hull Bay. Continue to the easternmost point on the peninsula at Pemberton Point, your destination. Across the Hull Gut stretch of ocean you can make out Fort Andrews on Peddocks Island, one of the Boston Harbor Islands.

The view across the water to downtown Boston is spectacular, particularly at sunset with the painted colors framing the city. In the evening the waterline is often ringed with parked cars of tourists and Hull residents alike savoring the breathtaking scene.

After you've drunk your fill and are ready to head back toward Scituate, follow Main Street and Spring Street back to Nantasket Avenue, keeping right onto Fitzpatrick Way for a last curve with an uninterrupted view of Hull Bay. Take Nantasket Avenue back along the main Hull beachfront strip, turning left onto Atlantic Avenue after the last beach parking lot. Follow Atlantic Avenue back to Jerusalem Road and on to Margin Street in Cohasset, then take a left onto Summer Street and then Border Street to cut back around Cohasset Harbor and across the line into Scituate. Turn left onto Otis Avenue and then right at Gardner Road to wind along Indian Trail through the wooded neighborhood stretch and emerge at Gannett Road and turn left. Take a right at Hatherly Road for the final leg back to Jericho Road. Turn left and ride to Museum Beach, where you began the ride.

MILES AND DIRECTIONS

0.0 From Museum Beach, ride northeast along Jericho Road, keeping the water to your right.

0.2 Turn right onto Lighthouse Road.

Scituate to Hull

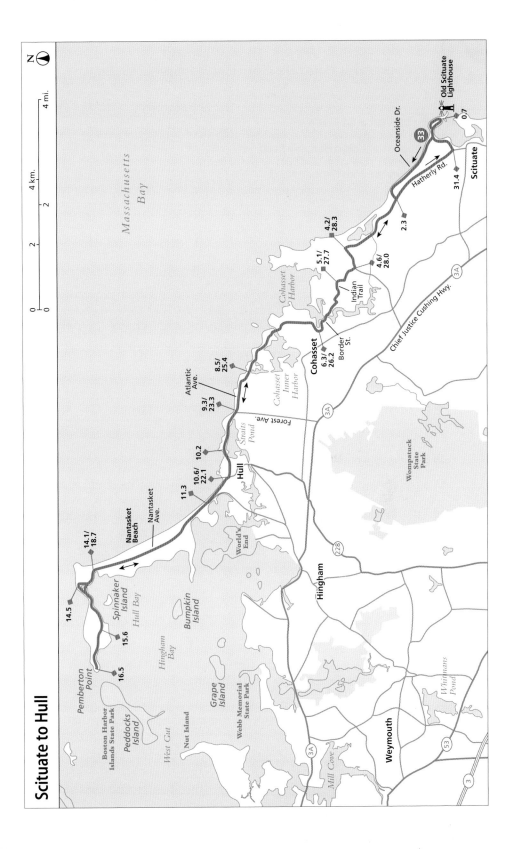

N

4 mi.

4 km.

Massachusetts Bay

Hingham Bay

Hull Bay

Boston Harbor Islands State Park

Pemberton Point

Peddocks Island

West Gut

Nut Island

Grape Island

Webb Memorial State Park

Bumpkin Island

Spinnaker Island

14.5

14.1/ 18.7

15.6

16.5

Nantasket Beach

Nantasket Ave.

11.3

10.6/ 22.1

10.2

Hull

World's End

Straits Pond

Atlantic Ave.

9.3/ 23.3

8.5/ 25.4

Forest Ave.

Cohasset Inner Harbor

Cohasset Harbor

5.1/ 27.7

4.2/ 28.3

Cohasset

6.3/ 26.2

Border St.

Indian Trail

4.6/ 28.0

2.3

Oceanside Dr.

33

Hatherly Rd.

31.4

Old Scituate Lighthouse

0.7

Scituate

Chief Justice Cushing Hwy.

3A

Wompatuck State Park

Hingham

228

3A

Weymouth

Mill Cove

Whitmans Pond

53

3

0.7 Continue onto Rebecca Road past the Old Scituate Lighthouse.

1.1 Continue straight onto Turner Road.

2.2 Turn left onto First Avenue.

2.3 Turn right onto Hatherly Road.

4.2 Turn left onto Gannett Road.

4.6 Turn right onto Indian Trail.

4.7 Keep right.

5.1 Turn right to stay on Indian Trail.

5.5 Turn left onto Otis Avenue.

5.6 Turn right onto Border Street.

6.3 Turn right onto Summer Street and right again onto Margin Street.

6.7 Keep left to continue onto Atlantic Avenue.

8.5 Keep right to continue onto Jerusalem Road.

9.3 Keep right and then left to continue along Atlantic Avenue.

10.2 Keep left to stay on Atlantic Avenue.

10.6 Turn right onto Nantasket Avenue.

11.3 Continue straight along Nantasket Avenue.

14.1 Keep right to stay on Nantasket Avenue.

14.5 Turn left to stay on Nantasket Avenue.

15.1 Turn left onto Spring Street.

15.6 Keep right onto Main Street.

16.5 Arrive at Pemberton Point and turn around.

18.2 Keep right onto Fitzpatrick Way.

18.7 Turn right onto Nantasket Avenue.

22.1 Turn left onto Atlantic Avenue.

23.3 Keep left to continue along Atlantic Avenue, which becomes Jerusalem Road.

25.4 Keep left to continue along Atlantic Avenue.

26.2   Keep right onto Margin Street, then turn left onto Summer Street and keep left onto Border Street.

27.0   Turn left onto Otis Avenue, then right onto Gardner Road.

27.7   Keep right to continue along Indian Trail.

28.0   Turn left onto Gannett Road.

28.3   Turn right onto Hatherly Road.

31.4   Turn left onto Jericho Road.

31.7   Arrive back at Museum Beach.

RIDE INFORMATION

Local Events/Attractions

Endless Summer Waterfront Festival: At the tail end of summer, this Hull tradition brings live music, food, and craft markets to Nantasket Beach in Hull. www.endlesssummerhull.com

Hull Lifesaving Museum: Explore Hull's long record of saving the lives of those shipwrecked and lost at sea. www.hulllifesavingmuseum.org

Scituate Heritage Days: One of the biggest South Shore events each summer, this celebration of Scituate highlights the town's history, cuisine, culture, and sites. www.scituatechamber.org

Restrooms

Start/finish: There are a number of shops and restaurants in Scituate with restrooms and water.

Mile 10.6 to 12.0 and 20.0 to 22.0: The boulevard along Nantasket Beach has many shops and restaurants with restrooms.

West of Boston

Larz Anderson Park is the largest park in Brookline and among the most beautifully landscaped areas in Greater Boston (Ride 35).

Just west of the city lie some of the region's secret gems. Within a half hour's ride from Kenmore Square and Fenway Stadium, you can circle the serene Chestnut Hill Reservoir near Boston College. Head even farther to the secluded Auburndale Park, then follow the upper reaches of the Charles River back toward the city. For a longer adventure, head to Wellesley or the Assabet River Rail-Trail, or follow the Boston Marathon route as it cuts from Hopkinton through Framingham to Heartbreak Hill and Copley Square.

Kenmore Square to Chestnut Hill Reservoir

One of the best things about Boston is its diverse landscape, which means that even a quick ride can lead from the flat Back Bay into hillier and greener areas. Those looking for an hour-long circuit can take this swift ride through Brookline to the Chestnut Hill Reservoir, one of the prettiest waterfront parks so close to the city. You'll pass ornate brownstones, churches, and temples along the way for a fascinating glimpse of the calm, serene suburbs that lie just a short pedal from downtown.

Start: Kenmore Square, Back Bay

Length: 7.8 miles

Approximate riding time: 45 minutes–1 hour with stops

Best bike: Road bike or hybrid

Terrain and trail surface: Well-paved roads and bike lanes with hard-packed gravel path around the reservoir

Traffic and hazards: Watch for traffic along Beacon Street, as well as joggers along the Chestnut Hill Reservoir path.

Things to see: Kenmore Square, Citgo Sign, Fenway Park, Ruggles Baptist Church, Audubon Circle, Coolidge Corner, Chestnut Hill Reservoir, Boston College, All Saints Parish, Chinese Christian Church, Temple Ohabei Shalom

Maps: USGS: *Boston South* and *Newton* quads; DeLorme: *Massachusetts Atlas & Gazetteer,* p. 41

Getting there: By car: There is street parking available along Commonwealth Avenue, Beacon Street, and Bay State Road near Kenmore Square. From downtown, take Commonwealth Avenue west to Kenmore Square. **By train:** The Green Line does not allow bikes, unfortunately. Take the commuter rail to Yawkey (check the timetable for schedule). Exit the station left onto Brookline Avenue and ride to Kenmore Square. GPS coordinates for starting point: N42 20.941' / W71 05.809'

THE RIDE

Begin the ride in Kenmore Square, in front of the New England School of Photography. Once a swampy backwater before the filling of Back Bay, today Kenmore Square is a major locus of activity in the metro area. The longest continuous road in the country, US 20, which has its western terminus at Newport, Oregon, on the Pacific Ocean, has its eastern endpoint in the square at Commonwealth Avenue. From your vantage point in front of the New England School of Photography you can see down Brookline Avenue to Fenway Park, iconic home stadium of the Boston Red Sox since 1912.

From Kenmore you'll ride west along Beacon Street into Brookline, passing the southern part of the Boston University campus with its brownstone dormitories and apartments. Just across the Massachusetts Turnpike overpass you'll come to Audubon Circle at the intersection with Park Drive, its square designed by Frederick Law Olmsted Sr. in 1887. The Ruggles Baptist Church on the northeastern corner of the circle, to your right as you ride through the intersection, was completed in 1914 by famed Boston architect Ralph Adams Cram, who also designed the Cathedral of Saint John the Divine in New York City. The ride west along Beacon Street is dotted with many notable churches, synagogues, and temples, of which the Ruggles Baptist Church is only the first.

Just past Audubon Circle you'll move into the town of Brookline, which was first settled in 1638 as part of Boston but incorporated as a separate entity in 1705. Brookline has successfully resisted several annexation attempts from Boston and remains so fiercely independent as to insist on being a part of Norfolk County instead of Suffolk County, which engulfs the town entirely. A few minutes on, just past St. Paul Street, you'll meet your first climb into Coolidge Corner, one of Brookline's core squares and its commercial center. The neighborhood is not named for President Calvin Coolidge, as is often assumed, but rather for the Coolidge Brothers general store that opened at the corner of Beacon Street and Harvard Street in 1857, and which has long since closed. Today, Coolidge Corner is much beloved for its mix of local shops,

Bike Shop

Superb Bicycle near Fenway is known for its custom builds and keen focus on the aesthetics of cycling. Superb is located at 842 Beacon St., Boston; (617) 236-0752; www.superbbicycle.com.

delis, and restaurants, as well for its independent movie house, the Coolidge Corner Theatre, a restored art deco building dating back to the 1930s that is consistently ranked among the best art-house theaters in the country.

Pressing on, Beacon Street rises for a few more blocks as you approach Cleveland Circle, which lies at the intersection of Chestnut Hill Avenue and

The Waterworks Museum across from the reservoir commemorates Chestnut Hill's historic role in keeping Boston's water supply safe and clean.

Beacon Street. Once a major railway hub when this part of Brookline was a "streetcar suburb," Cleveland Circle is now home to a mix of professionals and Boston College students. Continue through the intersection toward the Chestnut Hill Reservoir, whose high banks are straight ahead.

Turn into the reservoir parking lot and take the paved path to the right that slopes up toward the reservoir banks. Created in 1870 to supplement Boston's drinking supply, the reservoir is entirely within Boston city limits, another reminder of the deep historical annexation politics between Brookline and its larger neighbor. Like so much of Boston's green space, the reservoir was designed by landscape architect Frederick Law Olmsted. The reservoir is no longer a part of the city water supply, having been taken offline in 1978 and maintained primarily for recreation and as an emergency backup source. The Waterworks Museum across Beacon Street from the reservoir commemorates its contribution to Boston's clean water supply.

Turn left to take the gravel path around the reservoir, riding toward Boston College's Chestnut Hill campus. The gothic spires visible across the reservoir adorn Boston College's Glasson Hall, one of the principal academic and administration buildings of the private Jesuit college. Its campus straddles the Brighton and Chestnut Hill neighborhoods, and its students are a significant segment of the residential population nearby. Round the northwest shore of the reservoir, passing the Chestnut Hill Reservoir Garden and the deeply wooded northern banks. Exit the reservoir via the same paved path, returning to Beacon Street, where you'll turn left to begin your return route to Kenmore Square.

Ride again through Cleveland Circle, quickly passing two stone churches at Clinton Path, the Chinese Christian Church and All Saints Parish, two more

Kenmore Square to Chestnut Hill Reservoir

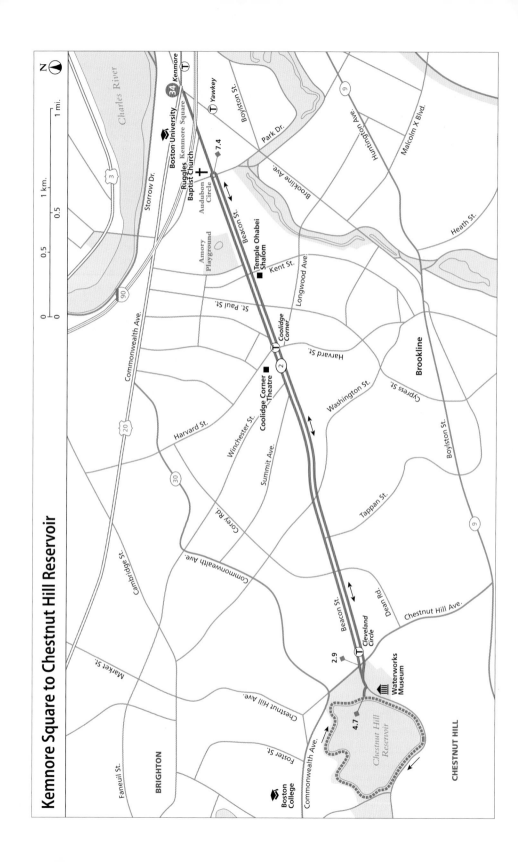

N

Charles River

Boston University

Storrow Dr.

3

Kenmore Square
Kenmore
34

Ruggles
Baptist Church

Audubon
Circle

Boston University

Yawkey
T

Boylston St.

Park Dr.

9

7.4

Beacon St.

Amory
Playground

Temple Ohabei
Shalom

Kent St.

Longwood Ave.

Huntington Ave.

Brookline Ave.

Malcolm X Blvd.

Heath St.

90

Commonwealth Ave.

St. Paul St.

Coolidge
Corner
T
2

Coolidge Corner
Theatre

Harvard St.

Brookline

20

Harvard St.

Winchester St.

Washington St.

Cypress St.

Boylston St.

30

Summit Ave.

Corey Rd.

Commonwealth Ave.

Tappan St.

Dean Rd.

9

Cambridge St.

Market St.

Faneuil St.

BRIGHTON

Beacon St.

Cleveland
Circle
T

2.9

Waterworks
Museum

Chestnut Hill Ave.

Chestnut Hill Reservoir

4.7

Chestnut Hill Ave.

Foster St.

Commonwealth Ave.

Boston
College

CHESTNUT HILL

0   0.5   1 km.

0   0.5   1 mi.

examples of the gothic and classicist architectural style of so many landmark buildings in Chestnut Hill. Follow Beacon Street back through Coolidge Corner, passing the ornate Temple Ohabei Shalom, the oldest Jewish congregation in Massachusetts and the state's first synagogue. Dedicated in 1925, the domed temple was modeled on the Hagia Sophia in Istanbul, and was originally designed to have a minaret, although this detail was never completed.

Follow Beacon Street back through Audubon Circle, where Fenway Park and Kenmore Square will come into view once again. From this perspective you're able to take in the massive Citgo sign, an icon of Kenmore first erected in 1940 and refurbished in 2005. The sign, which is visible even over the walls of Fenway Park, welcomes you back to Kenmore, where you began the ride.

MILES AND DIRECTIONS

0.0 Ride west out of Kenmore Square along Beacon Street, which is the center street straight ahead of the massive intersection.

2.9 Continue straight along Beacon Street past Chestnut Hill Avenue, then turn right into the reservoir parking lot and take the path up to the shore, where you'll head left around the water.

4.7 Turn left out of the reservoir, taking a left onto Beacon Street back toward Kenmore Square.

7.4 Continue straight on Beacon Street.

7.8 Arrive back to the starting point at Kenmore Square.

RIDE INFORMATION

Local Events/Attractions

Waterworks Museum: Explore the machinery and processes required to maintain a clean water supply in a complex metropolitan area like Boston. The museum is located at 2450 Beacon St., Boston; (617) 277-0065; www.water worksmuseum.org.

Restrooms

Start/finish: Many of the fast-food restaurants in Kenmore Square have public restrooms and water.
Mile 1.4 and 6.5: Many of the shops in Coolidge Corner have restrooms.
Mile 2.9 and 4.9: Many of the shops in Cleveland Circle have restrooms.

Brookline Loop and JFK Birthplace

The fiercely independent town of Brookline has resisted Boston's sprawl for over 300 years, persevering even as the city, block by block, annexed adjoining towns like Brighton, Roxbury, and Jamaica Plain. This ride explores Brookline's enviable greenery, hills, and cultural sites, cutting from Amory Park near Back Bay through Coolidge Corner to the idyllic Larz Anderson Park. You'll hook back north via the Brookline Reservoir and Aspinwall Hill, passing the preserved headquarters of famed landscape architect Frederick Law Olmsted as well as the birthplace of John F. Kennedy. By the end of this ride, you'll have no doubts about why its larger neighbor has a right to be jealous.

Start: Hall's Pond, Amory Playground, Brookline

Length: 8.7 miles

Approximate riding time: 1–1.5 hours with stops

Best bike: Road bike or hybrid

Terrain and trail surface: Paved roads and paved bike paths, with brief stretches of well-packed dirt paths

Traffic and hazards: Joggers, skateboarders, families with small children, and dog walkers frequent the parks along this ride. Be mindful of traffic along roads.

Things to see: Amory Playground, Hall's Pond Sanctuary, Coolidge Corner, Larz Anderson Park, Reservoir Park, Frederick Law Olmsted National Historic Site, John F. Kennedy National Historic Site

Maps: USGS: *Boston South* and *Newton* quads; DeLorme: *Massachusetts Atlas & Gazetteer*, p. 41

Getting there: By car: There is parking at Amory Playground, off Amory Street. From Kenmore Square, take Beacon Street west. Turn right onto Amory Street into Amory Playground. **By train:** The Green Line does not allow bikes, unfortunately. Take the 8, 9, 19, 57, 60, or 65

bus to Kenmore, or the commuter rail to Yawkey on the Framingham/ Worcester line. Check the commuter rail timetable for bike details. Exit the station left onto Brookline Avenue into Kenmore Square, then take Beacon Street west to Amory Street and turn right, then turn right again into Amory Playground. GPS coordinates for starting point: N42 20.796′ / W71 06.756′

THE RIDE

You'll start the ride in Amory Playground near Brookline's border with Allston. This grassy bowl that now holds athletic facilities and an open field was once wetland known as Cedar Swamp before being filled in and drained for development. The Hall's Pond Sanctuary on the park's eastern edge holds one of the town's two remaining natural ponds and is home to a variety or birds, including majestic blue herons and red-winged blackbirds. Brookline acquired the pond in 1975 in its first purchase of conservation land.

Ride south past the pond sanctuary and out of the park, turning right on Beacon Street. You'll pass the beautiful Temple Ohabei Shalom on your left as you climb to Coolidge Corner, one of Brookline's cultural and commercial centers. The neighborhood is not named for President Calvin Coolidge, as is often assumed, but rather for the long-closed Coolidge Brothers general store that occupied the corner of Beacon Street and Harvard Street through the late 1800s. Today Coolidge Corner is much beloved for its mix of local shops, delis, and restaurants, as well as for its independent movie house, the Coolidge Corner Theatre, which occupies a restored art deco building dating back to the 1930s. Turn left at Harvard Street to cut south through the Brookline Village neighborhood.

The Larz and Isabel Legacy

Beyond the park, Larz and Isabel's generosity is on display in a number of places around Boston and Brookline. The Larz Anderson Auto Museum, which holds one of the oldest collections of carriages and automobiles in the country, was also included in Ms. Perkins donation to Brookline upon her husband's death. The couple also had a strong impact on the Arnold Arboretum, whose Larz Anderson Bonsai Collection holds more than twenty dwarf trees that once belonged to the couple. The bronze eagle statue at Boston College once adorned their home in Tokyo and was donated to the college in 1954.

You may note that street signs here indicate that you are in Norfolk County, rather than Suffolk County. Brookline has resisted annexation not only by Boston but at the county level as well, stubbornly maintaining its allegiance to the Norfolk County seat despite being completely engulfed by Suffolk zip codes. A map of Norfolk County includes the vast swath from Wellesley in the north to Foxboro in the south and Quincy to the east, plus the island of Brookline, its town boundary 2 miles from the contiguous county line even at its closest point. Follow Harvard Street to Boylston Street and continue straight onto High Street, mounting the hill as you move deeper into the more suburban and affluent southern stretches of the town. Turn left onto Chestnut Street, taking the first exit out of the rotary to continue south and turn right at Perkins Street.

Follow Perkins Street along the northwestern shore of Jamaica Pond and past Hellenic College and Holy Cross Greek Orthodox School of Theology on your left. Keep left at the fork to take Goddard Avenue up a series of short but challenging hills. Your efforts will be rewarded as Larz Anderson Park comes into view just past the Park School on your right. Enter the park just after its main parking lot, and follow the paved trail past the athletic fields and around the small pond.

Larz Anderson Park was once the sprawling estate of Brookline socialite Isabel Weld Perkins and her diplomat husband, Larz Anderson. Larz attended Harvard and was a member of its famed Hasty Pudding Club before serving diplomatic posts in London, Rome, Belgium, and Japan. Larz and Isabel met in Rome and led a life of luxury, travel, and philanthropy, building up a trove of artifacts in their estate from journeys to five continents, including forays into places as distant as Tibet and Nepal. When Ms. Perkins died in 1948, she left the twenty-five room mansion and breathtaking grounds to the town. The mansion had fallen into such disrepair that it had to be torn down, but the massive Carriage House from the previous estate remains on the very southern edge of the grounds. The largest in Brookline, Larz Anderson Park is a recreational hub for locals looking for a picnic spot or community garden plot. Rounding the pond, you'll come to the Temple of Love gazebo, one of the estate's original hallmarks and an ideal vantage point to take in the park's gentle hills, peaceful waters, and elegant landscaping.

Continue along the pond's edge and exit the park, turning left onto Goddard Avenue once again. Take a right at Clyde Street to begin the return leg

Bike Shop

Superb Bicycle near Fenway is known for its custom builds and keen focus on the aesthetics of cycling. Superb is located at 842 Beacon St., Boston; (617) 236-0752; www.superbbicycle.com.

The Temple of Love gazebo is one of the remaining fixtures from Larz Anderson's gardens.

north. Winding through a residential stretch, continue onto Lee Street and stay left at the roundabout to ride north. Turn right at Dudley Street, where the bike lane allows you to ride along the southern shore of Brookline Reservoir despite the one-way motor traffic along the road. Unfortunately, bicycles are not allowed around the water's edge. This man-made pond was part of Boston's drinking supply until 1902, when the city sold the reservoir and surrounding land to Brookline. Today Reservoir Park is popular for jogging, walking, and fishing, but swimming is banned along with biking. A historic park on the national and state registers, the reservoir's granite gatehouse has some of the oldest extant architectural trappings made of iron in the country: Its roof, trusses, and cast-iron staircases are the oldest known structures of their kind in the United States that were made for public use.

Past the reservoir, you'll come to the Frederick Law Olmsted National Historic Site. This is the preserved headquarters of the famed landscape architect whose firm was responsible for crafting countless US suburbs, parks, and preservation lands, including Central Park and Prospect Park in New York as well as Boston's Emerald Necklace, Franklin Park, and many others. His preserved headquarters, called Fairsted, includes historical exhibits, self-guided tours, and archives of Olmsted's original park designs. It provides a fascinating look through the life and legacy of this under-recognized molder of the national aesthetic.

Take a left onto Warren Street and ride past Boylston Street onto Sumner Road and then Tappan Street, where you'll climb through the neighborhood of Aspinwall Hill before reaching Beacon Street. Turn right and ride back to Coolidge Corner, turning left onto Centre Street, just before Harvard Street, and then right at Shailer Street. Take a left at Harvard Street and then your first right onto Beals Street, where you'll find the John F. Kennedy National Historic Site on your right about halfway down the street. This unassuming house is JFK's birthplace, purchased by his father in 1914. After JFK's assassination, the Kennedy family repurchased the home from its private owner, and the president's mother restored the house to her recollection of how it appeared when her son was born in 1917. The home is open to the public for guided or self-guided tours of its artifacts and exhibits, including the nursery where JFK and all nine Kennedy children slept and the dining room where this powerful clan had their family meals.

Follow Beals Street to the end for the final stretch of the ride, which includes some quick turns along Brookline's one-way streets. Turn right at Gibbs Street, left onto Stedman Street, then right at Manchester Road, right at Babcock Street and left around Freeman Square onto Freeman Street. Follow Freeman Street back to Amory Playground, where you began the ride.

MILES AND DIRECTIONS

0.0 Begin in Amory Playground at the entrance to Hall's Pond Sanctuary and ride south through the park.

0.1 Turn right onto Beacon Street.

0.6 Turn left onto Harvard Street.

1.4 Continue straight onto High Street.

2.0 Turn left onto Chestnut Street.

2.1 Take the first exit out of the rotary to continue south along Chestnut Street.

2.2 Turn right onto Perkins Street.

2.7 Stay left onto Goddard Avenue.

3.6 Turn left into Larz Anderson Park, just after the main parking lot, to ride past the athletic fields and around the pond.

3.9 Turn left out of the park onto Goddard Avenue.

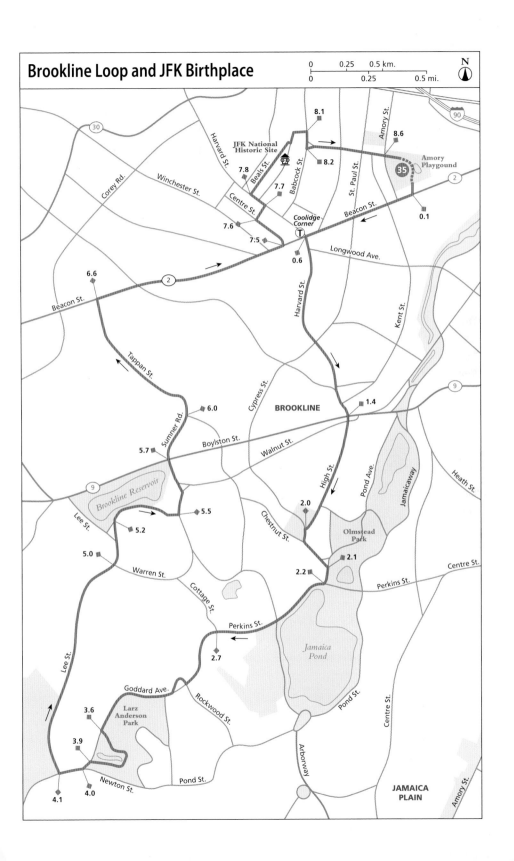

Brookline Loop and JFK Birthplace

| 0 | 0.25 | 0.5 km. |
| 0 | 0.25 | 0.5 mi. |

N

JFK National Historic Site

Amory Playgound

8.1

8.6

8.2

7.8

7.7

35

7.6

0.1

7.5

Coolidge Corner

0.6

Longwood Ave.

6.6

Beacon St.

Tappan St.

6.0

BROOKLINE

1.4

5.7

Boylston St.

Walnut St.

Brookline Reservoir

5.5

2.0

5.2

5.0

Olmstead Park

2.1

Warren St.

2.2

Perkins St.

Centre St.

Cottage St.

Perkins St.

Jamaica Pond

2.7

Goddard Ave.

Larz Anderson Park

3.6

Rockwood St.

3.9

Pond St.

4.1

4.0

Newton St.

Pond St.

Arborway

JAMAICA PLAIN

Amory St.

Harvard St.

Beals St.

Centre St.

Babcock St.

St. Paul St.

Beacon St.

Harvard St.

Kent St.

Winchester St.

Corey Rd.

Cypress St.

Sumner Rd.

High St.

Pond Ave.

Jamaicaway

Heath St.

Lee St.

Chestnut St.

Lee St.

Centre St.

Amory St.

30

2

9

9

2

90

4.0 Turn right onto Newton Street.

4.1 Turn right onto Clyde Street, which turns into Lee Street.

5.0 Keep left to stay on Lee Street, then turn right onto Dudley Street.

5.2 Turn right onto the bike path along Brookline Reservoir.

5.5 Turn left onto Warren Street.

5.7 Continue straight onto Sumner Road.

6.0 Stay left to continue along Tappan Street.

6.6 Turn right onto Beacon Street.

7.5 Turn left onto Centre Street.

7.6 Turn right onto Shailer Street.

7.7 Turn left onto Harvard Street.

7.8 Turn right onto Beals Street.

8.1 Turn right at Gibbs Street, then a quick left onto Stedman Street, right onto Manchester Road, and right onto Babcock Street.

8.2 Turn left onto Freeman Street.

8.6 Cross Amory Street into Amory Playground.

8.7 Finish at Amory Playground.

RIDE INFORMATION

Local Events/Attractions

Larz Anderson Auto Museum: Donated to the public along with Anderson's gardens, this museum just off the southern tip of Larz Anderson Park is home to one of the oldest car collections in the country. www.larzanderson.org.

John F. Kennedy National Historical Site: Daily tours and regular exhibitions of JFK's effects allow you to step back in time to the president's childhood and family home. www.nps.gov/jofi

Restrooms

Start/finish: Amory Playground has restrooms and water.

Mile 0.6 and 7.5: Coolidge Corner has a number of shops and restaurants with restrooms and water.

Mile 3.6: Larz Anderson Park has restrooms and water.

Auburndale Park and the Upper Charles River

Boston Common and the Public Garden are fantastic urban parks, and their location in the middle of Back Bay make them ideal for a quick fix of greenery. This ride takes you from the heart of the city in Kenmore Square to a true wooded retreat: Auburndale Park in Newton. Complete with deep forest and marshy lakes, it will make you forget just how close you are to a major city before following the tree-lined banks of the Charles River back to Boston along the Blue Heron Trail and the Esplanade.

Start: Kenmore Square, Boston

Length: 21.4 miles

Approximate riding time: 2.5–3 hours with stops

Best bike: Road bike or hybrid

Terrain and trail surface: Well-paved roads, with brief stretches of gravel and dirt path

Traffic and hazards: Watch for traffic along Commonwealth Avenue, particularly at Kenmore Square and Packard's Corner in Allston. Joggers, hikers, families with small children, and dog walkers frequent the trails and paths of Auburndale Park and the Upper Charles Reservation.

Things to see: Kenmore Square, Boston University, Boston College, Newton City Hall, Auburndale Park, Ware's Cove, Upper Charles River Reservation, Charles River Greenway, and Esplanade

Maps: USGS: *Boston South* and *Newton* quads; *DeLorme: Massachusetts Atlas & Gazetteer*, pp. 40–41

Getting there: By car: From Boston Common and the Public Garden, take Commonwealth Avenue west to Kenmore Square. There is street parking along Commonwealth Avenue, Bay State Road, or Beacon Street, or lot parking at VIP Parking at 120 Brookline Ave. in Fenway.

By train: The Green Line does not allow bikes, unfortunately. Take the 8, 9, 19, 57, 60, or 65 bus to Kenmore, or the commuter rail to Yawkey on the Framingham/Worcester line. Check the commuter rail timetable for bike details. Exit the station left onto Brookline Avenue into Kenmore Square. GPS coordinates for starting point: N42 20.942′ / W71 05.822′

THE RIDE

You'll start at Kenmore Square, beneath the iconic Citgo sign. Once swampy marshland before the filling of Back Bay, today Kenmore Square is a major commercial and cultural hub. From your vantage point in front of the New England School of Photography, you can see down Brookline Avenue to the far left to the Green Monster of Fenway Park, iconic home stadium of the Boston Red Sox since 1912. The middle road is Beacon Street, which cuts through Brookline toward Coolidge Corner and Chestnut Hill.

Take the street on the right, Commonwealth Avenue. For this initial stretch, Commonwealth Avenue is part of US 20, the longest continuous road in the country, which spans all the way from Kenmore Square to Newport, Oregon, on the Pacific shore. You'll follow Commonwealth Avenue all the way to Newton, first passing the Charles River campus of Boston University. Founded in 1839 as a Methodist seminary, BU has its roots in Beacon Hill but moved to its current location in 1937. The BU College of Arts and Sciences, its largest and oldest academic building, will be on your right, as will the infamous Warren Towers dormitory, the second-largest dorm in the country. A bit farther on is Marsh Plaza, adorned with the ornate Marsh Chapel and commemorative dove statue that honors Martin Luther King Jr., an alum of the BU School of Theology. Students strictly avoid walking over the large BU seal behind the statue, since a campus superstition holds that walking on the medallion curses you to delayed graduation.

Continue straight past the Boston University Bridge into Allston, where you'll keep left at Packard's Corner to stay on Commonwealth Avenue. Known as the college-student epicenter of Boston, the Allston neighborhood is also home to a diverse immigrant population and thriving arts scene. Underground music shows spring up across Allston every weekend during the school year, and a number of bands on the national scene got their start at Allston open mics.

A few hills on will bring you into the more suburban Brighton neighborhood of Boston, then the Chestnut Hill territory of BU's bitter rivals at Boston College. The Jesuit school was established in 1827 but was barred from incorporating

A cable bridge carries the Blue Heron Trail back across the Charles.

officially by the anti-Catholic Massachusetts legislature until 1863. The tall tower visible for miles around is Gasson Hall, named for BC president Thomas Glasson, who led the school's move to Chestnut Hill from the South End. The tower was built from stone quarried on-site for its 1913 opening. To this day, BC is home to one of the largest Jesuit communities in the world.

Past BC you'll enter Newton, consistently ranked among the top places to live in the country for its quality schools, safe neighborhoods, and close proximity to Greater Boston's cultural resources. First incorporated as Cambridge Village in 1688, Newton developed into a wealthy commuter suburb in the mid-1850s. Stay on Commonwealth Avenue as you come to the infamous Heartbreak Hill past Hammond Street, known as a particularly grueling segment of the Boston Marathon route. While the hill is pretty tame by bike, its ascent so late in the course has humbled thousands of marathoners since the race began in 1897. A couple of miles on along Commonwealth Avenue, you'll come to Bullough's Pond on the right, a former mill pond now popular with birders and ice-skaters in wintertime. Just across the street is Newton City Hall, which holds the city's war memorials in addition to its main administrative offices.

After crossing the I-90 overpass, turn right at Islington Road. The entrance to Auburndale Park is on your immediate right via the dirt path. This stretch of green was one of Newton's first purchases along the Charles River and includes a number of dirt paths through its heavily wooded preserve. Follow the main path straight through the woods, keeping the water and marsh to your right.

You'll briefly come to a breathtaking view of the Upper Charles at Ware's Cove, one of the most popular picnic destinations in the city. Fishermen and birders also flock to Auburndale Park for its abundant wildlife. Pressing on through the woods and across the small parking lot, you'll pass between two vast marshy expanses, one a dammed lake on your right and the other a curve in the Charles to your left.

As you leave the parkland, you'll enter the bordering city of Waltham, once known as Watch City for its numerous timepiece factories. Today the small city is a center for research and academics, home to Brandeis University and Bentley University. Aerosmith rented their "A. Wherehouse" space in

Bike Shops

Centre Ski and Bike has been supplying adventure sport needs in Boston since 1980 and offers a full-service shop as well as an extensive equipment selection. The shop is located at 1239 Washington St., Newton; (617) 332-0300; www.centreskiandbike.net.

Harris Cyclery has been serving Newton cyclists since 1952 with its expert sales and service team. The shop is located at 1353 Washington St., Newton; (617) 244-1040; www.harriscyclery.net.

International Bicycle has a full selection of new bikes, equipment, and apparel, plus a full-service department of expert technicians. The shop is located at 89 Brighton Ave., Allston; (617) 783-5804; www.internationalbike.com.

Landry's Bicycles has been a family-owned bike business since 1922, gaining the trust of avid cyclists at its four locations in Boston, Natick, Norwood, and Westboro. The Boston shop is close to the ride route at 790 Worcester St., Natick; (508) 655-1990; www.landrys.com.

Waltham from 1975 into the 1980s, often hosting artists like Boston and Ted Nugent at their complex on Pond Street.

Follow Woerd Avenue to Crescent Street and turn left, continuing as it curves east into Pine Street. Take a left at Elm Street, then turn right at McKenna Playground onto the Blue Heron Trail that runs along the river back toward Boston. At Farwell Street, follow the blue-painted heron tracks to the left across the bridge to continue right along the trail, which now leads into Watertown before crossing back into Newton a few minutes on via a cable bridge.

The Newton segment of the Charles River Greenway is particularly fantastic, its boardwalk segments through deep woods so serene and quiet and altogether too brief. As you leave the woods, the greenway trail winds once more into Watertown and jogs along the riverfront with only brief obstructions all the way to Soldiers Field and Christian A. Herter Park. Follow the trail under the Eliot Bridge and continue along the Charles to pass Harvard Business School and Harvard Stadium on your right. After the BU Bridge you'll come to the Esplanade, which you'll follow until the exercise area on the hill a few minutes in. Take the ramp on your right over Storrow Drive, then ride along Silber Way south to Commonwealth Avenue. Turn left and follow Commonwealth Avenue back to Kenmore Square, where the ride began.

MILES AND DIRECTIONS

0.0   From Kenmore Square head west along Commonwealth Avenue, toward Boston University.

1.4   Keep left at Packard's Corner to stay on Commonwealth Avenue.

3.4   Curve right around Chestnut Hill Reservoir along Commonwealth Avenue.

9.2   Turn right onto Islington Road, and then immediately into Auburndale Park.

9.9   Exit the park onto Forest Grove Road and then Woerd Avenue.

10.6   Turn left onto Crescent Street, which becomes Pine Street.

11.6   Turn left onto Elm Street.

11.7   Turn right at McKenna Playground onto the Blue Heron Trail.

12.6   Turn left onto Farwell Street and follow the blue-painted tracks across the bridge, turning right at the north shore to continue along the riverfront.

Auburndale Park and the Upper Charles River

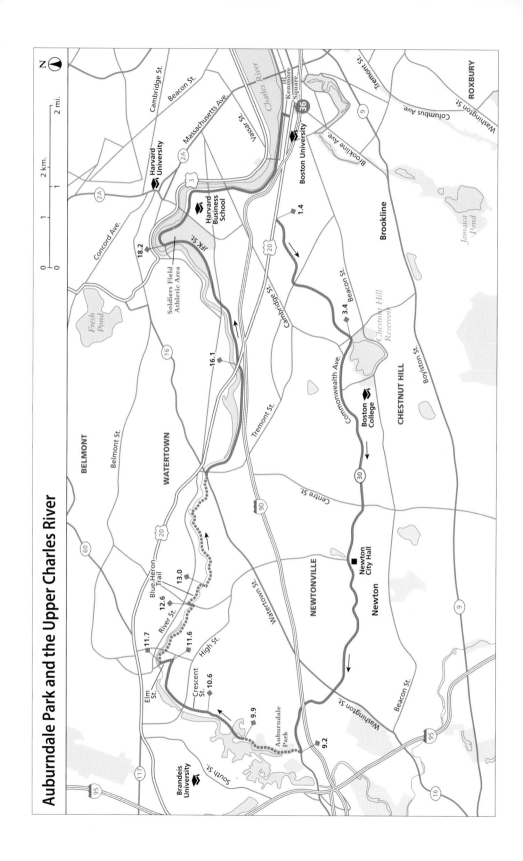

13.0 Cross back to the southern shore via the cable bridge.

16.1 Cross North Beacon Street.

18.2 Follow the path under the Eliot Bridge.

21.0 Exit the Esplanade via the footbridge over Storrow Drive and follow Silber Way to Commonwealth Avenue.

21.2 Turn left onto Commonwealth Avenue.

21.4 Finish at Kenmore Square.

RIDE INFORMATION

Local Events/Attractions
Auburndale Park: A favorite spot for fishing, kayaking, and picnics, Auburndale has amenities for all manner of recreational activities. www.newtonma.gov

Restrooms
Start/finish: Kenmore Square has a number of shops and cafes with restrooms and water, as does most of Commonwealth Avenue.
Mile 9.6: Auburndale Park has restrooms at the Cove Picnic Area.
Mile 17.5: Christian Herter Park has restrooms and water.

In Norfolk County to the southwest of Boston lies the picturesque town of Wellesley, famous around the globe as the home of Wellesley College and an incredibly well-educated populace to match. The hills and ponds of Wellesley make for a varied ride through natural landscapes and historic architectural districts, with a couple of decent climbs thrown in to keep things from becoming too academic. This loop will take you through forest stretches, along lakefront shores and bygone aqueducts for a jaunt around one of the most quintessentially New England towns in Massachusetts.

Start: Wellesley Farms commuter rail station

Length: 15.3 miles

Approximate riding time: 2–2.5 hours with stops

Best bike: Road bike, mountain bike or hybrid

Terrain and trail surface: A mix of paved roads and clear, hard-packed dirt trails, with occasional patches of uneven pavement or rocky terrain and a couple of steep climbs

Traffic and hazards: Watch for traffic at intersections and along Washington Street and Worcester Street in particular. Joggers and dog walkers frequent the Crosstown Trail and Aqueduct Trail.

Things to see: Wellington Farm Historic District, Morses Pond, Wellesley College, Cochituate Aqueduct, Olin College, Babson College

Maps: USGS: *Natick* quad; DeLorme: *Massachusetts Atlas & Gazetteer*, pp. 39–40

Getting there: By car: Parking is available at the Wellesley Farms station on the commuter rail. From Boston, take the I-90/Massachusetts Turnpike west. Take exit 15 to I-95/MA 128 toward Waltham, exiting at 21A. Turn left on Washington Street and right at Glen Road, which you'll follow to Wellesley Farms. **By train:** Take the commuter rail to Wellesley Farms station along the Framingham line. Check the commuter rail timetable for bike details. GPS coordinates for starting point: N42 19.422' / W71 16.350'

The Wellesley Farms neighborhood reflects the agrarian roots of Wellesley with its vast parcels, winding roads, and stone fences.

THE RIDE

First settled in the 1630s as part of nearby Dedham and Needham, Wellesley is a woodsy town centered around three campuses: Wellesley College, Babson College, and Olin College. You'll see all three in quick succession toward the middle of the ride, which you'll begin at the Wellesley Farms commuter rail station. Head west along Glen Road, riding through a hilly neighborhood full of vast parcels and a number of true mansions. Between Glen Brook Road and Pembroke Road you'll cross into the neighboring town of Weston, after which you'll pass Norumbega Reservoir before coming to the Wellington Farm Historic District at Glen Road's intersection with Wellesley Street. One of few working farms remaining in the Wellesley or Weston area, the Wellington Farm boasts a main house that dates back to 1760 and stone-lined fields that still produce hay for the horses boarded in its red barn complex.

Turn left onto Wellesley Street and take a right onto Radcliffe Road, which passes through a neighborhood with agrarian roots similar to those of the Wellington Farm but which has since left the hands of farm-minded owners. The first significant climb will come into view around the second bend in the road, after which you'll turn left onto Winter Street to pass the Rivers School, the college prep school where actor Jack Lemmon got his first taste for the stage in the 1930s. The school lies close to Nonesuch Pond, whose whimsical name harkens back to an old English word for "above all others," a lofty name for a pond less than a quarter mile across.

The town line for Natick lies just past the Rivers School, and you'll cross into it as you take another left at Rathburn Road. Follow Rathburn to Oak Street and turn left again. After a slight climb and a straight stretch you'll come to Worcester Street, which you'll follow left to the Crosstown Trail, which lies just off the main street past Stuart Road, just after you pass back across the town line into Wellesley. Ride the trail along the shore of Morses Pond, a man-made pond created in the mid-nineteenth century that once fueled a bustling local ice industry. The town bought the pond in 1931, after the invention of the refrigerator killed the ice harvesters' business and the Great Depression decimated land prices. The town created its first public beach along the pond's shore, which remains a popular summer destination today. Leaving the pond, you'll cross Turner Road to continue along the Crosstown Trail

Wellesley was founded as one of the original Seven Sisters Colleges, which included Radcliffe College (now a part of Harvard) in nearby Cambridge, Smith College in Northampton, and Mount Holyoke college in South Hadley, as well as Vassar College, Bryn Mawr College, and Barnard College.

through a stretch of dense forest, then turn right onto Weston Road and cross Central Street to arrive at the Wellesley College entrance.

One of the most prized liberal arts colleges in the world, Wellesley was founded in 1870. Originally the female parallel to the all-male Ivy League colleges, Wellesley now rivals the Ivies in academic reputation. After a fire devastated its sole building in 1914, Wellesley began a master renovation under the design of Frederick Law Olmsted Jr., who settled on a plan based on the rolling landscape of the 500-acre campus rather than the courtyard-and-quadrangle layout typical of other American campuses.

Follow the path past a parking lot to College Road, where you'll turn right toward the campus center where the magnificent Green Hall rises above the surrounding redbrick academic and dormitory buildings. Turn left at the hall to ride past the Houghton Memorial Chapel and short spires of Billings Hall toward Lake Waban. Make the loop and head back toward the campus center, turning right just before the chapel to ride along the lakeshore trail. Turn right at College Road, left at Washington Street to exit the campus, and then a quick right onto Dover Road.

Turn left at Benvenue Street to join the Aqueduct Trail, which follows the Cochituate Aqueduct that brought water from Lake Cochituate in Natick to the Brookline Reservoir from 1848 to 1951. Once the cornerstone of Boston's public water system but now disused, many of its gatehouses and granite bridges remain intact, making this segment a ride literally atop history. Turn right off of Benvenue Street just past Arden Road to continue along the Aqueduct Trail, winding through the woods and behind neighborhoods, until Great Plain Avenue, where you'll turn right and pass into the town of Needham just before the entrance to Olin College of Engineering.

A young addition to New England academia, Olin was founded in 1997 as a project-based engineering school without separate academic departments, and the college has quickly risen the ranks of the "New Ivies" as a small-but-mighty upstart. Turn left and take Olin Way to the campus center, which you'll cross to turn left onto Map Hill Drive. Already you've left the Olin campus and entered adjacent Babson College, a private business school founded in 1919. Consistently among the top MBA programs in the world, the Babson campus is centered around the famous Babson Globe, built in 1955 by founder, business theorist, and vocal prohibitionist Roger Babson at a then-staggering cost of $200,000. The globe originally rotated on its axis as well as its base, making it the largest rotating globe in the world for a time until disrepair claimed its rotation after decades of neglect.

Bike Shops

Landry's Bicycles has been a family-owned bike business since 1922, gaining the trust of avid cyclists at its four locations in Boston, Natick, Norwood, and Westboro. The Natick shop is close to the ride route at 790 Worcester St., Natick; (508) 655-1990; www.landrys.com.

Follow Map Hill Drive through the campus center and take the path between the athletic fields. Pass through the historic Babson gateway and merge onto Bryant Way, which becomes West Gate Road. Turn left onto Wellesley Avenue, following it until turning left after Wilson Street onto the paved Brook Path. Continue left at the fork at Smith Street, following the Brook Path as it winds around the Hunnewell Field, skirts Wellesley High School, and diverges right at Paine Street. At Phillips Park, exit the path onto Maugus Avenue and turn right onto Washington Street, which you'll follow toward the edge of Wellesley. Turn left on Glen Road and finish at Wellesley Farms station, where you began the ride.

MILES AND DIRECTIONS

0.0 Exit the station left onto Glen Road.

0.3 Keep left to stay on Glen Road.

1.4 Turn right to stay on Glen Road.

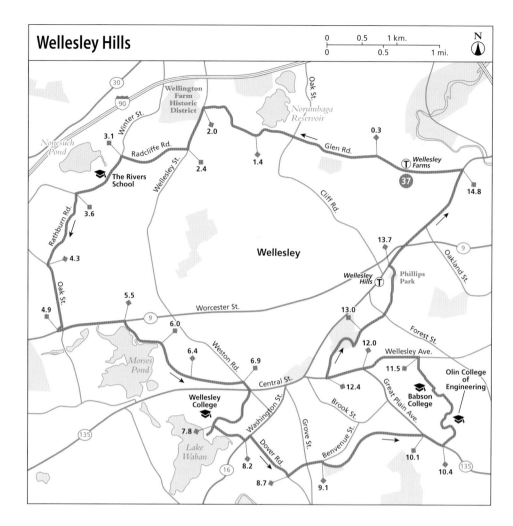

Wellesley Hills

2.0 Turn left at Wellesley Street.

2.4 Turn right on Radcliffe Road.

3.1 Turn left at Winter Street.

3.6 Turn left onto Rathburn Road.

4.3 Turn left onto Oak Street.

4.9 Keep left at the intersection to turn left onto Worcester Street.

5.5 Turn right just past Stuart Street onto the unpaved Crosstown Trail.

6.0 Continue across Russell Road to Kendall Road. The Crosstown Trail continues at the end of the pavement.

6.4 Cross Turner Road to continue along the Crosstown Trail.

6.9 Turn right onto Weston Road.

7.0 Cross to the Wellesley College entrance gate just past Central Street.

7.1 Follow the path past the parking lot to College Road,

7.3 Turn right onto College Road.

7.5 Turn left at Green Hall, following the road down toward the water. Make the loop back toward the center of campus.

7.8 Turn right just before the chapel to ride along the lakeshore trail.

8.2 Turn right at College Road, then left at Washington Street to exit the campus, then right onto Dover Road.

8.7 Turn left at Benvenue Street to join the Aqueduct Trail.

9.1 Turn right off of Benvenue Street just past Arden Road to continue along the Aqueduct Trail.

10.1 Turn right onto Great Plain Avenue.

10.4 Turn left into the Olin College campus.

10.8 Ride north through the Olin campus center to Map Hill Drive and turn left.

11.0 Follow the street left and continue straight through the athletic fields.

11.3 Continue on Bryant Way.

11.5 Turn left at Wellesley Avenue.

12.0 Stay right through the intersection to continue along Wellesley Avenue.

12.4 Turn right onto the paved Brook Path.

12.6 Continue past Smith Street, keeping left at the fork to follow the path around Hunnewell Field.

12.9 Turn left to follow Rice Street.

13.0 Turn right at Paine Street and continue along the Brook Path.

13.7 Cross Phillips Park and exit the path onto Maugus Avenue, then turn right onto Washington Street.

The Babson Globe at the top of Map Hill Drive was long the largest rotating globe in the world.

14.8 Turn left on Glen Road.

15.3 Arrive back at the starting point at Wellesley Farms station.

RIDE INFORMATION

Local Events/Attractions

Wellington Farm Historic District: This National Historic Landmark show-cases architectural styles from a number of historic and agrarian periods. www.westhistcomm.org

Hoop-rolling at Wellesley College: One day in late May, the women of Wellesley roll hoops down Tupelo Lane in a tradition dating back to 1895. The winner is carried away by her sisters and thrown into Lake Waban. www.wellesley.edu

Restrooms

Mile 4.9: There are a number of shops and restaurants along Worcester Street with restrooms.

Mile 7.0: There are a number of shops and restaurants along Central Street with restrooms.

Hemlock Gorge Reservation

Due west of Boston lies the quiet city of Newton. Consistently ranked among the top places to live in the country for its quality schools, safe neighborhoods, and close proximity to Greater Boston's cultural resources, Newton's hills are also popular destinations for cyclists. This ride cuts through Newton Centre from Brighton, passing beautiful Crystal Lake en route to Hemlock Gorge, whose steep canyon walls and rushing water from the upper Charles River transfix visitors crossing the landmark Echo Bridge. Between the tranquil sites, smooth ride, and handful of challenging hills, this route has it all!

Start: Cambridge Street and Brighton Avenue, Allston

Length: 14.5 miles

Approximate riding time: 1.5–2 hours with stops.

Best bike: Road bike or hybrid

Terrain and trail surface: Well-paved urban roads, with brief patches of dirt trail

Traffic and hazards: Watch for traffic along roads and for hikers along the Hemlock Gorge path.

Things to see: Allston, Brighton, East Parish Burying Ground, Boston College (Newton and Brighton campuses), Crystal Lake, Hemlock Gorge Reservation, Echo Bridge, Chestnut Hill Reservoir

Maps: USGS: *Boston South* and *Newton* quads; DeLorme: *Massachusetts Atlas & Gazetteer*, p. 40–41

Getting there: By car: From Kenmore Square, take Commonwealth Avenue northwest to Packard's Corner. Stay right to continue along Brighton Avenue, then keep right again onto North Beacon Street. There is parking available in the Stop & Shop parking lot off of Arthur Street, on the right. Exit the lot left onto Everett Street and turn left onto North Beacon Street then right onto Cambridge Street to arrive at the ride start. **By train:** Bikes are not allowed on the Green Line, unfortunately. From Kenmore Square, take the 51, 57, 64, or 66 bus to Union Square in Allston, near the ride start of the intersection of Brighton Avenue and Cambridge Street. GPS coordinates for starting point: N42 21.207′ / W71 08.275′

THE RIDE

You'll start at the intersection of Cambridge Street and Brighton Avenue in Allston. Known as the college-student epicenter of Boston, the Allston neighborhood is also home to a diverse immigrant population and thriving arts scene. Underground music shows spring up across Allston every weekend during the school year, and a number of bands on the national scene got their start at Allston open mics.

Follow Cambridge Street southwest past the Franciscan Hospital. Continue onto Washington Street as you enter the adjoining neighborhood of Brighton. Often lumped with Allston into "Allston-Brighton," Brighton has a distinctively more suburban vibe and was in fact one of the nation's first streetcar suburbs back in the days when the Green Line had an "A" branch. Once part of the farming community of Little Cambridge, Brighton was annexed to Boston in 1873. Turn left at Oak Square onto Tremont Street, which you'll follow across the city line into Newton.

Bike Shops

International Bicycle has a full selection of new bikes, equipment, and apparel, plus a full-service department of expert technicians. The shop actually has two locations along this route, one at 89 Brighton Ave. in Allston and the other at 71 Needham St. in Needham; (617) 783-5804 (Allston), and (617) 527-0967 (Needham); www.internationalbike.com.

Like Boston, Newton is a city of neighborhoods, its boundaries carved up into thirteen distinct villages. Consistently ranked among the country's top places to live for its quality schools, safe neighborhoods, and close proximity to Greater Boston's cultural resources, Newton developed into a wealthy commuter suburb in the mid-1850s and then into a minor manufacturing center into the mid-1900s. Fewer and fewer Newtonites commute to work in Boston these days.

Turn left again as Tremont Street comes to an end at Park Street, then right onto Vernon Street past the Presbyterian church and across Farlow Park. Ride left on Centre Street as you head south through the village of Newton

Charles Eliot christened Hemlock Gorge when he described its ledges as "clothed with hemlocks."

Corner. You'll mount a couple of decent hills as you head south past the East Parish Burying Ground. The cemetery dates back to the 1660s, when the first Europeans settled in this area and began establishing churches. Just across Centre Street from the cemetery lies Boston College's Newton campus, which holds the law school and freshmen dormitories. Continue along Centre Street past Commonwealth Avenue and into the village of Newton Centre, where you'll pass the Newton Centre Green on your left.

At Beacon Street, turn left onto Lake Avenue, staying left and then right as you pass Crystal Lake in the village of Newton Highlands.

Previously known as Baptist Pond and Wiswall's Pond in the colonial era, Crystal Lake is a natural lake and popular swimming and fishing spot. It received its current name from commercial ice harvesters in the 1800s, who sold the ice for refrigeration and thought the moniker more enticing for customers. The lake's frozen surface continues to draw ice-skaters during the winter even today, long after commercial interests yielded to public stewardship. Take Lake Avenue to Walnut Street, where you'll turn left and then right onto Lincoln Street.

Turn left at Woodward Street and ride past Boylston Street onto Elliot Street, which takes you through the village of Newton Upper Falls and across the small bridge on the city border with Needham. Take a right onto Reservoir Street and then right again on the dirt path that leads into the Hemlock Gorge Reservation and its Echo Bridge.

One of the reservations created by Charles Eliot as part of the Metropolitan Parks System during his time with the Frederick Law Olmsted Landscape Architectural Firm, Hemlock Gorge Reservation is a stunning retreat on the upper banks of the Charles River. The gorge's swift, foamy waters were once harnessed by colonists for their mills, which made Newton Upper Falls a small center for machinery and textiles.

Eliot named the gorge for the trees that line its ledges, which he wrote were "clothed with hemlocks." The stone arch of Echo Bridge was the second largest of its kind when first constructed in 1867, and quickly earned its name for acoustic peculiarities that make echoes from shouts up at the bridge platform reverberate with shocking strength. The bridge carries part of the Sudbury Aqueduct, part of Boston's backup water supply, and was designated a National Historic Landmark in 1982.

Walk your bike across the bridge back into Newton to Chestnut Street, where you'll turn left and ride north into the village of Waban. Turn right at Beacon Street and continue past the Coldspring Park and Newton Cemetery, pressing on through Newton Centre and into Chestnut Hill. Turn left at the reservoir onto Chestnut Hill Drive and ride past the main Boston College campus, passing Commonwealth Avenue to continue north on Lake Street, which forms part of the boundary between Newton and Brighton. You'll pass St. John's Seminary before coming once again to Washington Street. Turn right and continue onto Cambridge Street, which will take you back to the ride's start at the intersection with Brighton Avenue.

MILES AND DIRECTIONS

0.0 Start at the intersection of Brighton Avenue and Cambridge Street, and ride southwest along Cambridge Street, continuing west along Washington Street.

1.7 Turn left onto Tremont Street.

2.5 Turn left onto Park Street, then turn right onto Vernon Street.

2.7 Turn left onto Centre Street.

4.4 Stay right to stay on Centre Street.

4.6 Turn right onto Beacon Street.

4.9 Turn left onto Lake Avenue.

Hemlock Gorge Reservation

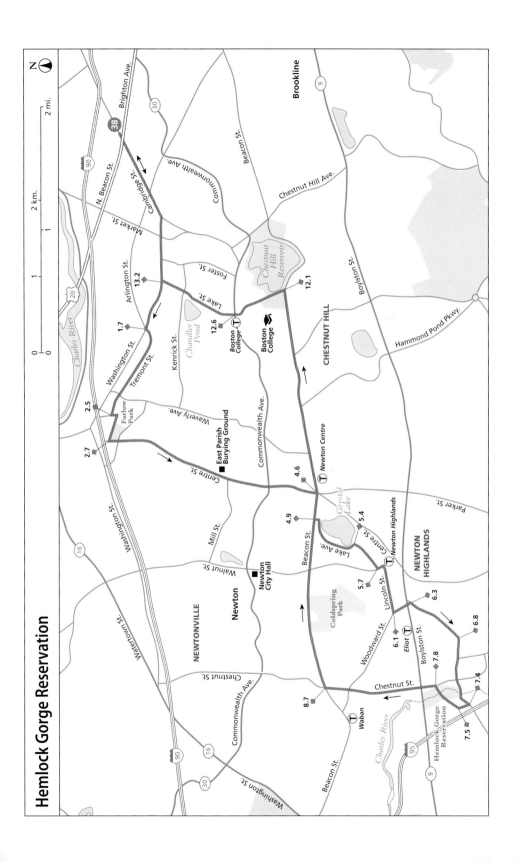

5.4 Stay left then right to continue on Lake Avenue.

5.7 Turn left onto Walnut Street, then right onto Lincoln Street.

6.1 Turn left onto Woodward Street.

6.3 Stay right past Boylston Street to continue onto Elliot Street.

6.8 Stay right to remain on Elliot Street.

7.4 Turn right onto Reservoir Street.

7.5 Turn right onto the Hemlock Gorge dirt path to Echo Bridge.

7.8 Exit the reservation and turn left onto Chestnut Street.

8.7 Turn right onto Beacon Street.

12.1 Turn left onto Chestnut Hill Drive, which becomes St.Thomas More Road.

12.6 Continue straight past Commonwealth Avenue onto Lake Street.

13.2 Turn right onto Washington Street.

14.5 End at the intersection of Brighton Avenue and Cambridge Street.

RIDE INFORMATION

Local Events/Attractions
Crystal Lake: A longtime Newton favorite spot for fishing and swimming. www.newtonma.gov.
Hemlock Gorge Summer Concert: A yearly tradition brings live music to Echo Bridge. www.hemlockgorge.org

Restrooms
Start/finish: Union Square in Allston has several shops and cafes with restrooms and water.
Mile 4.6 and 10.3: Newton Centre has several shops and cafes with restrooms and water.

Assabet River National Wildlife Refuge and Assabet River Rail-Trail

The Esplanade, Emerald Necklace, and Arboretum are all great for a quick fix of forest close to the city. But for a real taste of the wild woods, you have to head beyond the city line and even the suburbs. This ride goes for a loop around the deep forest of Stow's Assabet River National Wildlife Refuge some 20 miles west of Boston, then winds through the back woods along farm country and the Assabet River Rail-Trail toward Marlborough and back. Few routes hit this sweet spot of pristine and tranquil nature with such a smooth, even ride.

Start: Assabet River National Wildlife Refuge, Stow

Length: 23.3 miles

Approximate riding time: 2–2.5 hours with stops

Best bike: Road bike or hybrid

Terrain and trail surface: Mostly well-paved roads, with stretches of gravel and dirt path around the wildlife refuge

Traffic and hazards: Joggers and hikers frequent the Assabet River refuge, and the Assabet River Rail-Trail is a common destination for joggers, families with small children, and dog walkers. Be mindful of traffic along the roads between the refuge and rail-trail, particularly at curves.

Things to see: Assabet River National Wildlife Refuge, Puffer Pond, Massachusetts Firefighting Academy, Assabet River Rail-Trail

Maps: USGS: *Maynard, Hudson,* and *Marlborough* quads; DeLorme: *Massachusetts Atlas & Gazetteer,* pp. 39–40

Getting there: By car: There is parking at the Assabet River National Wildlife Refuge. From Boston, take the I-90W/Massachusetts Turnpike to exit 15. Take I-95N/MA 128 north toward Waltham, exiting at exit 26 onto US 20E (Boston Post Road) east toward Weston, turning right onto Cochituate Road and then left onto Hudson Road. Turn right onto Winterberry Way to arrive at the refuge. **By train:** Take the commuter rail to West Concord on the Fitchburg/South Acton Line. Check the commuter rail timetable for bike details. Exit the station right onto Main Street, which you'll follow straight onto Parker Street. Turn right at Fairbank Road and right again at Hudson Road, then take a left at Winterberry Way to arrive at the refuge. GPS coordinates for starting point: N42 23.734' / W71 28.127'

THE RIDE

You'll start at the parking lot of the Assabet River National Wildlife Refuge along Winterberry Way. Assabet is among the youngest wildlife refuges in the country, having opened in 2005. The refuge land has a long military history that stretches back to the Revolutionary War, when ammunition and supplies for the colonial army crisscrossed the area along the Concord-Marlborough Road. In 1942, the federal government seized the land under eminent domain to use for ammunition storage during World War II. A number of concrete-lined bunkers remain scattered throughout the refuge, which was closed off to the public behind razor wire and heavy patrols. Also remaining are sections of old railway tracks that connected some fifty ammunition bunkers to the Massachusetts Central Railroad. After the war the area remained under military control as a test station for military research. The army designated 2,230 acres for use as a wildlife refuge in 2000, and the current park opened in 2005 after extensive cleanup and restoration. It is one of eight national wildlife refuges in the Eastern Massachusetts National Wildlife Refuge Complex.

Nathaniel Hawthorne, who lived in nearby Concord for many years, once wrote of the Assabet River that a "more lovely stream than this . . . has never flowed on earth."

Take Winterberry Way deeper into the refuge, savoring the wildflowers and tall trees along the road. Assabet's critical mix of woods and wetland makes the refuge a prime breeding area for migratory birds, river otters, and a handful of rare freshwater turtle species. Where the road ends at the parking lot roundabout, continue straight onto the dirt path. Take care to remain on the trail, as bikes are allowed along a limited number of paths within the refuge.

You'll quickly pass Puffer Pond on your left, its marshy waters a fertile home for the refuge's many amphibious residents. Depending on the time of

Visitors regularly spot river otters in Taylor Brook, in addition to geese and turtles.

year, temporary watering holes called vernal pools may dot the forest along the path, as well. These pools made of snowmelt and rainwater from spring showers are a crucial component of the life cycle in the refuge before they dry up in late summer.

Follow the trail left at the edge of the park, making sure to keep right at the fork with Otter's Alley to stay on the bike-approved Taylor Way, which runs between the refuge's northeastern edge and Taylor Brook to your left. The pond to your right contains remnants of the refuge's military past, including some railroad ties that peek above the water's surface and scattered mossy and rusted telephone poles that once ran between the fort's ammunition storage bunkers.

Keep left where the path veers into a closed section of the refuge, taking White Pond Road to ride south, past stone fences that date back to the Revolution and open fields cleared during the land's military heyday. Turn left onto Patrol Road to ride back to the refuge entrance at Winterberry Road, completing your small loop around the park.

Turn right out of the park to head toward Hudson and the Assabet River Rail-Trail, keeping left past the Massachusetts Firefighting Academy and White Pond onto Sudbury Road, which becomes Main Street. Follow Main Street along the gentle hills and then one considerable incline as you near the main strip of Hudson.

Long a suburb of neighboring Marlborough, when it was known as "Fentonville," Hudson was incorporated as a separate town in 1866. This was once a shoe town, home to seventeen shoemaking factories, their machinery powered by the Assabet River's torrents. The town's industry attracted immigrant families, particularly those of Irish and Portuguese descent. The factories also brought railroads to the town, including the abandoned Marlborough Branch of the Fitchburg Railroad which was converted into the Assabet River Rail-Trail.

As Main Street spans the Assabet River, cross the street to join the Assabet River Rail-Trail. One of the smoothest and best-planned rail-trails in the Commonwealth, if not the country, the Assabet River Rail-Trail was begun in 2001 along the disused Marlborough railroad right-of-way, which had not been used in twenty years. Today, the paved rail-trail runs from Hudson all the way to Marlborough, with plans to extend it north past the wildlife refuge as far as South Acton. Follow the paved path parallel to Main Street, passing the restored blue caboose, an authentic Boston & Maine Railroad car from 1921. Follow the rail-trail as it curves south, passes through the intersection of Broad Street and South Street, and slopes upward and across the Assabet River via a wooden bridge. You'll pass behind homes and shops before crossing Washington Street into progressively deeper woods.

Bike Shop

Assabet River Bicycles has extensive experience repairing all types of bikes and also carries a range of equipment and apparel. The shop is located at 45 Main St., Hudson; (978) 568-0000; www.assabetbicycles.com.

As you emerge from the short tunnel that runs beneath MA 85, you'll see the marker designating the boundary between Hudson and Marlborough. Incorporated in 1660, Marlborough is a minor city and industrial center that grew during colonial times as a favored rest stop along the Boston Post Road, one of the first major highways in the United States that connected Boston to Manhattan. You'll curve around Assabet Valley Regional Technical High School and catch intermittent views of Fort Meadow Reservoir to the north before plunging south once again, passing right by the campus of Boston Scientific Corporation. Follow the rail-trail to its end at Lincoln Street, just blocks from the heart of Marlborough.

For the return leg, retrace the rail-trail to Hudson, exiting the path to turn right onto Main Street. Continue along Main Street across the town line back into Stow, keeping right at Sudbury Road and then Hudson Road. Turn left at Winterberry Road to arrive at the Assabet River National Wildlife Refuge, where the ride began.

Assabet River National Wildlife Refuge and Assabet River Rail–Trail

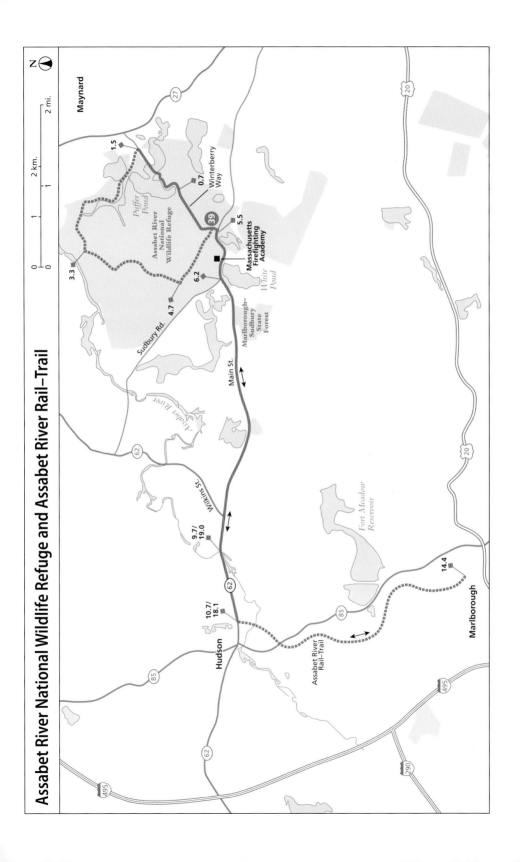

N

0   1   2 km.

0   1   2 mi.

Maynard

27

1.5

0.7
Winterberry
Way

Puffer
Pond

Assabet River
National
Wildlife Refuge

3.3

39

5.5

Sudbury Rd. 4.7

6.2

Massachusetts
Firefighting
Academy

White Pond

Main St.

Marlborough-
Sudbury
State
Forest

Assabet River

62

Wilkins St.

9.7/
19.0

62

10.7/
18.1

Hudson

85

85

62

Assabet River
Rail–Trail

Fort Meadow
Reservoir

20

14.4

Marlborough

495

20

495

290

MILES AND DIRECTIONS

0.0 Start at the Assabet River National Wildlife Refuge parking lot on Winterberry Way, and turn left into the park.

0.7 Continue straight past the small parking lot onto the gravel and dirt path.

1.5 Turn left at Taylor Road to continue along the northern edge of the refuge.

1.8 Stay right at the fork.

3.3 Turn left onto White Pond Road.

4.7 Turn left onto Patrol Road.

5.5 Turn right onto Winterberry Way, then right out of the refuge onto Hudson Road, continuing right on Sudbury Road.

6.2 Keep left at the fork onto State Road, which becomes Main Street.

9.7 Exit Main Street south onto the Assabet River Rail-Trail and head west.

10.7 Cross the triple intersection to continue along the rail-trail.

14.4 Come to the end of the rail-trail at Lincoln Street, where you'll turn around.

18.1 Cross the triple intersection to continue along the rail-trail.

19.0 Exit the rail-trail onto Main Street and turn right.

23.3 Turn left onto Winterberry Way and finish at the Assabet River National Wildlife Refuge parking lot.

RIDE INFORMATION

Local Events/Attractions

Historical walking tours of Assabet: Tour the bunkers and former military installations around the Assabet River National Wildlife Refuge. www.fws.gov/northeast/assabetriver

Restrooms

Start/finish: The Assabet River National Wildlife Refuge visitor center has restrooms and water.
Mile 9.7 to 10.7: This stretch of Hudson's main street has a number of shops and cafes with restrooms.

Boston Marathon Ride

One the the six World Marathon Majors, the Boston Marathon is the world's oldest annual marathon, founded in 1897 and run every year since. Its 26-mile, 385-yard route runs through eight communities from Hopkinton to Boston's Copley Square, passing ponds, woods, and hills, including the famous Heartbreak Hill near Boston College. The marathon route makes for a rewarding ride from the suburbs to the heart of Boston, a ride completed every year by hundreds of avid members of the Society of Spontaneity as part of its Midnight Marathon. Come trace the path run by hundreds of thousands of avid racers for the past hundred-plus years, a course now designated Boston Strong after the bombing of April 2013.

Start: Boston Marathon starting line, Hopkinton Green, 1 Ash St., Hopkinton

Length: 26.5 miles

Approximate riding time: 2.5–3 hours with stops

Best bike: Road bike or hybrid

Terrain and trail surface: Even paved bike lanes and roads with a number of challenging climbs.

Traffic and hazards: Watch for traffic along all roads, and take extra care at railroad track crossings.

Things to see: Hopkinton State Park, Framingham Reservoir, Cochituate State Park, Morses Pond, Wellesley College, Heartbreak Hill, Boston College, Chestnut Hill Reservoir, Coolidge Corner, Kenmore Square, Prudential Center, Copley Square, Boston Public Library, Old South Church

Maps: USGS: *Milford, Holliston, Framingham, Natick, Newton,* and *Boston South* quads; DeLorme: *Massachusetts Atlas & Gazetteer,* pp. 39–40, 41, 51

Getting there: By car: Street parking is available in the blocks surrounding the starting line. From Boston, take the Mass Pike (I-90) west to exit 12. Follow Turnpike Road to Cordaville Road and find parking near Hopkinton Green. **By train:** Take the commuter rail to Southborough (check the timetable for bike directions). Ride south from the station along River Street, passing through Hopkinton State Park to Main Street. Turn left toward the starting line at Hopkinton Green. GPS coordinates for starting point: N42 13.786′ / W71 31.096′

THE RIDE

A tiny town of around 15,000 people, Hopkinton has hosted the starting line at its town green since 1924, where the marathon starting-line pavilion is set up every year. The statue to the right of the starting line honors George Brown, the Hopkinton native who started the race for more than thirty years.

Continue to follow Main Street (MA 135) as it becomes Union Street between mile 4 and 5, where first female registrant Kathrine Switzer had her famous 1967 encounter with race manager Jock Semple, who attempted to rip off her number and force her from the course. Kathrine had registered under the listing "K.V. Switzer" in defiance of the marathon's exclusion of women; she went on to finish the race despite officials' opposition. The Boston Marathon first accepted women runners in 1972.

You'll pass the lower Framingham Reservoir as Union Street becomes Waverly Street, which winds through the center of Framingham. First settled in 1647, Framingham was a fixture in the abolitionist movement as the annual gathering place for the Massachusetts Anti-Slavery Society from 1854 to 1865, when prominent members like William Lloyd Garrison, Sojourner Truth, and

Bike Shops

Back Bay Bicycles is a Boston institution, with an experienced and friendly staff that will care for your equipment and can answer your maintenance questions. The shop also rents bikes by the day. Back Bay Bicycles is located at 362 Commonwealth Ave., Boston; (617) 247-2336; www.backbaybicycles.com.

Landry's Bicycles has been a family-owned bike business since 1922, gaining the trust of avid cyclists at its four locations in Boston, Natick, Norwood, and Westboro. The Natick shop is close to the ride route at 790 Worcester St., Natick; (508) 655-1990; www.landrys.com.

Superb Bicycle near Fenway is known for its custom builds and keen focus on the aesthetics of cycling. Superb is located at 842 Beacon St., Boston; (617) 236-0752; www.superbbicycle.com.

At the Hopkinton start line, *The Starter* commemorates George Brown, the Boston Athletic Association coach who shot the starting gun for the event from 1905 to 1937.

Henry David Thoreau would gather to develop strategy for abolishing slavery. Continue on West Central Street between Lake Cochituate on the southern end of Cochituate State Park and Fisk Pond on your right, after which you'll pass into the town of Natick near mile 10 of the marathon course.

In the language of the Massachusett Native American tribe, "Natick" means "place of hills," a foreshadow of what lies before you as you follow MA 135 between Morses Pond and Paintshop Pond at the edge of the Wellesley College campus. You'll pass along the northern edge of Wellesley's picturesque campus, which was designed by Frederick Law Olmsted Jr. after its sole building burned down in 1914. Follow Washington Street past the Wellesley Town Hall, into the Wellesley Hills and toward the Newton city limits. The hill that begins as you cross the Charles River, near mile 16 of the course, is considered by many to be the most difficult in the race. This marks the beginning of the four Newton hills, which continue as you turn right onto Commonwealth Avenue. The climbs culminate in the infamous Heartbreak Hill between the 20- and 21-mile marks. The hill got its name in 1936, when marathon defending champion Johnny Kelley overtook Ellison Brown with a condescending shoulder pat that spurred Brown to rally and pull ahead of Kelley, breaking his heart after thinking he had clinched another win.

40

Follow Commonwealth Avenue past the Chestnut Hill of Boston College, the private Jesuit university established in 1827 in Boston's South End. The anti-Catholic Massachusetts legislature barred BC's charter until 1863, and fifty years later the school moved to its new "college gothic" campus near the Chestnut Hill Reservoir. After the Evergreen Cemetery, turn right onto Chestnut Hill Avenue to round the reservoir and turn left onto Beacon Street at Cleveland Circle. Here you cross into the town of Brookline as the Boston skyline begins to come into view. Continue along Beacon Street past the historic Coolidge Corner, a local haven for foodies and film lovers for its gourmet options and the iconic Coolidge Corner Theatre. Ride through Audubon Circle at Park Street, making a brief climb into Kenmore Square.

Turn right onto Commonwealth Avenue and follow the Commonwealth Avenue Mall past Massachusetts Avenue. Turn right at Gloucester Street and then left onto Boylston Street at the Prudential Center Plaza. You'll make the final stretch toward the finish line at Copley Square along Boylston Street, passing the historic Lenox Hotel, once the tallest building in Boston at eleven stories when it was built in 1900. Judy Garland, a frequent guest, lived at the Lenox for three months in 1965. The finish line comes into view in front of the Boston Public Library, its ornate facade built in 1848 as the first publicly supported municipal library in the country. This finish line is crossed by 20,000 marathon qualifiers each year, all of whom doubtless share your same elation at completing the long path from Hopkinton.

A temporary memorial was erected in Copley to honor of the victims of the 2013 bombing, which has since been relocated to the Boston City Archives. A permanent memorial is still in the works as of this writing, but thousands of Bostonians and people from all across the world will run, walk, and bike the marathon route for years to come to commemorate the strength of common humanity over terror and tragedy.

Pulling a Fast One

In 1980, Rosie Ruiz was disqualified after taking the subway for part of the Boston Marathon track. Ruiz had clocked a time of two hours, thirty-one minutes, and fifty-six seconds, the fastest time ever for a woman in the race. When Ruiz was unable to recall key elements of the marathon course and competitors noticed she was not fatigued, officials began investigating her performance. A week later, the Boston Athletic Association officially disqualified Ruiz.

Boston Marathon Ride

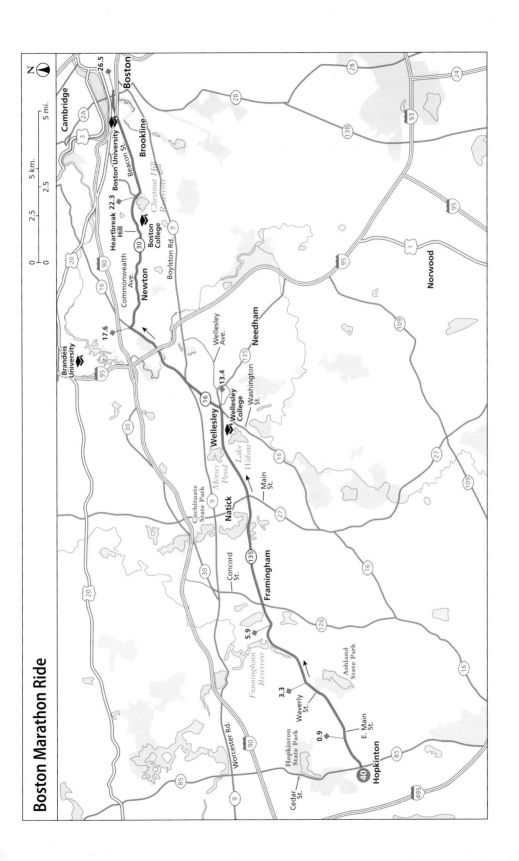

MILES AND DIRECTIONS

0.0 From the Hopkinton Green, ride northeast along East Main Street.

0.9 Stay right at the fork to continue on East Main Street.

3.3 Stay right at the fork to continue on East Union Street.

5.9 Keep left to continue on Waverly Street, which becomes Central Street, through Framingham and Natick.

13.4 Keep left at the fork to ride along Washington Street going through Wellesley.

17.6 Turn right onto Commonwealth Avenue.

22.3 Turn right at Chestnut Hill Avenue, then left through Cleveland Circle onto Beacon Street.

25.4 Merge onto Commonwealth Avenue.

26.0 Turn right at Gloucester Street.

26.2 Turn left onto Boylston Street.

26.5 Cross the finish line at Copley Square.

RIDE INFORMATION

Local Events/Attractions
Midnight Marathon Ride: Every year the night before the Boston Marathon (the Sunday before Patriots' Day in mid-April), Boston's Society of Spontaneity hosts this annual bike ride of the marathon course. www.bostonsos.org

Restrooms
Start: The gas station at Cedar Street and Main Street in Hopkinton has a public restroom.
Mile 5.9 to Mile 7.3: There are a number of fast-food restaurants and shops in Framingham with restrooms.
Mile 13.4 to Mile 14.9: There are a number of shops in Wellesley with restrooms.
Mile 22.3: Cleveland Circle has a number of shops and restaurants with restrooms.
Mile 26.5: The Boston Public Library has public restrooms.

Ride Index

About the Author

Shawn Musgrave, a journalist and investigative reporter, has written extensively for the *Boston Globe, The Phoenix, DigBoston,* and *Motherboard,* among other publications, on topics ranging from cycling culture and bike politics to privacy, civil liberties, and national security. As a former pedicabber, cycling advocate, and longtime bike commuter, he relishes finding great new routes around Boston and the metro area. Shawn lives in Cambridge, Massachusetts.

IMBA

INTERNATIONAL MOUNTAIN BICYCLING ASSOCIATION

You've just purchased, or are about to purchase, the mountain bike of your dreams. Where will you take your new steed? Who will you ride with? Joining IMBA's network of chapters, clubs and patrols taps you into a friendly network of experienced mountain bikers. They host rides for all skill levels, build trails and get together before and after rides to share stories and plan the next adventure. Find a local group by visiting imba.com/near-you.

Come Ride With Us!

FIVE RECENT ACCOMPLISHMENTS

1) *Built incredible trails.* IMBA's trailbuilding pros teamed with volunteers around the nation to build sustainable, fun singletrack like the 32-mile system at Pennsylvania's Raystown Lake.

2) *Won grants to build or improve trails.* Your contributions to IMBA's Trail Building Fund were multiplied with six-figure grants of federal money for trail systems.

3) *Challenged anti-bike policies.* IMBA works closely with all of the federal land managing agencies and advises them on how to create bike opportunities and avoid policies that curtail trail access.

4) *Made your voice heard.* When anti-bike interests moved to try to close sections of the 2,500-mile Continental Divide trail to bikes, IMBA rallied its members and collected more than 7,000 comments supporting keeping the trail open to bikes.

5) *Put kids on bikes.* The seventh edition of National Take a Kid Mountain Biking Day put more than 20,000 children on bikes.

FIVE CURRENT GOALS

1) *Host regional bike summits.* We're boosting local trail development by hosting summits in distinct regions of the country, bringing trail advocates and regional land managers together.

2) *Build the next generation of trail systems* with innovative projects, including IMBA's sustainably built "flow trails" for gravity-assisted fun!

3) *Create "Gateway" trails* to bring new riders into the sport.

4) *Fight blanket bans against bikes* that unwisely suggest we don't belong in backcountry places.

5) *Strengthen its network* of IMBA-affiliated clubs with a powerful chapter program.

FOUR THINGS YOU CAN DO FOR YOUR SPORT

1) *Join IMBA.* Get involved with IMBA and take action close to home through your local IMBA-affiliated club. An organization is only as strong as its grassroots membership. IMBA needs your help in protecting and building great trails right here.

2) *Volunteer.* Join a trail crew day for the immensely satisfying experience of building a trail you'll ride for years to come. Ask us how.

3) *Speak up.* Tell land-use and elected officials how important it is to preserve mountain bike access. Visit IMBA's web site for action issues and talking points.

4) *Respect other trail users.* Bike bans result from conflict, real or perceived. By being good trail citizens, we can help end the argument that we don't belong on trails.